ASSISTED SUICIDE
AND THE
RIGHT TO DIE

ASSISTED SUICIDE
AND THE
RIGHT TO DIE

THE INTERFACE OF SOCIAL SCIENCE, PUBLIC POLICY, AND MEDICAL ETHICS

BARRY ROSENFELD

AMERICAN PSYCHOLOGICAL ASSOCIATION
WASHINGTON, DC

Published by
American Psychological Association
750 First Street, NE
Washington, DC 20002
www.apa.org

To order
APA Order Department
P.O. Box 92984
Washington, DC 20090-2984
Tel: (800) 374-2721; Direct: (202) 336-5510
Fax: (202) 336-5502; TDD/TTY: (202) 336-6123
Online: www.apa.org/books/
E-mail: order@apa.org

In the U.K., Europe, Africa, and the Middle East, copies may be ordered from
American Psychological Association
3 Henrietta Street
Covent Garden, London
WC2E 8LU England

Typeset in Goudy by Stephen McDougal, Mechanicsville, MD

Printer: Data Reproductions, Auburn Hills, MI
Cover Designer: Berg Design, Albany, NY
Technical/Production Editor: Rosemary Moulton

The opinions and statements published are the responsibility of the authors, and such opinions and statements do not necessarily represent the policies of the American Psychological Association.

Library of Congress Cataloging-in-Publication Data

Rosenfeld, Barry.
   Assisted suicide and the right to die : the interface of social science, public policy, and medical ethics / Barry Rosenfeld.
       p. cm.
   Includes bibliographical references and index.
   ISBN 1-59147-102-8 (alk. paper)
   1. Assisted suicide—Moral and ethical aspects. 2. Right to die—Psychological aspects. 3. Right to die—Social aspects. 4. Euthanasia—Psychological aspects. 5. Euthanasia—Social aspects. 6. Death—Psychological aspects. I. Title.

   R726.R64 2004
   179.7—dc22   2004000157

British Library Cataloguing-in-Publication Data
A CIP record is available from the British Library.

Printed in the United States of America
First Edition

Death don't have no mercy in this land.

CONTENTS

ASSISTED SUICIDE
AND THE
RIGHT TO DIE

INTRODUCTION

As the 20th century drew to a close, a relatively new legal issue emerged in American courtrooms and dining rooms: Do individuals have a legal right to determine how and when they die? Questions regarding the ethics, legality issues and the morality of end-of-life issues such as physician-assisted suicide and euthanasia brought these questions squarely into the forefront of public and political debate. Although numerous journal articles, books, and newspaper editorials have been written about such issues, few have attempted to integrate this rapidly growing literature into a coherent overview of the legal and scientific issues involved. This book attempts to fill this void, providing a comprehensive review of scientific research, case law, and social history to inform the future research and policy decisions that will inevitably arise.

Attempting to achieve the central goals of this book—to summarize, interpret, and elaborate on a growing scientific literature devoted to understanding assisted suicide and related end-of-life decisions—feels a bit like the struggle of Sisyphus. In a rapidly expanding research area, any attempt to present a review of scientific research findings runs the risk of being outdated even before it is published. New results emerge even as these very pages are being printed and bound. Because an exhaustive review is virtually impossible, a more modest goal seems appropriate: to address and discuss the most important scientific elements of the clinical, legal, and social policy issues that surround physician-assisted suicide and, to a lesser extent, end-of-life care in general. Indeed, this goal is sufficiently broad as to perhaps exceed the limitations of a contemporary research analysis and will hopefully raise issues—methodological, theoretical, and ethical—that remain vital even after the present scientific literature has become somewhat outdated.

In this book, I have attempted to use the assisted suicide debate as a vehicle for analyzing a wide range of issues that are central to mental health clinicians and other professionals who work in health care settings. Among them are topics as diverse as informed consent, Do Not Resuscitate (DNR) orders, surrogate decision making, clinical assessment of depression, and the competency of patients to make decisions. Each of these issues has direct relevance for clinicians and researchers of virtually every discipline. In addition, the attention to legal and ethical issues and the history and current status of assisted suicide might help frame the ethical issues that are interwoven with clinical practice and research for virtually all psychologists. Indeed, I hope (and expect) that most clinicians and social scientists will find this book to be relevant and useful even if they do not consider themselves to be ethicists, behavioral medicine specialists, or forensic psychologists. Moreover, I anticipate that this book would be particularly useful to researchers and graduate students who seek to contribute to the growing body of research addressing the important issues covered in this volume. The chapters on methodological issues, depression and psychosocial influences, and end-of-life decision making (to name a few) highlight a number of areas in which important research needs remain unfulfilled. My hope is that this book helps guide the next generation of researchers who want to contribute to this important literature.

OVERVIEW OF THE BOOK

This book is divided into 11 chapters (including this one), beginning with 2 chapters devoted to the historical and legal background of assisted suicide and the "right-to-die" debate. These chapters provide the necessary backdrop against which to understand the contemporary ethical, legal, clinical, and research issues that are described in the chapters that follow. These chapters will also be of particular interest to policymakers and others interested in examining the legal and ethical history of assisted suicide and other end-of-life policies.

Chapter 4 describes DNR orders, living wills, surrogate decision making, and other end-of-life issues that are at the heart of clinical practice with the terminally ill. Chapters 5, 6, and 7 describe methodological issues and the scientific literature on depression, psychosocial factors, pain, and other medical symptoms that are most pertinent to the assisted suicide and right-to-die debates. Chapter 8 is particularly important for clinicians, because it describes an area that has increasingly emerged at the forefront of clinical practice in palliative care: assessing the decision-making abilities of patients around end-of-life issues. To date, few psychologists have been asked to evaluate a patient's request for assisted suicide, but I expect that this situation will occur more frequently; it is a thorny issue with which few clinicians feel comfortable. This chapter highlights distinctions between decision-making capacity and competence as well as the psychological factors that influence patient decision making.

Chapters 9 and 10 describe the practice of assisted suicide in two areas in which it has been legalized: the Netherlands and Oregon. These experiences provide insight that links back to the research and clinical issues described in the previous chapters and illuminates some of the dark corners of the debate on assisted suicide and the right to die. The final chapter summarizes what I believe to be the central issues that need to be examined empirically and clinically by social and behavioral scientists, policymakers, and clinicians who seek to contribute to this growing and critically important field.

TERMINOLOGY AND DEFINITIONS

Despite the widespread use of terms such as *physician-assisted suicide* and *euthanasia*, both the general public as well as many health care professionals often misunderstand what is meant by these terms. Confusion abounds, for example, regarding how, or even whether, physician-assisted suicide and euthanasia differ. As a result, discussions of these end-of-life issues are often based on incorrect assumptions and perceptions. Questions arise as to whether these terms are appropriate to describe any instance of hastened death,[1] or refer only to a particular (in the minds of many people, improper) subset of death-hastening actions. Because an informed discussion of end-of-life medical interventions requires an adequate understanding of the terms and issues involved, it is only fitting that this volume begin with a thorough explication of the various terms that appear in these pages.

Perhaps the most commonly used term to describe hastened death, *euthanasia*, is also one of the most widely misunderstood. The lay interpretation of this term often differs from that intended by legal scholars and bioethicists, often confusing euthanasia with genocide or eugenics.[2] The most widely

---

[1]The term *hastened death* has been used to encompass physician-assisted suicide, euthanasia, and various other interventions or treatment decisions that can result in the more rapid decline and death of a medically ill individual than would otherwise be expected.

[2]This confusion is likely rooted in the adoption of the term *euthanasia* by the Nazi regime to describe the systematic murder of any population deemed "undesirable" by their leaders (e.g., Jews, homosexual individuals, mentally handicapped individuals). *Eugenics*, another term adopted by the Nazis to justify the extermination of "undesirable" populations, refers to the elimination of the "genetically inferior," typically (but not always) through sterilization (thereby ending reproductive potential).

accepted definition of *euthanasia* is the administration of a medication or other toxic substance, typically (but not necessarily) by a physician, with the specific intent of causing the death of the individual.[3] Note that this definition of euthanasia might include actions taken by other health care professionals (e.g., nurses, nurse practitioners) or even friends and family members, and it is presumably distinguished from murder on the basis of the actor's intent: to relieve suffering in a terminally ill individual rather than kill for personal or social gain. This distinction is based on the principal of *beneficence* (defined as "doing good"), which is a well-known tenet of health care practice and refers to any decision that is intended to directly benefit the patient's physical or mental health.

Many writers make a further distinction between *voluntary euthanasia* and *nonvoluntary euthanasia*, with the former term referring to instances in which the patient has specifically requested that a substance be administered to end his or her life. Nonvoluntary euthanasia, on the other hand, involves the same action on the part of the medical professional but without any explicit request on the part of the patient. Nonvoluntary euthanasia could be instigated at the request of a family member acting on behalf of a patient who is presently unable to communicate (but may have expressed this desire in the past) or even by a physician who believes that death is in the patient's best interest but has received no explicit request to hasten death from anyone involved in the person's care. Nonvoluntary euthanasia, which accounts for a modest proportion of cases of hastened death in the Netherlands, has rarely been the subject of debate in the United States, because few proponents of legalization have advocated this option. Nevertheless, anonymous surveys of physicians and nurses have shown that nonvoluntary euthanasia occurs periodically, even in the United States, typically in cases where the patient is extremely ill or otherwise unable to participate in a meaningful discussion of end-of-life options (e.g., comatose or in a persistent vegetative state).[4]

Physician-assisted suicide (often referred to simply as *assisted suicide*) differs from euthanasia in that the principal actor is the patient rather than a physician, another health care professional, or friend or family member. In cases of assisted suicide, physicians provide guidance and assistance, such as a prescription for a lethal medication, along with instructions on how to use this substance. In the United States most of the legal and medical attention has focused on physician-assisted suicide because this option appears to maxi-

---

[3]See, e.g., Matersvedt et al., "Euthanasia and Physician-Assisted Suicide: A View From an EAPC Ethics Task Force," *Palliative Medicine*, 17 (2003): 97–101.

[4]See, e.g., D. A. Asch, "The Role of Critical Care Nurses in Euthanasia and Assisted Suicide," *New England Journal of Medicine*, 334 (1996): 1374–1402; Back et al., "Physician-Assisted Suicide and Euthanasia in Washington State," *Journal of the American Medical Association*, 275 (1996): 919–925; Meier et al., "A National Survey of Physician-Assisted Suicide and Euthanasia in the United States," *New England Journal of Medicine*, 338 (1998): 1193–1201.

mize patient autonomy and minimize the involvement (and legal responsibility) of other parties. Indeed, the retired pathologist Jack Kevorkian, who many credit with having brought the issues of euthanasia and assisted suicide into public awareness, was repeatedly acquitted of abetting suicide (despite the enactment of laws specifically in response to his actions) before ultimately being convicted of second degree murder after a publicly televised demonstration of euthanasia. His eventual conviction highlights the importance placed on the distinction between euthanasia and assisted suicide in the United States.

In addition to physician-assisted suicide and euthanasia, other end-of-life interventions that hasten death include terminal sedation, withdrawal of life support, and refusal of artificial nutrition and hydration. Although these interventions have also been debated in legal arenas and medical journals, they are considerably less controversial than euthanasia and assisted suicide. These acts are sometimes referred to as *passive euthanasia* because death is secondary to another medically or ethically justified action, and they are contrasted with active euthanasia, both voluntary and nonvoluntary. *Terminal sedation* typically refers to cases in which a physician provides a dosage of pain medication that effectively allows the individual to sleep through the remaining hours (or days or weeks) of life. Although this action is ostensibly taken to control pain or other troubling symptoms, it is acknowledged to hasten the patient's death by hindering respiratory functioning. Other potential treatment decisions, such as the cessation of life-support (mechanical ventilation), the refusal or discontinuation of artificial nutrition and hydration (stopping intravenous feeding and saline), or refusal of dialysis (for patients with renal failure) also hasten an inevitable death for terminally ill patients or for patients with unrelenting suffering, but these medical options have not been subjected to the same intense public scrutiny as have euthanasia and physician-assisted suicide because death results from the underlying illness or disease.

Although all of the above methods of hastening death share some similarities (e.g., hastening a terminally ill patient's death), significant differences among them have led to varying degrees of acceptance by the lay public. Among the most clearly drawn distinctions along moral and legal lines have been between the passive refusal of interventions which might sustain life (i.e., mechanical ventilation, cardiopulmonary resuscitation [DNR orders are discussed in chap. 4], intravenous hydration and feeding) and the active provision or administration of a substance that causes death (i.e., euthanasia, assisted suicide and, to a lesser extent, terminal sedation). Perhaps more ambiguous are the distinctions drawn among the active death-hastening interventions: euthanasia, physician-assisted suicide, and terminal sedation. Of these three, terminal sedation has also been distinguished from physician-assisted suicide and euthanasia by the presence of an alternative motivation beyond hastened death: pain or symptom control. However, whether symptom control is truly the primary goal of terminal sedation or is simply a pretext for hastening death often depends on the particular circumstances of the case. Nevertheless, many of the same theorists who oppose euthanasia and physician-assisted suicide acknowledge that hastened death is a common, even expected, outcome of terminal sedation and maintain the legitimacy of this intervention. To some extent, the distinctions between lessening suffering by hastening death and relieving pain through terminal sedation may be more semantic than genuine. In some cases, physicians may nod to one another when justifying the prescription of high doses of narcotics for their terminally ill patient knowing full well that their actions are motivated by a desire to help their patient end suffering in general, not to help them avoid pain per se.

Ethical and legal distinctions between physician-assisted suicide and euthanasia are perhaps more subtle than distinctions among other death-hastening methods. This distinction is perhaps most clearly evidenced by the almost exclusive focus on physician-assisted suicide in the current debates in the United States about legalization of hastened death. Several states have held referendums on legalizing physician-assisted suicide (discussed in more detail in chap. 3), but legalization of euthanasia has rarely been suggested as an option. This relative acceptance of assisted suicide may be more an artifact of American cultural values (i.e., the premium placed on individual liberty and autonomy) rather than an objective assessment of the difference between the two options. In the Netherlands, euthanasia has been much more common than physician-assisted suicide, despite the equal legal status afforded to both, suggesting that culture may influence the perceived appropriateness of the method.

Assisted suicide may be more readily accepted in the United States because of the emphasis Americans place on individual rights. Indeed, arguments for legalization of physician-assisted suicide have often focused on the "right" of one to control one's death. The "right to die" argument can be viewed as a logical extension of patient autonomy, the gradual transition of ultimate medical decision making from physicians to patients that began with the first legal recognition of the informed consent doctrine (discussed in more detail in chap. 8). Euthanasia, on the other hand, has more often been the focus of debate in European countries (and has now been legalized in Belgium as well), where physicians continue to be seen as the primary decision makers acting on the behalf of their patients. Data from the Netherlands, where both options have long been decriminalized (but only recently legalized), consistently show far greater use of euthanasia and relatively fewer individuals requesting or using physician-assisted suicide (see chap. 9).[5]

---

[5]Although many individuals mistakenly equate decriminalization with legalization, significant differences exist. Legal policy in the Netherlands dictated, for many years, that although euthanasia and physician-assisted suicide were illegal, cases were not prosecuted when appropriate health care

Whether this difference reflects actual cultural differences in the physician–patient relationship or is an outgrowth of other legal or social factors is unclear, but the history of euthanasia and physician-assisted suicide debates in the United States and Europe have clearly taken a markedly different path over the past few decades. Chapter 2 presents a historical account of the debates about euthanasia and physician-assisted suicide.

ARGUMENTS FOR AND AGAINST LEGALIZATION OF PHYSICIAN-ASSISTED SUICIDE

One important context for interpreting the scientific literature reviewed in this book is the ongoing legislative, policy, and ethical debates regarding legalization of assisted suicide. Although initiatives to legalize assisted suicide may have slowed in recent years, interest in this issue has certainly not subsided and the importance of scientific input is clear.

Advocates of legalization of assisted suicide typically begin with the principal of autonomy. There is little dispute that personal autonomy, the right to make decisions for oneself and to control one's destiny, is a central principal of American law. Hence, arguments for legalization of assisted suicide typically begin by asserting that patients should have the right to end their lives when and if they so choose.[6] Perhaps more importantly, advocates of legalization buttress their case on the basis of compassion. Given the unfortunate but undeniable fact that some patients suffer great physical as well as emotional or spiritual pain, the desire to help ease their suffering is understandable. A related assumption by many advocates of legalization is that decisions to hasten death are often a logical reaction to an incurable disease and unresolvable suffering. This stance, that suicide can be a "rational" solution to one's problem rather than the outcome of depression or otherwise distorted decision making, is a cornerstone of the advocacy position. As such, proponents of legalization often acknowledge that assisted suicide should be quite infrequent, given that relatively few patients actually experience untreatable suffering. However, the reassurance provided by knowing that hastened death is an option if one's condition were to worsen may be a source of emotional support for a great many terminally ill patients (see Table 1.1).

---

policy regulations were followed (discussed in detail in chap. 9). Despite decades of acceptance, euthanasia was only legalized in the Netherlands recently. Prior to this legal change, physicians were simply required to follow a series of procedural requirements in order to avoid prosecution (i.e., seeking a medical second opinion, confirmation of the "terminal" status of the patient, filing necessary documents with the Solicitor's Office). When these required procedures were not followed, physicians were vulnerable to criminal prosecution for their role in cases of euthanasia, although prosecution appears to have been quite rare.
[6]The principal of autonomy is more clearly applicable in cases of suicide, or even assisted suicide, where the patient is essentially ending his or her own life rather than euthanasia, where a physician is the primary actor.

TABLE 1.1
Arguments for and Against Legalization of
Physician-Assisted Suicide (PAS)

Arguments For	Arguments Against
■ PAS is consistent with personal autonomy–liberty	■ Killing is morally unacceptable
■ Not all suffering can be relieved by palliative care	■ Adequate palliative care will eliminate virtually all requests
■ The desire to hasten death is often rational	■ Many PAS requests are due to depression
■ PAS can be safely administered without abuse	■ Legalization will impede efforts to improve palliative care
■ The availability of PAS is reassuring to many terminally ill patients	■ Determinations of who is eligible for PAS and when will gradually expand (the "slippery slope")
■ PAS allows for better safeguards against misuse	

This topic is discussed further in the context of the psychosocial literature (chap. 6) and emerging data from Oregon (chap. 10).

Opponents of legalized assisted suicide offer several arguments to support their position, beginning with the Hippocratic Oath. This oath, discussed in chapter 2, bars physicians from treatments that are not intended to help extend life or alleviate symptoms. This argument is essentially an ethical one. Opponents of physician-assisted suicide also argue that with adequate palliative care, patients may not want to hasten death. Thus, requests for assisted suicide are often viewed as a cry for help by patients who are not receiving sufficient symptom relief (whether the symptoms are physical, such as pain, or psychiatric, such as depression) rather than a "rational" request. Many experts argue that adequate palliative care, which is still not available to many terminally ill patients, will be even less available if assisted suicide provides a less expensive and more expedient option. The presumption that the demand for assisted suicide is linked to inadequate palliative care leads many writers to express concern that disenfranchised populations, who have even less opportunity to receive adequate palliative care, may feel that assisted suicide is their only viable option. Finally, opponents of legalization often express concern that legalization for extreme cases of untreatable pain or symptom distress may lead to a gradual expansion of the criteria of who is eligible to hasten death and under what circumstances. This so-called *slippery slope* argument is discussed in detail in the context of the Netherlands, where the practice of euthanasia has indeed expanded from terminally ill patient to populations who have a psychiatric disorder but are physically healthy. Concerns that the practice of physician-assisted suicide and euthanasia will gradually expand, and that the sanctity of life will be further eroded, are a central aspect of the argument against legalization.

Some elements of the advocacy for or against legalization of assisted suicide are amenable to scientific study whereas others are not. Questions such as whether untreated pain or depression indeed fuel requests for assisted suicide, or the extent to which fears of the slippery slope are justified, are examined in the chapters that follow. On the other hand, ethical concerns do not necessarily fall in the domain of science. How these various concerns should be viewed and balanced is the purview of ethicists, scientists, and clinicians in concert. My hope is that focusing on how science can inform these issues, and reviewing and synthesizing what research has uncovered thus far, will be helpful to professionals in all disciplines.

1

HISTORY OF EUTHANASIA AND PHYSICIAN-ASSISTED SUICIDE: PHILOSOPHICAL, RELIGIOUS, AND CLINICAL CONTEXTS

One might think, after reading some of the many newspaper articles, editorials, and medico-legal writings on the topic of assisted suicide that have appeared in the past decade, that physician-assisted suicide and euthanasia reflect "modern thinking" about an age-old problem of trying to improve the quality of one's death and dying. Perhaps previous generations have simply not considered the possibility that the same medical advances that are used to save or extend lives might also be used to hasten death. Indeed, many an introduction to the topic of end-of-life decision making frames the emergence of the assisted suicide debate as a reaction to the growing availability of life-extending medical interventions. But the perception of assisted suicide and euthanasia as recent concepts in medicine could not be less accurate. History is replete with discussions of euthanasia and physician-assisted suicide. In fact, the most glaring differences between past discussions of hastened death and the contemporary debates around legalization of assisted suicide pertain to the methods used to end life and society's response, not the overarching principles or ethical concerns. Public debates regarding legalizing assisted death have existed for centuries, waxing and waning with the social climate. Documented discussions, recollections, and descriptions of assisted death date to pre-Christian eras, with assisted death figuring prominently in ancient Greek and Roman writings. However, it was not until the 19th century that the specific types of assisted death currently under debate, physician-assisted suicide and euthanasia, began to take on their current form.

EUTHANASIA IN ANTIQUITY AND THE CHRISTIAN ERA

Although the term *euthanasia* has been found in the writings of ancient Greek and Roman scholars, the meaning ascribed to this term in antiquity differed somewhat from its modern usage (see chap. 1 for a discussion of current definitions). Roman and Greek philosophers used the term *euthanasia* to refer to a pleasant state of mind at the time of one's death, with no reference to the speed or timing of death per se (Fye, 1978). Thus, euthanasia implied an easy or happy death, but not necessarily a hastened death. A quote from the *Lives of the Caesars*, cited by Gillon in his 1969 review of the history of euthanasia, captures this usage: "As often as Caesar Augustus heard that someone had died quickly and without suffering he prayed for euthanasia for himself" (Gillon, 1969, p. 173). However, whether euthanasia was something one prayed for or directly requested, many ancient philosophers found no moral or philosophical objection to the concept of hastened death.

The acceptance of assisted death in the face of illness or suffering was rooted in several philosophical principles common to Greek and Roman society. Perhaps the most central was the virtue of being physically healthy; physical fitness was considered "an ideal, indeed the highest good, set above beauty, wealth and inner mobility" (Amundsen, 1978, p. 24). Even the writings of Hippocrates and his followers, who were among the earliest opponents of assisted death, reflected this ideal of physical health. This perspective is best exemplified in a statement from the Hippocratic Corpus: "nothing avails, not money or any other thing without health" (Admunsen, 1978, p. 24).

The emphasis placed on physical health was bolstered by a general approval of suicide as a morally acceptable act among many (not all) Greek and Roman scholars. Although suicide among the physically healthy was not condoned and was seen by many as an insult to the gods, it was generally accepted as an appropriate response to many unpleasant circumstances. Plato, in *The Republic*, asserted that the medically ill should be allowed to refuse interventions that might lengthen life when the quality of life would suffer and their usefulness to the State had lapsed. The Aristotelian and Epicurean schools of philosophy also condoned suicide at times: "death was considered morally neutral and sometimes it was preferable to life, sometimes not" (Gillon, 1969, p. 174). According to Greek legend, Zeno of Citium (336–

264 B.C.), the founder of the Stoics, reportedly committed suicide in response to an agonizing foot injury (Carrick, 1985). Greek legend also describes the acts of Hegesias, who was so persuasive a proponent of suicide that King Ptolemy banned him from speaking on the subject because too many of his listeners killed themselves after his speeches (Gillon, 1969). The Romans, too, often approved of suicide, even at times as a form of entertainment. Peregrinus reportedly declared his intent to kill himself simply in order to gain fame and notoriety and subsequently threw himself onto the pyre at the Olympic games (Barry, 1995).

Greek and Roman philosophers were supported in their acceptance of suicide by the laws of their time, which did not include suicide as a punishable offense unless the individual was a soldier or slave. In fact, suicide was only prohibited for soldiers and slaves because their bodies belonged to the State or their owner, not themselves. However, according to Roman law, individuals who committed suicide without legitimate justification did forfeit their property and estate. This practice, which continued in most Judeo-Christian cultures at least until the 18th century, has typically been attributed more to avarice than any criticism of suicide per se (Amundsen, 1978). Nevertheless, not only was there no punishment imposed on individuals who attempted to commit suicide, but those who assisted another person in committing suicide were also not considered legally responsible. Pliny the Younger, whose letters documented Roman daily life in the 1st century A.D., characterized the moral status of suicide in his description of Titus Aristo, a man afflicted with a painful illness:

> He asked me and a few special friends to consult the physicians, his intention being voluntarily to depart from life if the illness was incurable, while if it were merely to be difficult and tedious he would bear up and bide his time . . . for the sake of his wife, daughters and friends. Such conduct I consider eminently high and praiseworthy . . . deliberately to weigh the motives for and against and then, as reason advises, to accept or reject the policy of life or death, that is the conduct of great soul. (Pliny, cf. Gillon, 1969, p. 187)

Just as the decision of whether to commit suicide was left to the individual, physicians in Greek and Roman times were free to assist in the death of a dying patient, a practice that occurred with some frequency (Admunson, 1978). Roman literature records numerous references to physicians helping their patients die, either through providing poisons or cutting veins, to facilitate a quick and relatively painless death (Edelstein, 1943/1967). At times, physicians were even praised for applying their knowledge of poisons to help develop combinations that would produce quick and peaceful deaths.

It was not until Hippocrates and his followers began to offer a "modern" perspective on medicine that Greek and Roman physicians began to question the acceptability of suicide as a response to medical illness. Hippocrates is considered the first physician to have advocated a "medical" understanding of illness rather than attributing ailments to divine causes, and he is generally acknowledged to have been the first physician to advocate a direct physical examination of the patient. Because of their emphasis on alleviating pain symptoms and improving the well-being of their patients, physicians from the Hippocratic school explicitly banned all types of assisted suicide. The well-known Hippocratic Oath that is still used in most major medical schools is often cited in support of this prohibition against physician-assisted suicide: "I will neither give a deadly drug to anybody, not even if asked for it, nor will I make a suggestion to this effect" (Edelstein, 1943/1967, p. 6). Although the precise date of the original formulation of the Oath is unknown, the influence of Hippocrates spread slowly and was not widely accepted by Roman physicians until well into the Christian era.

During the second and third centuries A.D., the acceptability of euthanasia and assisted suicide and other forms of hastened death began to wane in Europe. This perspective on assisted death was bolstered by Church doctrines that emphasized the sanctity of human life over human suffering. By the Middle Ages, when Christianity dominated the legal and moral thinking of Western societies, the practice of euthanasia was viewed as an unthinkable act, a perspective that has persisted for centuries (Fye, 1978). In fact, in the third century, Christian teachings dictated that suicide delayed the soul's passage into the afterlife, and by the fifth century suicide began to be seen as an unforgivable sin, even in the face of painful illness. This evolution was fueled by the writings of St. Augustine, who clearly articulated the Roman Catholic Church's stringent opposition to suicide, an opposition that dramatically curtailed this practice (Crone, 1996).

The Renaissance saw a rebirth of education, the arts, and critical thinking, as well as a renewed perspective on euthanasia and assisted suicide. Philosophers began to break free from the shackles of Christian doctrines and to propose that the goal of moral philosophy is to produce free and educated citizens. Some of these Renaissance philosophers offered opinions that were considered at the time to be quite radical, such as the permissibility of euthanasia (Gillon, 1969). For example, in his 1516 book, *Utopia*, Sir Thomas More wrote:

> If a disease is not only incurable but also distressing and agonizing without any cessation, then the priest and the public officials exhort the man, since he is now inequal to all of life's duties, a burden to himself and a trouble to others, and is living beyond the time of his death, to free himself from this bitter life as from prison and the rack, or else voluntarily to permit others to free him. In this course he will act wisely since by death he will put an end not to enjoyment but to torture. (More, 1516/1965, p. 187)

In another passage, More wrote: "Should life become unbearable for these incurables the magistrates and priests do not hesitate to prescribe euthanasia" (More, 1615/1965, p. 187). A century later, Francis Bacon declared that the physician's duty was "to mitigate pains and dolors, and not only when such mitigation may conduce to recovery, but when it may serve to make a faire and easy passage" (Bacon, 1937, p. 182). Perhaps the most influential philosopher to voice his approval of assisted suicide was David Hume, who wrote:

> If suicide be supposed a crime it is only cowardice can impel us toward it. If it be no crime, both prudence and courage should engage us to rid ourselves at once of existence when it becomes a burden. It is the only way that we can be useful to society—by setting an example which, if imitated, would preserve to everyone his chance for happiness in life and would effectually free him from all danger of misery. (Hume, 1771/1980, p. 104)

Despite the acceptance of suicide and euthanasia among many philosophers, however, the practices of physicians do not appear to have been influenced by these philosophical writings. Both popular opinion as well as medical practice continued firmly to oppose the practice of euthanasia or physician-assisted suicide throughout the 17th and 18th centuries (Gillon, 1969). Indeed, the philosophical approach to medicine originally attributed to Hippocrates, including his emphasis on the patient's well-being as the primary concern of doctors, continued to dominate western medicine for several centuries.

THE 19TH CENTURY: EUTHANASIA RE-EMERGES

Moral and legal opposition to suicide and assisted death began to undergo change in tandem with a number of developments in the practice of medicine in the 19th century. Although contemporary writers often cite the tremendous advances in medical technology during the late 20th century as an influence in generating interest in euthanasia and physician-assisted suicide, the level of progress in medical technology in the 19th century may have been far more substantial, particularly given the state of medicine during previous generations. Fye (1978) cited several developments in medical practice that facilitated the 19th-century revival of the euthanasia debate. These included advances in medical diagnosis, including more accurate prognostic assessments; the development of analgesic medicines and in particular, the discovery of anesthesia; and perhaps most important, the emergence of Darwin's theory of evolution and the impact it had on science in general.

One of the most significant advances that occurred during the late 18th and early 19th centuries was the marked increase in diagnostic and prognostic accuracy. By the middle of the 19th century, physicians were able to offer far more accurate predictions of the course of many illnesses than had ever before been possible. The ability to determine, with some degree of accuracy, whether an illness was likely to result in death perhaps naturally led to the consideration of whether one's remaining life was indeed worthwhile. For the first time in history ill individuals were able to know whether they were likely to survive their illness. Like current medical practice, the accuracy of prognostic assessments was highly variable when it came to individual patients. Nevertheless, considerations of whether the amount of time remaining was "worthwhile" could for the first time be debated both by individual patients as well as by their physicians.

A second major change during the 19th century that fostered discussions of assisted death was the development of effective analgesics. Morphine, which was first manufactured in 1819, as well as the invention of the hypodermic syringe that helped administer analgesics more accurately, allowed for rapid and effective pain relief for many patients. This ability to treat pain, along with the subsequent discovery of anesthesia, enabled physicians to consider the extent to which pharmacologic interventions could or should be used to help dying patients. Most 19th century physicians encouraged the use of these medications, but they were largely opposed to giving "a large dose that might be hazardous," instead arguing that these medications should only be used to prolong life (Bullar, 1866, p. 11). Nevertheless, the availability of techniques that could end life in a rapid, painless manner provided a crucial element that would later be incorporated into the public and political debates regarding the legalization of euthanasia.

Darwin's theory of evolution may have had a more profound influence on the subsequent euthanasia debates than the medical advances. His book, *Origin of the Species*, led to revolutionary changes in scientific thinking and allowed the euthanasia debate to be disentangled from the moral and religious dogma that had previously hindered any real discussion of these issues. The confluence of these developments in medical technology and scientific thinking fostered a renewed acceptance of assisted death as a possible option (Emanuel, 1994).

It is not a physician but a British schoolmaster and essayist, Samuel D. Williams, Jr., who is credited with initiating the 19th century public debate over euthanasia. In an 1870 lecture to the Birmingham Speculative Club, Williams presented what many consider to be the first public argument of the modern era directly focused on the issue of euthanasia (Emanuel, 1994; Fye, 1978). His position, published in subsequent writings, was as follows:

> In all cases of hopeless and painful illness it should be the recognized duty of the medical attendant, whenever so desired by the patient, to administer chloroform, or such other anesthetics as may by and by supercede chloroform, so as to destroy consciousness at once, and put the sufferer at once to a quick and painless death; all needful precautions being adopted to prevent any possible abuse of such duty; and means being taken to establish beyond any possibility of doubt or question, that

the remedy was applied at the express wish of the patient. (Williams, 1873, cited in Emanuel, 1998, pp. 180–181)

The boldness of Williams's essay is reflected in his argument that all willing patients with incurable and painful disease should be allowed to seek euthanasia and that it was the "duty of the medical attendant" to provide assistance. Williams also vehemently opposed religious doctrines regarding the sanctity of life, instead asserting that "life is a thing to be used freely and sacrificed freely" (Emmanuel, 1994). His stance sparked widespread public debate in Britain and the United States, with his original essay being published several times over the next few years in journals and books. However, it was not until Williams's essay and other writings were reviewed and quoted in a popular magazine *Popular Science Monthly*, that 19th century physicians began to enter the euthanasia debate. One of the first published reactions to Williams's argument from the medical community appeared in 1873 in the form of an editorial published in the *Medical and Surgical Reporter*. This editorial acknowledged that issues related to euthanasia and assisted death had existed for many years but had largely remained unspoken.

> Generally we dodge the responsibility of answering, and at the same time meet the requirements of the case by prescribing such a dose of opium or other narcotic that will certainly plunge the patient into a profound sleep, whence he may or may not come forth . . . [W]e have often been asked— and we presume our experience is by no means singular—by friends of the sick and by the patient himself, to administer some potent drug that would close the fearful struggle. (Williams, 1873, p. 122)

In 1879, the South Carolina Medical Association became the first group to publicly debate the issue of euthanasia. It considered a wide array of potential factors including medical, religious, moral, and legal issues. The Association concluded, after vigorous private discussions, that "in the present state of society, the practice of Euthanasia was illegal, and could only be regarded as the practice of murder" (South Carolina Medical Association, 1879, c.f. Emanuel, 1994, p. 797). Not surprisingly, the content of the debate as well as the conclusions were representative of the views of physicians throughout the United States and England. Numerous other medical groups who entered into similar discussions regarding the appropriateness of euthanasia and assisted suicide reached virtually identical conclusions, characterizing euthanasia and physician-assisted suicide as inappropriate and illegal (Emanuel, 1994). Nevertheless, individual physicians were forced to confront issues of euthanasia and assisted suicide with increasing frequency and many of them seem to have acceded to their patient's (or family's) requests.

By the end of the 19th century, however, opinions regarding the acceptability of euthanasia began to change. As a growing number of articles began to document the practice of euthanasia, a number of writers began to acknowledge the appropriateness of the intervention for some terminally ill individuals. Along with the growing acceptance of euthanasia among the medical professionals, debates regarding its appropriateness started in legal circles as well. By the 1890s, many attorneys began to argue for greater patient rights, including the right to die. One particularly influential lawyer, Albert Bach, who was vice president of the New York Medico-Legal Society, publicly advocated legalized euthanasia and physician-assisted suicide. His argument focused on the excessive authority that the medical profession exercised over patients and insisted that patents should have the right to end their own lives if they so choose (Emanuel, 1994). In a speech at the 1895 Medico-Legal Congress, Bach stated:

> There are also cases in which the ending of a human life by physicians is not only morally right, but an act of humanity. I refer to cases of absolutely incurable, fatal and agonizing disease or condition, where death is certain and necessarily attended by excruciating pain, when it is the wish of the victim that a deadly drug should be administered to end his life and terminate his irremediable suffering (c.f. Emanuel, 1994, p. 184)

The arguments put forth by Bach and his contemporaries were not well received by most physicians, many of whom argued that legalizing euthanasia would bring disgrace to the profession. Nevertheless, the growing demand for patient rights espoused by the legal profession, including the right to euthanasia and physician-assisted suicide, continued well into the early 20th century.

THE 20TH CENTURY: EUTHANASIA ENTERS THE LEGAL ARENA

The trends of the 1890s continued into the early 20th century, with many legal scholars calling for increased patient autonomy, particularly regarding issues of euthanasia and physician-assisted suicide. Most physicians, on the other hand, continued to firmly oppose these practices, despite occasional acknowledgments by individual physicians of engaging in euthanasia or assisted suicide. This opposition was no doubt sustained by adherence to many of the principals originally outlined by Hippocrates, as well as a long-standing resistance by physicians to the increased demands for patient autonomy (Faden & Beauchamp, 1986).

One of the more significant catalysts of the early 20th century euthanasia debates was a speech by a renowned Harvard University professor, Charles Eliot Norton (Emanuel, 1994). Norton's speech inspired a wealthy socialite, Anna Hill, to campaign for legalization of euthanasia. Her efforts culminated in a bill before the Ohio legislature entitled "An Act Concerning Administration of Drugs, Etc. to Mortally Injured and Diseased Persons" (c.f. Emmanuel, 1994). This bill, which drew widespread opposition in medical journals as well as the public press, was soundly defeated in 1905. Following the defeat of this legislation, and a similar bill in Iowa, interest in euthanasia in the United States diminished rapidly. Although occasional editorials continued to appear in medical journals throughout the first half of the 20th century, these writings were virtually unanimous in their opposition to the practice of euthanasia.

As interest in euthanasia and physician-assisted suicide waned in the United States, it was steadily increasing in Germany. A number of German scholars published treatises supporting "mercy killing," beginning with Adolf Jost's 1895 book entitled *The Right to Death*. German interest in euthanasia, however, was intertwined by the growing acceptability of eugenics, as many German writers advocated for the termination of life for "incurable idiots . . . [who] are a fearfully heavy burden both for their families and for society" (Binding & Hoche, 1992, p. 241).

Indeed, as economic depression worsened in Germany following World War I, the emphasis on potential economic benefits from euthanasia and mercy killing began to dwarf the initial emphasis on containing human suffering. By the early 1930s, euthanasia debates resurfaced in British medical circles, this time with much stronger support from legal professionals. One of the most well-known British physicians of the 1920s and 1930s, C. Killick Millard, even proposed a model for legislation legalizing euthanasia in Britain (Emanuel, 1994). A number of prominent British physicians founded the Voluntary Euthanasia Legislation Society, which emerged as a leading force supporting the right of terminally ill individuals to seek euthanasia. Public debates regarding this issue were also extensive throughout Britain, as evidenced by the frequent editorials published in leading newspapers and magazines. The efforts of the Voluntary Euthanasia Legislation Society culminated in a bill before the House of Lords that was debated in 1936 and was defeated, largely because of the opposition of two physician members of the House of Lords (Emanuel, 1994).

Shortly after the defeat of this bill, the growing awareness of German atrocities, many of which were carried out by physicians who had previously advocated euthanasia, helped stifle further discussions of euthanasia or physician-assisted suicide in almost every country. It was not until the 1950s that British and American scholars renewed their discussions of the ethics of euthanasia. Public interest in euthanasia and assisted suicide grew steadily throughout the 1950s, 1960s, and 1970s (Blendon, Szalay, & Knox, 1992). Another bill to legalize euthanasia was introduced in the British Parliament in 1969, but this proposal fared no better than the 1936 bill. Nevertheless, public interest in and support for the legalization of euthanasia and physician-assisted suicide has continued to grow over the last 30 years, both in Europe and the United States. The Netherlands became the first country to permit euthanasia, albeit in an "unofficial" manner in 1984 when the Dutch Supreme Court ruled that a physician could invoke the defense of "justification" in cases where their patient's suffering was "unbearable and hopeless." Since that time, specific guidelines have been spelled out for the practice of euthanasia and physician-assisted suicide (e.g., regarding proper medical procedures and documentation), with the proviso that prosecution will not occur if these guidelines are adhered to. But it was not until April 2001 that euthanasia was officially legalized in the Netherlands, nearly 20 years after this practice was first decriminalized (Griffiths et al., 1998).

The most recent rekindling of the public debate about euthanasia and physician-assisted suicide in America was sparked by a 1988 letter published in the *Journal of the American Medical Association* entitled "It's Over, Debbie." (Anonymous, 1988). This letter documented a case of euthanasia and, for the first time in decades, brought the issue of euthanasia back into the forefront of medical ethics. Not long afterwards, Jack Kevorkian, a retired Michigan pathologist, began his public physician-assisted suicide practice using his infamous "suicide machine." In fact, Dr. Kevorkian, who has often been criticized for obscuring the ethical and legal debates with his crusade, was the impetus behind a Michigan law specifically criminalizing physician-assisted suicide (Angell, 1998). Nevertheless, he was acquitted three times by three different juries in trials held both before and after the passage of Michigan's law. He was eventually convicted of second degree murder after performing euthanasia on a man with amyotrophic lateral sclerosis (ALS) that was nationally televised on the program *60 Minutes*. These high-profile events have spurred to action advocates as well as opponents in their efforts to focus legislative attention on euthanasia and physician-assisted suicide. This legal history is discussed in chapter 2.

The highly publicized actions of Dr. Kevorkian have perhaps overshadowed the actions of countless physicians around the country who have engaged in assisted suicide and euthanasia with some regularity. A number of surveys of physicians and other health care professionals have shown that assisted suicide and euthanasia are not as rare as commonly believed (e.g., Back, Wallace, Starks, & Pearlman, 1996; Meier, Emmons, Wallenstein, Quill, Morrison, & Cassel, 1998). Other forms of hastened death have become even more frequent during recent decades, such as the refusal or termination of life-sustaining interventions and prescription of opioid medications at dosages that hasten death. The legal developments that have laid the groundwork for these changes in health care practices are discussed in the next chapter; however, the impact of these changes in health care practices on the growing acceptance of assisted suicide should not be underestimated. Indeed, a common criticism of legalization of assisted suicide rests on this very same premise, namely, that increased utilization of hastened death will lead to increased acceptance of this alternative and that in turn will eventually fuel even greater demand for hastened death. Whether this anticipated spiral is likely or reflects the fears of opponents of physician-assisted suicide is simply not known at this time.

UNDERSTANDING THE RISE AND FALL OF INTEREST IN PHYSICIAN-ASSISTED SUICIDE

Attempts to explain the fluctuation of interest in euthanasia and assisted suicide over the past 150 years have resulted in a number of differing theories and opinions. Ezekiel Emanuel, one of the leading scholars on the history of euthanasia, has argued that interest in euthanasia increases during periods of economic depression, where self-interest and Social Darwinism lead individuals to seek rapid, cost-efficient means of coping with death and disease (Emanuel, 1998). More liberal social policies, on the other hand, which typically promote social welfare and improved health care, are thought to hinder interest in assisted death. The economic assumptions of this theory, however, which may have been plausible when Emanuel first proposed it in the early 1990s, did not appear as credible in the late 20th century when the public acceptance of assisted suicide was at an all-time high at a time of sustained economic prosperity. Nevertheless, the possibility that social and economic factors that are theoretically independent of the developments in health care practice are responsible for this shift in public acceptance warrants further investigation.

Another "explanation" for the fluctuating interest in physician-assisted suicide and euthanasia pertains to the ongoing developments in health care practices. The first wave of interest, in the late 19th century, followed the emergence of "modern" medicine that, for the first time, allowed physicians a greater degree of control over the dying process. Along with these developments came the possibility that patients might live far longer than they had in past generations, but not necessarily with the same quality of life that they had come to expect. Many writers have speculated that interest in assisted suicide and euthanasia reflect a reaction to these developments, as patients become disenchanted with the prospect of extending life with severe pain or disability. This theory may help explain the gradual rise in interest in physician-assisted suicide and euthanasia during the 20th century, but it does little to explain the ebb and flow in interest over the preceding decades.

A more significant factor in the continuing euthanasia debates, at least during recent decades, may be the importance placed on patient autonomy and individual rights in determining the course of one's life and medical treatment options. In particular, as Americans struggle to identify the contours of their "rights" in both legal and medical areas, the desire for unrestricted decision making has steadily grown. The gradual change in patient and physician roles that began a century ago but has become increasingly pronounced in recent decades may be a much more relevant catalyst than economic concerns or medical progress. In fact, many proponents of legalization focus on the "right to die" as a justification for legalization. This issue is not likely to be resolved in the foreseeable future, and the need for guidance in helping develop informed social and legal policies will no doubt continue. These issues are the focus of the chapters that follow.

SUMMARY

The history of assisted suicide and euthanasia is far more extensive than many current theorists and clinicians assume. Despite pockets of "acceptance" of euthanasia during ancient times, these practices have been largely rejected by physicians, philosophers, and ethicists through much of the past two millennia. Interest in hastened death regained support from some sectors of the medical and scientific communities in the late 19th century, but these populist movements were relatively short-lived. The modern interest in assisted suicide began to increase in the 1980s, although the groundwork for this interest was probably rooted in the growing emphasis on patient autonomy that has characterized the last half-century of American medicine. Where this evolution will lead, however, is still unclear.

2

LEGAL STATUS OF EUTHANASIA AND PHYSICIAN-ASSISTED SUICIDE

To fully understand the legal issues related to euthanasia and physician-assisted suicide, one must first consider the status of suicide laws more generally. Suicide has long been recognized as a criminal offense in the United States and most developed countries, punishable (assuming the suicide attempt was unsuccessful) to varying degrees in different jurisdictions. The roots of this common law history can be found in Roman law, which treated most suicides as a form of felony. Although the early Romans considered suicide acceptable under some circumstances, suicide among the physically healthy was typically prohibited. In fact, the Romans, like many other early societies, refused to allow a proper burial for suicide deaths although the "punishment" imposed varied according to the circumstances of the suicide. The Greeks too prohibited suicide among the physically healthy and punished the offender by amputating the right hand of the deceased and denying traditional burial rituals (Gorsuch, 2000).

The legal status of suicide in medieval England was detailed in the writings of Henry de Bracton, a 13th-century English legal scholar who outlined the following conditions:

1. If a man has slain himself after having committed a felony, and for the purpose of evading the punishment therefore, his lands escheat and his chattels [wealth] are forfeited.
2. If he has brought death on himself "without any cause, through anger or ill will, as when he wished to hurt another, and could not fulfill what he wished," he is likewise to be punished with escheat of lands and forfeiture of goods.
3. If he commits suicide "from weariness of life or impatience of pain," his lands descend to his heir and his chattels only are to be confiscated.
4. If he was insane when he did the act that caused his death, or if he did it by accident, he is to be held guiltless, and forfeits nothing. (cited in Alesandro, 1994, p. 825)

Thus, an individual whose suicide was driven by pain or "weariness of life" would forfeit the wealth that would ordinarily pass to his descendents, but the descendents would not lose the land or title that would have been inherited. This treatment of suicide as a wrong that necessitated some form of punishment remained common practice in both England and many other medieval countries for many centuries. In fact, the punishment for suicide increased as the power of the Catholic Church grew. By the 15th and 16th centuries, individuals who committed suicide were denied a proper church burial and were often laid to rest in places designed to convey a lack of respect for the dead (e.g., alongside the highway).

William Blackstone, the principal chronicler of early British law, summarized the applicable punishments for suicide similarly:

> on the deceased's reputation . . . by an ignominious burial in the highway, with a stake driven through his body; on [his fortune], by a forfeiture of all his goods and chattels to the king: hoping that his care for either his own reputation, or the welfare of his family, would be some motive to restrain him from so desperate and wicked an act. (Blackstone, 1765/1992, p. 189)

Laws in the 13 colonies largely followed the practices of England, prohibiting suicide and punishing the offender through both reputation and estate. For example, a 1672 summary of the General Laws and Liberties of the Commonwealth of Massachusetts declared that an individual who commits suicide "shall be buried in some Common Highway where . . . a Cart-load of Stones [shall be] laid upon the Grave as a Brand of Infamy and also as a warning to others to beware of the like Damnable practices" (cited in Gorsuch, 2000, p. 632). Although most of the original colonies held similar opinions of suicide as a criminal offense, this attitude began to fade in the 18th century. The first step in this process began when Pennsylvania officially removed any criminal sanctions for a suicide in 1701 and, within a short period, most of the colonies had followed suit (Gorsuch, 2000). England was somewhat slower to remove criminal sanctions, waiting until the early 19th century to eliminate the practice of burying those who commit suicide by the highway with a stake driven through the body. Instead these individuals were allowed a burial in churchyards or other cemetery but occasionally without the usual religious ceremonies that accompanied most burials.

The long-standing treatment of suicide as a criminal act is important in understanding the culpability associated with aiding or assisting another person to commit suicide. According to English law, the aider or abettor to any crime, as either principal or accessory, was subject to the same punishment as the perpetrator of the crime (Alesandro, 1994). Because suicide was considered not only a felony but also a type of murder, the individual who assisted in a suicide was subject to punishment for the crime of murder as well. However, English law treated the abettor who was present during the offense quite differently than the abettor who was not. If the person who assisted in a suicide was present when it occurred, he was considered guilty of murder; if he was not present he was simply considered an accessory before the fact. However, because English law declared that an accessory could not be tried before the principal actor was tried, and the principal actor was deceased (if the suicide was successful), the individual who assisted in a completed suicide could not be tried. An unsuccessful suicide, on the other hand, was subject to prosecution, leaving the individual who assisted in a legally vulnerable position.

CASE LAW

If English law was somewhat inconsistent in its treatment of those who assisted in a suicide, early American law was even less clear. In the 18th century, the American states practiced neither the ignominious burial practice nor the forfeiture of goods in cases of suicide. In fact, an individual who committed suicide was not punished by the American court system in any significant manner. Nevertheless, the courts continued to punish acts such as the attempt to commit suicide or assisting in a suicide. The first recorded U.S. prosecution for the crime of abetting suicide occurred in the early 19th century in Massachusetts (*Commonwealth v. Bowen*, 1816). The defendant in this case, Bowen, was accused of assisting in the "self-murder" of another man, Jewett, who had himself been convicted of murder and was sentenced to death. Bowen was alleged to have "feloniously, wilfully, and of his malice aforethought" counseled Jewett to kill himself. Bowen's attorneys argued that the suicide was not murder within the meaning of the applicable statute, but the prosecuting attorney, citing the writings of Blackstone, "insisted that the adviser of one who commits a felony of himself is a murderer" (p. 358) Chief Justice Parker noted a sufficient correspondence between suicide and murder to permit the case to go to the jury; his instructions to the jury focused solely on the question of causation—whether Bowen's advice actually influenced Jewett to kill himself or merely engaged him in "idle talk." Bowen was eventually acquitted by the jury, apparently because it was unclear whether his advice was a sufficient cause of Jewett's death.

Treatment of assisted suicide as possible murder was common in many of the original 13 states. For example, early common law in the state of New York declared that an individual who assisted in the suicide of another could be indicted with murder even if the accused was not present when the suicide occurred (Alesandro, 1994). In 1828, the state of New York enacted the first statute explicitly prohibiting assisting in a suicide, although this law effectively reduced the offense from murder to manslaughter in the first degree. This law remained in effect even after the 1881 Penal Law revision declared that suicide attempts were no longer a punishable offense.

In 1953 the Supreme Court of Oregon addressed the relationship between suicide and assisted suicide in *State v. Bouse* (1953). In this case, Thomas Bouse had been convicted of murder in the first degree and sentenced to death for drowning his wife in a bathtub. The State had contended that Bouse had murdered his wife whereas Bouse claimed that his wife "wished to commit suicide, and that he . . . merely assisted her toward that end" (p. 803). The appellate court noted that although evidence of his wife's willing participation in her own death might have some bearing upon the punishment, it would not necessarily reduce the defendant's crime from murder to manslaughter. Furthermore, the court indicated that the verdict might have been different if the defendant's participation in his wife's death consisted only of (for example) running the water and helping her to get into the bathtub. Such actions would have fallen within the state's definition of manslaughter rather than murder. Actually holding her under the water was seen as a different kind of act.

Despite the widespread, and long-standing, prohibition against assisted suicide, several states throughout much of their legal history had no common law or statutes prohibiting assisting a suicide. In the wake of the growing national attention on assisted suicide, however, bills to regulate assisted suicide have been introduced in most of these states in the past few years. For example, in the early 1990s a bill proposing to legalize physician-assisted suicide in Vermont was defeated whereas legislation to criminalize assisted suicide was successful in Maryland, and legislation establishing civil liability for physicians participating in assisted suicide was passed in Virginia (cited in *Washington v. Glucksberg*, 1997).

Much of the current interest in physician-assisted suicide has been spurred by Jack Kevorkian, a retired pathologist who has publicly acknowledged assisting in the deaths of more than 100 individuals. After several unsuccessful prosecutions in Michigan in the early 1990s for participating in suicide deaths of his "patients" (with whom he did not have an ongoing treatment relationship but was merely providing a service upon request), Dr.

Kevorkian was ultimately convicted of second-degree murder after a 1998 act of euthanasia. This event, which was televised on CBS's 60 *Minutes* program, involved the administration of a lethal injection to Thomas Youk, a 52-year-old man diagnosed with amyotrophic lateral sclerosis (ALS; also known as Lou Gehrig's disease). Whereas Dr. Kevorkian's actions certainly fueled public interest and generated considerable publicity for end-of-life issues, the criminal cases against him have had relatively little legal significance. Rather, the primary case law surrounding the legality of physician-assisted suicide in the United States, and the existence, if any, of a "right to die" have been derived from a series of important state and federal cases. The four most important cases in U.S. legal history, Quinlan, Cruzan, Quill, and Glucksberg, are discussed next.

In the Matter of Karen Ann Quinlan

Perhaps the single most important case in the history of right-to-die legislation was the New Jersey Supreme Court's decision regarding the withdrawal of life-sustaining treatment for Karen Ann Quinlan (*In Re Quinlan*, 1976). In April 1975, Karen Quinlan, a 21-year-old woman, lost consciousness and stopped breathing for reasons that have never been completely clear. Despite attempts to provide mouth-to-mouth resuscitation, Karen suffered severe brain damage as a result of lack of oxygen. She fell into a permanent vegetative state and required assistance breathing with a mechanical respirator. Three months later, after being informed that she would never regain consciousness, her parents asked that the respirator be removed to allow their daughter to die. Hospital staff, however, opposed this request because Ms. Quinlan was not dead according to accepted medical or legal standards, which focused primarily on physical rather than cognitive functioning.

Making an unprecedented request to the New Jersey Superior Court, Ms. Quinlan's parents sought legal guardianship for their daughter to terminate the mechanical ventilation that was preserving her life. The Quinlans' petition was opposed by State officials as well as a Guardian Ad Litem who had been appointed to make decisions on Karen's behalf, all of whom agreed with the hospital staff's position that life-sustaining interventions should continue. The Superior Court rejected the Quinlans' contention that their daughter had a constitutionally protected right to die and refused to grant their petition for guardianship. However, the New Jersey Supreme Court overturned the lower court's decision, appointing Karen's father Joseph to be her legal guardian and supporting his right to make treatment decisions on behalf of his daughter.

The Quinlans' argument was rooted in a number of constitutional provisions including freedom of religion, protection against cruel and unusual punishment, and right to privacy. The Court rejected the first two of these arguments, but agreed that the Quinlans' right to privacy allowed them the privilege of making treatment decisions on their daughter's behalf. The Court opined that the right to privacy, which is not explicitly mentioned in the Constitution but is clearly assumed in numerous Supreme Court decisions, under certain specified circumstances, outweighed the State's interest in preserving the lives of its citizens. The Court wrote:

> [W]e have no hesitancy in deciding . . . that no external compelling interest of the State could compel Karen to endure the unendurable, only to vegetate a few measurable months with no realistic possibility of returning to any semblance of cognitive or sapient life. (p. 663)

Furthermore, the Court added:

> [T]he State's interest weakens and the individual's right to privacy grows as the degree of bodily invasion increases and the prognosis dims. Ultimately there comes a point at which the individual's rights overcome the State interest. (p. 664)

More important, the Court specifically refuted the Attorney General's contention that any action that hastened the death of another individual would constitute a criminal homicide:

> We conclude that there would be no criminal homicide in the circumstances of this case. We believe, first, that the ensuing death would not be homicide but rather expiration from existing natural causes. Secondly, even if it were to be regarded as homicide, it would not be unlawful. . . . There is a real . . . distinction between the unlawful taking of the life of another and the ending of artificial life support systems as a matter of self-determination. (pp. 669–670)

However, contained within the New Jersey Supreme Court's decision is the assumption that not all circumstances in which an individual might seek to refuse medical treatment and hasten his or her death would be viewed similarly. For example, the Court distinguished Quinlan's case from those in which the invasiveness of the procedure was minimal and the chances of recovery high. The Quinlan court also rejected the presumption that their decision constituted a precedent for some sort of "right to die." Likewise, the Court rebuffed the assertion that the refusal of life-sustaining or life-saving treatment constitutes attempted suicide ("suicide means something quite different in the law"). Following the Supreme Court's decision appointing her parents legal guardians, Karen was taken off the respirator which had been keeping her alive. Surprisingly, terminating this "life support" mechanism did not result in her immediate death; she remained alive and unconscious for another eight years.

Reaction to the Quinlan decision was rapid and widespread. More than 100 subsequent legal decisions extended the Quinlan ruling across the country, and numerous state statutes have been passed concerning end-of-life decision making, many in direct response to the Quinlan case (Angell, 1998).

These statutes fall under three primary types: advance directive statutes, surrogate decision-making statutes, and DNR order statutes. The details, and impact, of these statutes are discussed in the following chapter. The accumulated case and statutory law form a clear legal consensus that allowing an individual to die by refusing life-saving or life-sustaining interventions is acceptable even where no authoritative appellate case has yet been recorded. Three cornerstones form the basis of this legal consensus: there exists a legal right of autonomy or self-determination by which competent individuals have the right to refuse medical treatment, even if death results; persons who have lost decision-making capacity have a right to have their families decide to withhold or withdraw medical treatment; and there is a clear distinction between the refusal of treatment that results in death and more active methods of hastening death.

Although the Quinlan case generated national attention, the legal implications were limited because the case never reached the U.S. Supreme Court. (The Supreme Court denied *certiorari*, the mechanism by which lower court decisions are reviewed by a higher court, in 1976.) It would take nearly 15 years before a "right-to-die" case would reach the U.S. Supreme Court. This case, *Cruzan v. Director, Missouri Department of Health* (1990), firmly established the foundation for patient rights around a number of important issues such as refusal of treatment, advance directives, and the right to terminate life-sustaining interventions.

Cruzan v. Director, Missouri Department of Health

In January 1983, Nancy Cruzan, a 25-year-old Missouri woman, suffered massive injuries as a result of an automobile accident. Like Karen Ann Quinlan, Nancy Cruzan also suffered permanent, irreversible brain damage as a result of anoxia and fell into a permanent vegetative state. Several weeks later, at the request of her then-husband, hospital staff inserted a feeding tube to provide artificial nutrition and hydration. Nancy's condition remained essentially unchanged for the next several years, as the artificial nutrition and hydration provided her with ample nourishment to sustain her physical survival. It was not until May 1987 that her parents, who had assumed the role of her legal guardians, requested that the hospital withdraw the feeding and hydration tube and allow her to die. The hospital refused and the Cruzans subsequently filed suit against the director of the Missouri Department of Health.

The Jasper Missouri County Circuit Court ruled in favor of the Cruzans, asserting that Nancy's "right to liberty" outweighed the State's interest in preserving her life, and ordered that all life-sustaining interventions ("death prolonging procedures"; p. 2843) be terminated. The court's decision was based in part on testimony provided by a former roommate of Nancy's who stated that Nancy had told her, in essence, "if she were sick or injured she would not wish to continue her life unless she could live at least half-way normally" (p. 2843).

However, upon appeal to the Missouri Supreme Court, this decision was overturned, finding the friend's testimony "unreliable for the purposes of determining her intent" (p. 268). The Supreme Court asserted that Missouri law required "clear and convincing evidence" before a decision to terminate life support could be made on behalf of an incompetent person. Moreover, the Court disputed the contention that the right to refuse life-sustaining treatment was in any way absolute. Of note, the application of the "clear and convincing evidence standard" was virtually unique to Missouri, as every other state (except New York) that had established a legal standard for decision making on behalf of incompetent individuals accepts a "preponderance of the evidence" as the threshold for decision making. The Missouri Supreme Court wrote in *Cruzan*:

> [T]he argument made here, that Nancy will not recover, is but a thinly veiled statement that her life in its present form is not worth living. Yet a diminished quality of life does not support a decision to cause death. (p. 422)

In 1989, the U.S. Supreme Court granted *certiorari*, agreeing for the first time to hear arguments regarding the "right to die" that had begun to accelerate in response to the Quinlan case. In June 1990, the U.S. Supreme Court affirmed the Missouri decision in a 5 to 4 vote, stating that the "clear and convincing" provision was indeed constitutional. However, Judge Rehnquist, writing for the majority, stated "the principle that a competent person has a constitutionally protected liberty interest in refusing unwanted medical treatment may be inferred from our prior decisions" (p. 2270). Thus, despite refusing to support the family's request to terminate life-support measures, the *Cruzan* opinion appeared to bolster the position that some life-terminating actions can be a constitutionally protected right. Citing early case law requiring a patient's consent to any medical treatment, the Court quoted New York State Justice Benjamin Cardozo, who stated that "every human being of adult years and sound mind has a right to determine what shall be done with his own body" (*Schloendorff v. Society of New York Hospitals*, 1914, pp. 129–130). However, despite the clear support for patient autonomy in its opinion, the Court also granted considerable leeway to individual states in determining what standards and procedures were required in decisions regarding incompetent patients and refusal of life-sustaining interventions.

Not all members of the Supreme Court agreed with the position that termination of life-sustaining interventions was a constitutionally protected right. Among the most vocal opponents to this "right" was Justice Scalia, who, despite siding with the majority, strongly disputed the contention that termination of life-sustaining treatment differed in any meaningful way from suicide. Justice Scalia criticized the distinction between passive methods of hastening death and more active methods such as physician-assisted suicide, writing "[i]t would not make much sense to say that one may not kill oneself by walking into the sea, but may sit on the beach until submerged by the incoming tide" (p. 2861). Furthermore, he argued that "starving oneself to death," even in the context of a terminal illness or permanent vegetative state, is "no different from putting a gun to one's temple as far as the common-law definition of suicide is concerned" (p. 2861).

Despite Justice Scalia's opposition to the prospect of legitimizing methods of hastening death, a more common reaction to the *Cruzan* decision was to suggest that a similar right to hasten death under intolerable circumstances should be extended to all terminally ill individuals. Indeed, this reaction formed the basis for Timothy Quill's argument to the New York State Court of Appeals, described in the section *Vacco v. Quill*, following his conviction for participating in the assisted suicide of a terminally ill patient. Likewise, in *Compassion in Dying v. Washington* (1996), the 9th Circuit Court of Appeals ruled that the liberty interest in refusing life-sustaining treatment acknowledged by the *Cruzan* Court was analogous to a liberty interest in ending one's life through physician-assisted suicide. The legal decisions that followed from these cases are discussed further below.

Following the U.S. Supreme Court's decision, the Cruzans' suit was returned to the original circuit court with the standard of "clear and convincing evidence" now affirmed. In December 1990, after hearing new "clear and convincing evidence" about Nancy Cruzan's wishes, the court again ruled in favor of the Cruzans. The Missouri Health Department subsequently withdrew their opposition and terminated all life-sustaining treatments. Nancy Cruzan died 12 days later, nearly 7 years after the accident that caused her injuries.

Washington v. Glucksberg

The surge of interest in euthanasia and physician-assisted suicide brought the "right to die" issue squarely into the legal spotlight. Two cases that reached the U.S. Supreme Court simultaneously directly challenged the status quo, but from slightly different legal perspectives (*Vacco v. Quill*, 1997; *Washington v. Glucksberg*, 1997). The first of these came in the form of a civil lawsuit filed by Compassion in Dying, a Washington-based nonprofit organization established to counsel and assist terminally ill patients in ending their lives. Their suit challenged the constitutionality of the Washington Promoting Suicide Law that made assisting in a suicide a criminal act. Joining in the suit were three terminally ill patients (none of whom survived the litigation) and five physicians with extensive experience treating terminally ill individuals, all of whom had received requests from patients for assistance in ending their lives. The basis for their argument, which sought to strike down a law established in 1854, was that a prohibition against assisted suicide violated the Due Process and Equal Protection Clauses of the 14th Amendment of the U.S. Constitution.

The plaintiffs argued that because a terminally ill individual who requires life-sustaining medical treatment was permitted to hasten death by refusing interventions, the refusal to allow another terminally ill individual to hasten his or her death through physician-assisted suicide simply because they didn't require life-sustaining interventions constituted a violation of the Equal Protection Clause.[1] In addition, the suit argued that by making physician-assisted suicide illegal, the State statute placed an excessive burden on terminally ill patients and their physicians in the exercise of their constitutionally protected liberty interest (a violation of the Due Process Clause). They cited previous Supreme Court decisions that deemed many personal decisions, such as abortion, procreation, and the right to refuse medical treatment, to be so fundamental to personal liberty as to be either totally or largely free from government interference. The plaintiffs argued that the decision to commit suicide should be included among these personal decisions.

Washington State's Attorney General countered the plaintiff's arguments, asserting that the State's interest in preserving life and preventing suicide outweighed these infringements on the Equal Protection and Due Process Clauses. In May 1994, however, the U.S. District Court for the Western District of Washington ruled in favor of the plaintiffs, finding that the Promoting Suicide Law was an unconstitutional violation of the 14th Amendment by placing an undue burden on terminally ill patients and physicians in exercising their right to liberty and treating different groups of terminally ill individuals differently. The State of Washington appealed this decision to the 9th Circuit Court of Appeals, which initially reversed the District Court's decision in a 2 to 1 decision. However, the plaintiffs appealed for a rehearing on the basis of the extraordinary importance of the case (*Washington v. Glucksberg*, 1997). Following extensive oral arguments, presented to an 11-judge panel, the Court reversed its earlier decision, affirming the District Court's decision that found the Promoting Suicide Law to be unconstitutional. However, the 9th Circuit based its decision only on the Due Process Clause, finding no violation of the Equal Protection Clause. In his opinion for the 9th Circuit, Justice Stephen Reinhardt wrote:

> In order to answer the question of whether the Washington statute violates the Due Process Clause insofar as it prohibits the provision of certain medical assistance to terminally ill, competent adults who wish to hasten their own deaths, we first determine whether there is a liberty

---

[1]The Equal Protection Clause of the 14th Amendment declares, in essence, that all similarly situated individuals must be afforded equal rights and protections. The Due Process Clause, on the other hand, states that the government cannot interfere with the expression of any individual's rights.

interest in choosing the time and manner of one's death—a question sometimes phrased in common parlance as: Is there a right to die? Because we hold that there is, we must then determine whether prohibiting physicians from prescribing life-ending medication for use by terminally ill patients who wish to die violates due process rights. . . . *Casey* and *Cruzan* provide persuasive evidence that the constitution encompasses a due process liberty interest in controlling the time and manner of one's death—that there is, in short, a constitutionally recognized "right to die." (pp. 798–799)

This case, which was appealed to the U.S. Supreme Court, was decided in conjunction with the New York State right-to-die case, *Vacco v. Quill.*

Vacco v. Quill

In March 1991, Dr. Timothy Quill, of Rochester, New York, went public with an account of the suicide of one of his patients. Dr. Quill had prescribed barbiturates for his patient Diane, in part for pain relief, and in part to make it possible for her to end her life. Diane was suffering from acute leukemia and she had made the decision to refuse treatment in order to maximize the quality of her remaining life by avoiding the unpleasant effects of treatment. In the final phases of her illness, Diane took the barbiturates and ended her life (*Vacco v. Quill*, 1997). Following the publication of his article and the disclosure of Diane's identity by an anonymous source, the Monroe County (Rochester, New York) District Attorney submitted the case to a grand jury, but the grand jury did not indict Dr. Quill despite the clear prohibition against assisted suicide in New York State law.[2] Likewise, the New York State Board for Professional Medical Conduct concluded that a charge of professional misconduct was not warranted in Dr. Quill's case. Although Dr. Quill's public disclosure prompted extensive discussion, the conclusions of the grand jury and the Board for Professional Medical Conduct in Dr. Quill's case had no precedential value for cases involving physician-assisted suicide.

Three years later, Dr. Quill and two other physicians, along with three terminally ill patients, sued the state of New York, citing the same issues that were raised in *Washington v. Glucksberg*. Quill and company alleged that the State's prohibition against physician-assisted suicide, referred to as the "Aiding and Promoting Suicide Laws," violated the 14th Amendment's Equal Protection and Due Process Clauses. Like the suit filed by Compassion in Dying, the plaintiffs alleged that because terminally ill patients who relied on life-sustaining interventions were allowed to hasten their deaths through the refusal of life-sustaining interventions but terminally ill patients who did

---

[2]New York law declares "A person is guilty of manslaughter when he intentionally aids another person to commit suicide" (McKinney's Consolidated Laws of New York, 1993).

not require life-sustaining interventions were not permitted, under State law, to hasten their deaths, this discrepancy constituted unequal treatment under the law and was therefore a violation of the Equal Protection Clause (*Compassion in Dying v. State of Washington*, 1996). They also claimed that the failure to allow individuals to choose the manner and timing of death, which they argued was a constitutionally protected liberty, was a violation of the Due Process Clause.

The Federal District Court in which this suit was first heard rejected the plaintiffs' arguments, ruling that there was no fundamental liberty interest in physician-assisted suicide and that therefore the Due Process Clause was not applicable. Judge Griesa also ruled that the New York State Aiding and Promoting Suicide Laws were constitutional and therefore were not in violation of the Equal Protection Clause. Two years later, however, in April 1996, the 2nd Circuit Court of Appeals reversed this decision, holding that the differential legal status of competent terminally ill patients who wish to hasten their deaths by taking lethal medication versus those who seek to end their life by terminating life-support mechanisms was indeed a violation of the Equal Protection Clause (*Quill v. Vacco*, 1996). The Court ruled that, despite the assisted suicide ban's apparent general applicability,

> New York law does not treat equally all competent persons who are in the final stages of fatal illness and wish to hasten their deaths . . . [because] those in the final stages of terminal illness who are on life support systems are allowed to hasten their deaths by directing the removal of such systems; but those who are similarly situated, except for the previous attachment of life sustaining equipment, are not allowed to hasten death by self administering prescribed drugs. (p. 724)

This case was subsequently appealed to the U.S. Supreme Court.

The Supreme Court Rules

In January 1997, the U.S. Supreme Court heard arguments regarding both *Washington v. Glucksberg* and *Vacco v. Quill*. Both cases essentially argued that a "right-to-die" exists for terminally ill, competent individuals and that laws prohibiting physician-assisted suicide were therefore unconstitutional. Whereas the legal claims in both cases were rooted in the 14th Amendment, the 2nd and 9th Circuits differed as to the precise reason for their decisions. *Washington v. Glucksberg* argued that the State's anti-suicide law violated the Due Process Clause of the 14th Amendment, whereas *Vacco v. Quill* based their argument on that amendment's Equal Protection Clause.

The Supreme Court, in a unanimous opinion, described the 700-year history of legal precedents supporting the prohibition of assisted suicide, beginning with the writings of the medieval English legal scholar Henry de Bracton (described in the beginning of this chapter). This history, the Court noted, was significant in that Due Process claims have typically been applied to fundamental rights and liberties that are "deeply rooted in this Nation's history and tradition" (*Vacco v. Quill,* 1997, p. 2271). The right to hasten one's death, although consistent with the Cruzan decision, has never been considered a "right" per se. Indeed, although hastened death was certainly an expected outcome of Cruzan, the Court's decision in that case focused principally on the right to refuse unwanted medical treatments, not the right to end one's life. Likewise, an analysis of Due Process claims required the Court to consider whether Washington's prohibition of assisted suicide served some legitimate State interest. They ruled affirmatively, asserting that Washington has an "unqualified interest in the preservation of human life" and that the prohibition against assisted suicide served that end.

With regard to the New York State law prohibiting assisted suicide, the Court offered a somewhat different explanation for overturning the 2nd Circuit's decision, which was based on the Equal Protection Clause rather than the Due Process Clause. The Court wrote:

> [N]either New York's ban on assisting suicide nor its statutes permitting patients to refuse medical treatment treats anyone differently than anyone else or draw any distinctions between persons. *Everyone,* regardless of physical condition, is entitled, if competent to refuse unwanted medical lifesaving treatment; *no one* is permitted to assist a suicide. Generally speaking, laws that apply evenhandedly to all "unquestionably comply" with the Equal Protection Clause. (*Vacco v. Quill,* 1997, p. 2295; emphasis in original)

Thus, the Court essentially ruled that although the Equal Protection Clause requires that state laws treat similar cases in the same manner, it is permissible to allow differential treatments when cases are distinguishable in some meaningful way. Terminally ill individuals who are dependent on life-sustaining interventions were thus deemed to represent a class distinct from terminally ill individuals who do not require such interventions, making discrepancies among the alternatives available to these two groups acceptable.

Perhaps the most significant aspect of the Court's decisions in *Washington v. Glucksberg* and *Vacco v. Quill* came not in the justification for these unanimous decisions but rather in Chief Justice Rehnquist's commentary, which accompanied the decisions. Although these cases obviously supported the right of individual states to prohibit assisted suicide, the possibility of legalizing assisted suicide was clearly intimated as well. Chief Justice Rehnquist, writing for the Court majority, wrote: "[t]hroughout the Nation, Americans are engaged in an earnest and profound debate about the morality, legality, and practicality of physician-assisted suicide. Our holding permits this debate to continue, as it should in a democratic society" (p. 2275).

Despite concurring with the majority opinion, Justice O'Conner also implied that the possibility of legalization was not unrealistic. She cited an early opinion of Justice Brandeis, who wrote that "the . . . challenging task of crafting appropriate procedures for safeguarding . . . liberty interests is entrusted to the 'laboratory' of the States . . . in the first instance" (p. 2303). This opinion, coupled with those of Justice Rehnquist and others, has been viewed as supportive of the potential legalization of assisted suicide.

"RIGHT-TO-DIE" LEGISLATION

Following the resurgence of public interest in physician-assisted suicide and euthanasia, it was perhaps to be expected that state legislatures and the general public would begin to debate the possibility of legalization. The first public referenda of the modern era occurred in Washington and California, in 1991 and 1992, respectively. In 1991, the Washington chapter of the Hemlock Society (an organization dedicated to eliminating prohibitions against assisted suicide and euthanasia) sought to amend that state's Living Will law to include decisions regarding physician-assisted suicide and euthanasia. Initiative 119, as this proposal was called, asked voters the following question: "Shall adult patients who are in a medically terminal condition be permitted to request and receive from a physician aid-in-dying?" Some writers have criticized the Washington initiative for its ambiguous wording of assisted death, using the term *aid-in-dying*, which might reasonably be construed to imply palliative care measures as well as measures to hasten death (Annas, 1994), although the initiative defined aid-in-dying as "a medical service, provided by a physician, that will end the life of a conscious and mentally competent qualified patient, when requested voluntarily by the patient through a written directive" (Annas, 1994, p. 1421). Not surprisingly, proponents of this initiative argued that terminally ill patients should have the right to choose hastened death under certain circumstances. Opponents, on the other hand, argued that the proposal had inadequate safeguards and suggested, through advertising campaigns, that physicians would essentially have a license to kill patients whose lives they felt were not worthwhile. Although voters rejected Initiative 119 by a margin of 54% to 46%, the legislation did approve changes in the state's Natural Death Act of 1979 (Annas, 1994) that facilitated the use of advance directives to refuse or withdraw life-sustaining interventions. Moreover, the defeat of Initiative 119 led to the emergence of Compassion in Dying, the Washington-based organization that led subsequent challenges to the state's law prohibiting assisted suicide.

Another public initiative, Proposition 161, the Humane and Dignified Death Act, was brought before California voters in 1992 (Annas, 1994). This initiative was a revised version of an earlier proposal, also sponsored by the Hemlock Society, which did not qualify for placement on the 1988 ballot. The language of Proposition 161 was similar to that used in Washington's Initiative 119, but it defined "aid-in-dying" somewhat more explicitly ("a medical procedure that will terminate the life of the qualified patient in a painless, humane and dignified manner, whether administered by the physician at the patient's direction or whether the physician provides the means to the patient for self-administration" (Annas, 1994, p. 1242). Proposition 161 also addressed many of the concerns raised regarding the Washington initiative, including clearer safeguards to prevent potential abuses. Like Washington's Initiative 119, Proposition 161 defined *qualified patients* as those with a life expectancy of 6 months or less and specified special requirements of oversight for requests coming from residents of skilled nursing facilities. Despite these added protections, California's Proposition 161 was defeated by the same margin as Washington's Initiative, 54% to 46%.

It was not until November 1994, when Oregon voters approved the Death with Dignity Act, that a ballot initiative supporting legalized assisted suicide garnered majority approval. This proposal, Ballot Measure 16, which passed by a relatively narrow margin (52% to 48%), supported legislative changes permitting physicians to prescribe a lethal medication to competent, terminally ill individuals for the purpose of ending their lives. Despite passing in 1994, the Oregon Death with Dignity Act (1996; also known as the ODDA or DWDA) was not enacted until 1997 after a second ballot reaffirmed it and a civil case (*Lee v. Haclerod*, 1997) challenging the act as unconstitutional failed. Since 1997, researchers and clinicians have been monitoring this law closely to assess the extent to which this act has fulfilled its goals. The impact of the Oregon statute is the focus of chapter 9.

After the Oregon law was passed, proposals to legalize assisted suicide were introduced in a number of other states (Alaska, Arizona, California, Colorado, Connecticut, Illinois, Maine, Maryland, Massachusetts, Michigan, Mississippi, New Hampshire, New Mexico, New York, Nebraska, Rhode Island, Vermont, Wisconsin), but none has been successful to date (N. M. Gorsuch, 2000). To the contrary, several states have enacted laws specifically prohibiting assisted suicide, either clarifying existing legislation or making new law where no explicit prohibition had previously existed (e.g., Iowa, Maryland, Rhode Island, Virginia). Nevertheless, stimulated by a growing body of research and evolving policy debates, a general consensus has emerged that, although a "right-to-die" may not be constitutionally protected, assisted suicide legislation may be legally acceptable nonetheless.

SUMMARY

This review of the legal history of assisted suicide and other methods of hastening death reveals a gradual evolution in the thinking and acceptability of these interventions. Although early laws were rigid in their treatment of individuals who assisted in the suicide of another individual, more recent developments have gradually expanded the boundaries and defined the conditions under which hastened death can occur. In the United States, this process began with the *Quinlan* case, which upheld the right to terminate life-sustaining interventions. Subsequent Supreme Court cases such as *Cruzan*, *Glucksberg*, and *Quill* have further clarified the parameters of interventions to hasten death. The most dramatic legal shift, however, occurred in 1997, when Oregon enacted the first legislation to permit assisted suicide. The impact of this legislation and the thorny legal and medical issues it raises are described in detail in chapter 9.

3

DO NOT RESUSCITATE ORDERS, LIVING WILLS, AND SURROGATE DECISION MAKING

The debates regarding the legalization of physician-assisted suicide and euthanasia have not occurred in a vacuum. On the margin of these debates, mechanisms have been developed that can influence and often expedite the dying process. These mechanisms, such as DNR orders, Living Wills, Durable Power of Attorney, and other legal instruments have been increasingly sought by medically ill individuals who are not necessarily interested in ending their lives immediately yet want to exert some control over their deaths. For example, patients may use advance directives to avoid unwanted but potentially life-sustaining interventions such as artificial nutrition and hydration or dialysis or to withdraw interventions that have already begun such as mechanical ventilation. There are many obvious reasons why patients want to avoid unpleasant health states such as the irreversible coma that characterized the last years of Karen Quinlan and Nancy Cruzan. But the right to avoid such situations, and availability of mechanisms for doing so have been relatively recent developments in health care law. This chapter focuses on several of the major developments in health care law that pertain to the end of life, many of which represent important alternatives or adjuncts to the issues of physician-assisted suicide and euthanasia that are the primary focus of this book.

DEFINITIONS AND DISTINCTIONS

A number of methods now exist which enable patients to specify in advance how treatment decisions will be made during the final stages of their life. Of these various methods, all of which fall under the general umbrella of *advance directives*, DNR orders and living wills have received the most attention in medical and scientific circles and therefore comprise the primary focus of this chapter. Other, related issues, however, such as surrogate decision making and Durable Power of Attorney assignments, are discussed as well. The DNR order is the most limited type of advance directive, because it simply dictates a decision preference (to refuse) a single intervention (cardiopulmonary resuscitation; CPR). Because CPR is the principal method for restoring life after heart failure, DNR orders specifying that this intervention should not be undertaken essentially inform medical personnel that the individuals wish to be allowed to die when their hearts fail. Living Wills, on the other hand, have a wide range of scope and complexity and therefore have the potential to offer far more detail about which interventions are desired and which are not and under what circumstances particular medical decisions (e.g., removal of life-support) should be made.[1] More recently, several states have adopted a more portable form of advance directive, termed the *Physician Order for Life Sustaining Treatment*. These orders enable physicians to readily understand and implement the patient's preferences for life-sustaining interventions through the use of a universally accepted, standardized legal instrument. The instruments are listed in Table 3.1.

However, when a patient loses the capacity to make treatment decisions (discussed in more detail in chap. 7), a surrogate decision-maker is typically asked (or required) to make treatment decisions. This appointment can be formal (e.g., through a Durable Power of Attorney for health care decision making or a "Health Care Proxy), both of which are legal mechanisms for appointing a particular individual as proxy decision-maker in case of later incompetence, or it can be informal, when health care providers ask family members to act as surrogates without seeking a legal determination of incompetence. Conflicts may arise as a result of these methods of decision making; an appointed surrogate may not wish to follow the directions speci-

---

[1]Note that many writers refer to living wills and advance directives synonymously although in fact, living wills are a specific type of advance directive whereas the term *advance directive* encompasses any legal dictate specified by the patient prior to becoming incompetent (e.g., including appointing a surrogate decision-maker; Winick, 1998).

TABLE 3.1
Advance Directive Mechanisms

Method	Scope	Specificity
Do Not Resuscitate order	Narrow	High
Living Will	Variable	Variable
Values History	Broad	Low
Health Care Proxy	Broad	None
Durable Power of Attorney	Broad	None
Physicians Order for Life-Sustaining Treatment	Broad	High

fied in the patient's Living Will. Despite limitations and difficulties inherent in each of these approaches (and perhaps because of them), there has been slow but steady growth in the use of all types of advance directives over the past three decades, presumably reflecting a growing desire on the part of patients to control not only their lives but their deaths as well.

Although patient autonomy in health care decision making increased steadily throughout the 20th century, interest in advance directives catapulted into the public spotlight in response to the highly publicized cases of Karen Quinlan and Nancy Cruzan. As discussed in the preceding chapter, both of those cases involved requests to discontinue life-support mechanisms by the parents of young women who were in a persistent vegetative state (i.e., coma). Although both cases ultimately supported the right to refuse life-sustaining interventions, they each reaffirmed the importance of clearly documenting a patient's preferences in advance. In fact, the U.S. Supreme Court's decision in *Cruzan* essentially offered a direct endorsement of living wills and other advance directives as a mechanism for expressing such wishes, but nevertheless indicated that decision-making autonomy might be limited when such documentation was absent. The *Cruzan* decision characterized the use of advanced directives as a mechanism to ensure that one's constitutionally protected right to privacy, the underpinnings of self-determination, would be maintained in the event of incapacity. In response to these and other legal decisions, and spurred by the emergence of diseases such as HIV/AIDS, which initially appeared to result in a gradual but inevitable physical and mental deterioration leading to death,[2] medically ill and elderly individuals began considering writing advance directives as a way to avoid an unpleasant and unnecessarily prolonged death.

---

[2]Recent treatment innovations have dramatically slowed or altered the course of HIV/AIDS, and many have begun to characterize this illness as a chronic rather than fatal disease. However, at present there is little evidence to contradict the assumption that the long-term course of HIV/AIDS is one of inevitable deterioration leading to death.

THE PRINCIPLE OF SELF-DETERMINATION

The right to control the course of one's medical treatment (and by extension the dying process) has become increasingly accepted as a general ethical principle in health care (see, e.g., the President's Commission for the Study of Ethical Problems in Medicine and Biomedical and Behavioral Research, 1982). Whether the desire to determine the course of one's illness and treatment reflects a psychological need for control or a cultural value we place on privacy and autonomy (e.g., as evidenced by the importance accorded the constitutional right to privacy by the Supreme Court) or some combination of these and other factors, patient autonomy has consistently grown over the past century (Faden & Beauchamp, 1986). This movement culminated in the 1990 Patient Self-Determination Act, legislation that required institutions reimbursed by Medicare (hospitals, nursing facilities, hospices, etc.) to inform patients of their right to participate in medical decisions and complete advance directives (Winick, 1998). In addition to establishing legal standards for many advance directives, the Patient Self-Determination Act specifically required that each institution must (a) provide information concerning an individual's statutory right to make decisions concerning medical care, including the right to accept or refuse treatment and to formulate advance directives, (b) provide a copy of the institution's written policies with respect to the implementation of such rights, and (c) document in the medical record whether the patient has signed an advance directive.

Although this legislative support for patient autonomy certainly bolstered, and formalized, the medical community's attention to advance directives, the Patient Self-Determination Act may have been merely an exclamation point on a sentence that was already written. Interest in and utilization of advance directives consistently grew during the 1970s and 1980s. Many writers have attributed this trend to the increasing availability of life-extending medical interventions, which presumably heightened fears of an unpleasant or undignified death. Whether or not this explanation is correct, advance directives have become an important aspect of health care and patient well-being both at the end of life as well as in the years leading up to death.

DO NOT RESUSCITATE ORDERS

Once considered a miracle of modern medical science, the practice of CPR has changed dramatically over the past several decades. For many years after its discovery, CPR was routinely applied in virtually any instance of sudden death. However, the long-term results of these "life-saving" interventions were often disappointing, leading many to question the real utility of CPR (Schonwetter, Teasdale, Taffet, Robinson, & Luchi, 1991). Research has consistently documented that relatively few patients experience meaningful recovery after CPR, particularly when the patient is elderly or has significant medical problems. In fact, most studies of CPR have found that less than 10% of resuscitated patients survive long enough to be discharged from the hospital after a cardiac arrest (Murphy, Murray, Robinson, & Campion, 1989). Moreover, many patients who are resuscitated suffer adverse consequences from the CPR itself. Physical injuries (e.g., broken ribs), hypoxia, or the need for mechanical ventilation to continue breathing are all too common results of CPR, each of which can markedly diminish the patient's overall quality of life.

Given the potential for so many adverse consequences associated with CPR, it was perhaps inevitable that physicians would become increasingly reluctant to apply this intervention in cases where recovery seemed unlikely (e.g., with elderly, seriously ill individuals). Initially, this reluctance emerged in an informal, ethically questionable manner, using "slow codes" (a term applied to cases in which CPR was deliberately delayed, withheld, or applied in a half-hearted manner long after the potential for success had passed). Eventually, like most areas of medical decision making, patients themselves became more involved in decisions regarding when or whether to use CPR. Because CPR decisions arise in emergency situations, however, informed and thoughtful decisions regarding whether to have CPR applied must necessarily be made in advance. The need for a mechanism to convey patient preferences for CPR (or, more accurately, preferences to have CPR withheld when cardiac failure has occurred) led to the first widespread form of advance directives, the DNR order.

DNR orders were made legal in the 1980s, but they were not used widely until the early 1990s. In New York State, DNR orders were officially recognized in a 1988 amendment to the State's Public Health Laws (Misbin, O'Hare, Lederberg, & Holland, 1993). This provision allowed patients or their legal surrogates to authorize medical professionals to withhold resuscitation in the event of a cardiopulmonary arrest. Following this amendment, hospitals throughout New York began using DNR orders for many elderly or terminally ill patients, although the implementation of DNR orders varied widely across different facilities (Misbin et al., 1993).

The question as to who is authorized to make decisions regarding DNR orders has been less clear than the law might imply. In one research study, patients hospitalized with a medical illness unanimously agreed that decisions regarding DNR orders should only be made by patients themselves (Wolf-Klein, Wagner, & Silverstone, 1992). Hospital staff, on the other hand, were far more likely to recommend that family members participate in DNR decisions. This discrepancy may reflect the hospital staff's awareness that family members actually participate in many end-of-life decisions, or it may simply reflect the discomfort many health care professionals feel when forced to discuss end-of-life issues with their patients. Some writers have offered an alternative suggestion, proposing that hospital review panels or ethics committees be charged with the responsibility of making DNR decisions rather than leaving the decision to patients or families, particularly given the numerous ethical concerns that arise in these situations (Preston, 1995). But despite these varied opinions, the principle of patient autonomy has mandated that patients or their legally appointed surrogates be the sole decision-makers in this area.

The tendency of physicians to avoid end-of-life discussions is well known among health care professionals and medical ethicists. In fact, avoidance of end-of-life decisions is often cited as a primary reason for the underuse of DNR orders. Early studies consistently noted that DNR discussions between physicians and their terminally ill patients were relatively uncommon, occurring only in 15–30% of cases despite the obvious relevance of the matter for all terminally patients (L. L. Emanuel & Emanuel, 1989). Attempts to better understand this apparent underuse of DNR orders has generated several alternative explanations, encompassing both emotional and pragmatic reasons. For example, several commentators have cited time as a substantial obstacle to DNR discussions; patient–physician discussions regarding advance directives are rarely reimbursed by insurance providers (L. L. Emanuel & Emanuel, 1989). For busy physicians, the amount of time required to engage in meaningful discussions of DNR and other end-of-life issues might exceed the amount of time they have allotted to spend with their patient on a particular day. Thus, the need to give priority to treatment-related discussions against discussions regarding end-of-life care options, with the latter being obviously more difficult and uncomfortable for many physicians, presents a significant obstacle to full use of available alternatives such as DNR orders.

A number of emotional factors have also been cited as potential obstacles to open physician–patient discussions of DNR. For example, a recent report from the American Medical Association's (AMA) Council on Ethical and Judicial Affairs (1998) described the process of obtaining DNR orders in particularly cynical terms. The report suggested that DNR discussions were often assigned to medical students or nurses, with most physicians using any means available to avoid discussing issues related to death and dying (e.g., the advantages and disadvantages of cardiopulmonary resuscitation) with their patients. When doctors were unable to avoid the topic of resuscitation, DNR discussions often occurred under urgent circumstances, when death was imminent. Moreover, because the process of obtaining a DNR order from a patient is so laden with framing biases (a tendency to present information in a manner that emphasizes the physicians' best judgments rather than an objective rendering of the facts), the eventual decision was often more a reflection of the physician's desires than the patient's. (AMA, 1988).

Perhaps the most troubling aspect of the DNR "revolution" has been the concern, on the part of patients, family members, and medical professionals, that DNR orders might be misinterpreted to mean that patients want no further interventions of any type. Although this fear may be exaggerated by physicians wary of engaging in DNR discussions, several studies have suggested that patients with DNR orders are more likely to be denied intensive care beds, receive less nursing attention, and not be presented with potentially available interventions (e.g., Shelley, Zahorchak, & Gambrill, 1987). However, such findings are not unique to the DNR order. Similar results have been observed for elderly patients in general, a group that often receives less aggressive medical care regardless of the existence of DNR orders (Shelley et al., 1987). Some writers have explained these findings by suggesting that the provision of interventions such as CPR is often inappropriate, even if desired by the patient or family members, when the patient has an extremely poor prognosis.

The belief that available interventions with a low probability of success should not be offered to patients has led to a new struggle within health care decision making, with health care providers often seeking to limit excessive resource use by dying patients. Considerable debate has focused on the issue of refusing to provide treatments that the patient desires if the likelihood of success is low, often couching this debate in discussions of "medical futility." The construct of medical futility is discussed later in this chapter. But regardless of whether medical interventions are considered appropriate in any particular circumstance, there is little doubt that the presence of a DNR order says nothing about an individual's preferences for other forms of treatment, particularly when one considers that many medical interventions are aimed at comfort care rather than extending life. Nevertheless, reports of physicians or other health care professionals choosing to withhold interventions (e.g., CPR) have appeared with some regularity, highlighting the difficulty many medical professionals have in accepting patient autonomy as the determining principle guiding medical treatment decisions.

One response to the growing concern regarding the implementation of DNR orders has been to increase the detail and specificity of advance directives. Increased specificity has the potential to explicitly document an individual's preference for a wide range of medical interventions rather than simply specifying preferences for DNR and leaving other medical decisions untouched. This need for greater breadth and specificity eventually led to the emergence of "living wills" as a mechanism for providing advance directives for a range of end-of-life health care decisions.[3] Potential treatment options such as dialysis, artificial hydration and nutrition, chemotherapy and antibiotics, and virtually any other possible intervention can be specified in a Living Will, with detailed documents enabling the writer to specify the

---

[3]Although Living Wills have existed for several decades, very little attention was focused on these legal instruments prior to the 1980s. Since that time, physicians, bioethicists, and legal scholars have become increasingly enamored with the Living Will as a mechanism for bolstering autonomous decision making even after the patient has lost the ability to make an independent decision.

conditions under which each should be applied or withdrawn. In fact, the emergence of Living Wills and related legal instruments (e.g., Durable Power of Attorney or Health Care Proxy designations) has led to dramatic changes in the way that health care decisions are made for medically ill and terminally ill individuals.

LIVING WILL AND HEALTH CARE PROXY LEGISLATION

Although the emphasis on advance directives did not fully take hold until after the widely publicized *Quinlan* and *Cruzan* cases, the first Living Will legislation emerged in the 1940s, when the movement toward patient autonomy first began to gather steam in the United States. However, this early interest in Living Wills had little impact on medical practice, as the general perception during the middle of the 20th century was that Living Wills were analogous to euthanasia, a practice that most people firmly opposed (Blendon et al., 1992). Not until 1976, when California enacted the Natural Death Act (Meisel, 1999), did a systematic method exist for safeguarding patient autonomy in the face of severe medical illness. Since that time, Living Will legislation has been passed in 47 of 50 states, and case law supports the use of Living Wills in the remaining three states (Meisel, Snyder, & Quill, 2000). Most of these statutes specifically permit the use of advance directives to be executed in other jurisdictions (i.e., "portability"), with relatively little concern for the actual format of the documents themselves. In some cases, even oral statements have been recognized as legitimate indicators of patient preferences, although verbal statements are obviously less desirable than written documents.[4] Advance directive forms that are recognized by the legal system as valid are much more likely to be adhered to, particularly when the decisions at issue are somewhat contentious, but even unverified oral statements can be offered as evidence of a patient's preferences under some circumstances.

The primary focus of advance directives such as the Living Will is to provide a mechanism for preserving patient autonomy after decision-making capacity has deteriorated. By documenting an individual's preferences about treatment options that are either presently available or may become available in the future, decision making can proceed in an informed rather than speculative manner. However, these documents offer other potential benefits beyond simply bolstering patient autonomy. Many clinicians have suggested that patients can experience profound psychological benefits from discussions about, and completion of, advance directives, because these steps often alleviate much of the anxiety that typically surrounds the dying pro-

---

[4]The *Cruzan* Court specifically criticized the reliability of oral expressions of treatment preferences.

cess. For example, Smucker and colleagues (1993) found that elderly patients showed an improved mood and felt that their physician had a greater understanding of them following a physician-initiated discussion of advance directives. Patients who simply discussed health-related issues with their physicians (the control condition) showed no such improvements in mood or comfort with their physicians. Other studies have shown that patients often feel grateful for the opportunity to provide advance directives, because of their desire to maintain decision-making autonomy and to help family members avoid having to make difficult medical decisions on their behalf (e.g., Henderson, 1990; Stephens, Babb, & Castleman, 1991).

The benefits of advance directives also extend beyond the individual patients themselves. Several studies have shown decreased medical expenses at the end of life for patients with advance directives compared to other patients. In a study of Ontario nursing home residents, Molloy et al. (2000) compared institutions in which aggressive educational outreach and staff training regarding advance directives was offered to a set of "control" institutions in which no such intervention was offered. They found that both the rate of completion of advance directives and the sophistication of those completed was markedly higher in the study institutions. More important, the study institutions had dramatically lower health care costs per patient (50% lower than the control institutions), despite having comparable death rates and equal numbers of days hospitalized per patient. Thus, financial incentives may exist to support increased utilization of advance directives to reduce the use of expensive, unnecessary, and unwanted interventions. Family members too may feel less burdened in their role of caring for a dying loved one when advance directives minimize their role in decision making. Thus, not only can advance directives sustain decision-making autonomy and prevent unwanted interventions, they also may offer significant psychological benefits for patients and family members as well as financial benefits for the health care system.[5]

Despite the seemingly obvious benefits of advance directives, many elderly people or medical patients seem to be unaware of these options. In a recent study of nearly 3,000 individuals admitted to nursing homes, only 11% had advance directives upon their initial assessment (shortly after admission), and only 17% had DNR orders (Suri, Egleston, Brody, & Rudberg,

---

[5]Not all studies of advance directives have been quite so optimistic. Coppola and colleagues (Coppola, Ditto, Danks, Houts, & Smucker, 2001) found that the accuracy of primary care physicians and family member's judgments regarding the treatment preferences of elderly adults was not significantly better for those individuals with existing advance directives compared to those without advance directives. Moreover, rates of agreement between patients and either family members or physicians were disappointingly low. The authors concluded that advance directives alone are clearly insufficient to guarantee that decision-making autonomy will be maintained.

[6]Although these utilization rates might seem to contradict the tendency toward increased utilization noted earlier, even these modest rates represent a substantial increase from the rate of DNR orders and other advance directives a decade earlier.

1999).[6] Moreover, of those individuals who did not have advance directives upon their initial assessment, relatively few completed these directives during their nursing home stay. Only 6% of the remaining patients completed an advance directive during the ensuing months, and 15% obtained a DNR order. Interestingly, older (over age 85) and Caucasian residents were significantly more likely to have an advance directive upon admission. Although the former finding is to be expected, given that advance directives are often more relevant for older patients, the racial disparity suggests a potential source of bias. It is not clear whether the under-utilization of advance directives by minority individuals reflects the reluctance of ethnic minority patients to rely on legal documents to guide health care treatment or a failure on the part of health care providers to inform minority patients of the options available to them. But regardless of the explanation for this racial disparity, this finding is nevertheless disconcerting.

Even more troubling is the evidence that a substantial proportion of advance directives are ignored by health care providers. Winick (1998) estimated that at least 25% of advance directives are ignored by medical professionals; other estimates have been even higher. One explanation offered for this seemingly disturbing finding is that many advance directives are overly vague; they do not indicate clearly and unambiguously what the patient's preference might be in any specific circumstance. Legal scholars and physicians have responded to such critiques by suggesting improved and clearer formulations of advance directives.[7] At minimum, they should provide detailed information regarding preferences for CPR and DNR orders, treatment withdrawal, intravenous hydration and nutrition, and other end-of-life procedures that are likely to be used in the course of an advanced or terminal illness. Yet overly specific advance directives can at times be problematic, especially when medical treatment options are rapidly changing. For example, the numerous treatment advances for persons with HIV/AIDS could not have been specified in advance, yet these interventions might be consistent with a person's long-standing wishes and values. This issue is highlighted by the recent interest in advance directives for research, as scholars are increasingly attentive to the prospect of establishing preferences for research participation in the event of later incompetence (Rosenfeld, 2002).

The 1990 Patient Self-Determination Act, which requires institutions to provide information regarding advance directives and document them when they do exist, stops short of requiring physicians (or any other health care professional) to discuss advance directives with patients. Moreover, advance directive legislation has typically excluded any sanctions for health care professionals who fail to adhere to the patient's requested course of action (Meisel,

---

[7]An extensive discussion of the form and content of advance directives, along with examples of model text, is available from the American Medical Association (http://www. ama-assn.org/public/booklets/livgwill.htm).

1999). Rather, some statutes explicitly protect health care professionals from liability when they fail to follow the advance directive. These policies likely reflect the continued reluctance of many physicians to cede decision making to patients, despite decades of well-established legal precedent supporting patient autonomy in health care decision making.

Nevertheless, most commentators agree that advance directives offer an important opportunity to retain decision-making autonomy and are grossly under-utilized by the very patients who could most benefit from them. As such, interventions designed to increase the completion and utilization of advance directives have become increasingly popular, and the early results have generally been encouraging. In one study intervention, a communitywide attempt to increase completion of advance directives resulted in a marked increase in the rates of completed advance directives. Although only 15% of newly deceased individuals had completed advance directives during the period preceding the study intervention, 85% of the sample completed them following a 2-year educational intervention (Hammes & Rooney, 1998). These data, along with other studies reporting similar improvements in advance directive completion (e.g., Molloy et al., 2000) demonstrate the ability to increase utilization of advance directives through systematic, systemic interventions.

Are Advance Directives the Answer?

Despite the compelling logic behind advance directives, philosophers and legal scholars have occasionally questioned their appropriateness and social science researchers have questioned their effectiveness. Philosophical objections are based on the observation that the incompetent individual for whom the advance directive is meant to apply is not necessarily the same person who initially executed the directive. This position, rooted in Person Identity Theory that was first described in the 1980s, suggests that the defining characteristic of an individual is psychological continuity or connection between past, present, and future cognitions (Rich, 1998). By becoming incompetent, whether through cognitive deterioration (e.g., dementia), coma, or psychological disorder, the individual's continuous sense of self has been disrupted and he or she becomes, psychologically speaking, a different person. These theorists argue that the decisions made by the competent person (e.g., to forego all further medical treatments) may not necessarily be in the best interest of the incompetent individual.[8] Indeed, it is this same logic, the

---

[8]Ben Rich (1998) described the hypothetical case of Margo, a woman with Alzheimer's disease who appears genuinely happy despite her severe cognitive limitations. Had this woman signed a Living Will indicating that no life-extending interventions should be allowed if she were permanently incompetent to make treatment decisions, even a simple but potentially fatal infection would be left untreated and she would be allowed to die. Rich argued that such an advance directive, although technically legal, does not reflect the best interest of the woman in her current mental state, and he suggested that the woman is sufficiently different from the person who drafted the Living Will as to render the document meaningless.

belief that an advance directive is not in the patient's best interest, that often leads health care providers to ignore advance directives.

A second level of criticism leveled on advance directives pertains to whether the decisions taken by appointed surrogates satisfies the requirements of informed consent, particularly when these decisions are based on the incomplete and hypothetical information such as that typically contained in advance directives. Because many of the details regarding risks, potential benefits, and other relevant information cannot be known in advance, most advance directives do not meet the requirements for valid informed consent.[9] This criticism is easily resolved when advance directives are regarded as guidelines for surrogate decision making rather than an expression of the patient's decision per se. Surrogates might still fulfill the patient's wishes but without having to adhere to each specific instruction. Nevertheless, this interpretation of advance directives, as a guide to decision making rather than a mandate, is not necessarily the same understanding that the patient may have had when completing the directive.

A related criticism of advance directives (and a possible explanation for the frequency with which they are disregarded) is the inadequacy of their contents. For example, an elderly patient might state that in the event of a terminal illness and decisional incompetency he or she should not receive any "heroic measures" to sustain his or her life. Yet terms such as *heroic measures* or *extraordinary treatments* that were common in early advance directives can be interpreted quite differently by physicians or family members; for example, is CPR a "heroic measure" or a routine intervention? Moreover, physicians are often unclear about when an illness has reached the "terminal" stage (typically defined as having less than 6 months to live) and this condition is present in many advance directives (e.g., that no further interventions occur if an illness has been determined to be "terminal").[10] The inclusion of conditions that cannot be clearly defined transforms many seemingly clear directives into essentially subjective instruments as to when and what action should be taken. Indeed, even in seminal cases such as those of Karen Ann Quinlan and Nancy Cruzan, where the need for advance directives seemed so obvious, a requirement of terminal illness might have excluded these women from having some forms of advance directive take effect because the nature of their illnesses were not necessarily terminal (although their incompetence was clearly permanent).[11]

---

[9]The doctrine of informed consent, a legal principle rooted in decades of case law, dictates that any health care decisions must be *knowing, voluntary, and competent* in order to be considered valid.
[10]Similar criticisms have been levied at assisted suicide legislation, often requiring a prognosis of less than 6 months, as is the case in Oregon). Proponents of these laws, however, accept the significant margin for error in prognostic judgments as unavoidable.
[11]Note that the requirement of a terminal illness is not necessarily a legal mandate, but rather refers to a common phrasing for advance directives that could easily be clarified by patients who are aware of this potential source of confusion.

The ambiguity of many advance directives is echoed in the standardized advance directive form distributed by the American Association of Retired Persons in collaboration with the American Medical Association and the American Bar Association (Cantor, 1998). The document states (in relevant part): "I don't want treatment . . . when the treatment will not give me a meaningful quality of life." Other sections specify that treatment should be withheld under circumstances such as "complete or near complete loss of ability to think or communicate with others." Although this document conveys the individual's desire to avoid life-sustaining treatment when the quality of his or her life has deteriorated, it fails to clearly specify when such conditions have been met. The seminal SUPPORT study (the Study to Understand Prognoses and Preferences for Outcomes and Risks of Treatments, 1995), that attempted to assess and improve end-of-life care, found that the vast majority (87%) of advance directives were "uninformative," either appointing a proxy decision-maker without providing any information regarding treatment preferences or giving only general information without specific details about the patient's preferences.

Emanuel and Emanuel (1989) published a lengthy, highly complex model advancing directives specifically aimed at addressing many of these problems. This document provides a mechanism to appoint one or more proxy decision-makers and specifically addresses issues such as whether the proxy should be permitted to override the preferences expressed in the advance directive. In addition, the advance directive describes four clinical scenarios (irreversible coma, coma with small chance of recovery, terminal illness with some brain damage causing incompetence, and brain damage causing incompetence without terminal illness) and presents a series of 12 medical interventions that might arise under each of these conditions. Patients are asked if they would want each of these interventions, with the option to indicate that they would definitely want the intervention, would not want the intervention, or are undecided. Alternatively, patients can indicate that a particular intervention should be tried for a specified period of time and then discontinued if no improvement occurred. Unfortunately, this model advance directive, although obviously thorough and complex, still contains a number of vague or potentially confusing terms (e.g., "invasive diagnostic tests") and frequently fails to adequately explain in lay terms the meaning or implications of many decisions. Despite the length and complexity of their model advance directive, Emanuel and Emanuel found that it required only 14 minutes to complete (on average), contradicting the frequent criticism that advance directives are excessively time consuming (L. L. Emanuel, Barley, Stoeckle, Ettelson, & Emanuel, 1991).

Are Advance Directives Effective?

Rapid completion of advance directives may be possible, but it is not necessarily advisable. Patients may have different opinions after having considered (or more clearly understood) the choices offered. This important issue, the stability of preferences expressed in advance directives, has rarely been the subject of systematic investigation but has clear implications for the validity of the entire process. Several studies (e.g., Danis, Garrett, Harris, & Patrick, 1994; Gready et al., 2000) have suggested that the preferences for life-sustaining treatments may vary considerably over time. For example, Gready et al. interviewed 101 elderly community residents regarding their preferences for life-sustaining interventions under a number of hypothetical conditions (e.g., Alzheimer's disease, coma, terminal cancer). When they contacted the residents 2 to 3 years later, they found a modest degree of stability in these preferences; 70–75% of the decisions were the same at both time points although some types of decisions appeared more variable than others. Interestingly, patients perceived their preferences to have been much more stable than they were; most patients did not recognize when their opinion had changed. Although few would suggest that a 25–30% rate of inconsistency should invalidate advance directives in general, it certainly raises questions about the extent to which advance directives fulfill their stated mission of safeguarding patient autonomy.

The AMA (1998) Council on Ethical and Judicial Affairs has also raised concerns regarding the validity of advance directives. The Council noted that unlike most mechanisms for gathering information, advance directives have never been subject to any form of empirical validation, a process that is clearly necessary before any document can be considered an accurate representation of patient preferences. Similar concerns have been raised about other mechanisms for articulating preferences such as the Values History, which has been suggested as an alternative to traditional Living Wills (Cantor, 1998). Like Living Wills, the Values History offers a format for patients to document their preferences and values regarding a number of different health-related issues but does not necessarily provide specific details regarding what treatments would (or would not) be desired in particular sets of circumstances. Instead, the intent of a Values History is to provide details regarding an individual's values and goals in order to assist surrogate decision-makers in making more informed decisions when faced with unanticipated situations.

Regardless of the type of advance directive used, a central concern for many health care providers is the possibility that they may be placed in the uncomfortable position of being obligated to carry out the wishes of a patient, including wishes they may not agree with, without the ability to discuss the decision under the *specific circumstances* in which the decision arises (i.e., because of patient incompetence). As noted earlier, many physicians are reluctant to adhere to the preferences expressed in advance directives, often because they believe that health care decisions should be made by medical professionals rather than patients. In fact, physicians and other health care providers (e.g., hospital administrators, insurance companies) have become increasingly reluctant to offer treatments when they perceive little or no potential for benefit and have justified this position by invoking the concept of medical futility. The *medical futility* argument refers to situations in which meaningful recovery is unlikely and frames the decision to withhold treatment in economic terms, as a justification for rationing health care services that have become increasingly expensive and often insufficient.

The concept of medical futility is probably best exemplified in the recently defeated Oregon proposal to limit Medicaid payments for some treatments that might otherwise have been provided (Batavia, 2002). These "rationing" decisions were based on the belief that terminally ill patients, who utilize a disproportionate share of health care resources, should not be entitled to expensive interventions that have little likelihood of improving their condition. Although rejected, this proposal generated intense scrutiny, both because of the fear that gaps between the treatments available to wealthy and poor individuals might widen and because of concern that interventions that are not curative (e.g., palliative care interventions) might be withheld because of pejorative assumptions as to what constitutes a reasonable quality of life. Though debates continue about how to define medical futility and toward what end, any such definitions have the potential to erode patient autonomy (Batavia, 2002).

SURROGATE DECISION MAKING

Until recently, responsibility for surrogate decision making typically fell upon the nearest family member willing to take on the responsibility of deciding what should be done for their ill relative.[12] However, along with the emergence of autonomy as a guiding principle in health care decision making, ethicists and legal scholars have increasingly clarified mechanisms for surrogate decision making. Instead of automatically turning to family members, Health Care Proxy designations and Durable Powers of Attorney have enabled medically ill individuals to select the person they most trust to make treatment decisions on their behalf. These alternatives became increasingly popular in the 1980s, spurred in part by the HIV epidemic that left many severely ill individuals seeking to appoint a friend or partner as surrogate decision-maker, assuming that the individual they selected would be better able to make treatment decisions that they would have chosen. Regardless of who is appointed as surrogate decision-maker, his or her ability to mimic the decisions the patient would have made hinges on the extent to which the surrogate is aware of the patient's preferences.

---

[12]Some states have a specific hierarchy of surrogate decision-making authority with the patient's spouse, if available, typically having the highest standing followed by children, parents, siblings, and more distant relatives. In fact, the omission of non-relatives from these legal standards was a central influence driving the emergence of health care proxy legislation.

This transition toward asking surrogate decision-makers to mimic the decisions that a patient would have made if competent also reflects a substantial shift from earlier practices. For many years, surrogate decision making followed what has become known as the *best-interest standard*, an attempt to base decisions on an assessment of what was best for the patient. As the importance of maintaining patient autonomy has increased, however, surrogate decision-makers have increasingly moved toward a "substituted judgment" approach, attempting to determine what decision the patient would have made if he or she were competent. However, the ability of surrogates to actually use the substituted judgment standard has been questioned by many clinicians and researchers (e.g., Coppola et al., 2001). Not only is there a substantial risk of misinterpreting the patient's wishes and values, but the ambiguity in patient preferences (i.e., advance directives) leaves considerable room for subjective interpretations.

Not surprisingly, surrogate decision-makers often readily acknowledge that they rely on their own experiences, values, and beliefs in making proxy decisions for their incompetent relatives. But different surrogate decision makers may have different types of biases in their approach to surrogate decision-making. For example, family members typically emphasize emotional factors in decision making (e.g., quality of life, dignity), often relying on other family members to support the decisions they have made. Health care professionals, on the other hand, are typically more "objective" in their approach to surrogate decision making, emphasizing the medical appropriateness of various alternatives such as the likelihood of success or failure of a particular procedure (Larsen, 1999). Researchers have questioned the ability of surrogates to accurately infer the decisions their relatives would have made. Uhlmann, Pearlman, and Cain (1988) observed little concordance between patient preferences and the spouse's predictions of what he or she would choose in a series of hypothetical scenarios. Unfortunately, physicians were no better at predicting what decision their patients would make, but they also were not noticeably worse than the spouses.

Ditto and his colleagues (2001) have conducted a series of studies aimed at understanding the discrepancies between patient and surrogate treatment decisions. They compared the preferences of elderly patients and their surrogate decision-makers (i.e., the decisions they predicted the patient would make), and asked surrogate decision makers to indicate their own preferences as well. They found that predicted decisions more closely approximated the surrogate's own preferences rather than those of patients. They interpreted this finding as evidence of a self-based bias whereby surrogates overestimate the extent to which others share their beliefs and values, essentially projecting their own values onto others. Furthermore, they noted that the concordance between patient and surrogate decisions was no stronger when an advance directive was provided versus decisions made without any formal guidance (even when the surrogate and patient had the opportunity to discuss the advance directive shortly before making the hypothetical decisions). Nevertheless, Ditto et al. concluded that decisions based on projection were more accurate than decisions that contradicted this tendency (i.e., counterprojection), suggesting that despite limitations, surrogate decision making is preferable to alternative mechanisms for decision making.

As noted earlier, surrogate decision making is difficult because patient preferences often change over time. Using a longitudinal design, Lee and colleagues (M. A. Lee, Smith, Fenn, & Ganzini, 1998) observed substantial changes in the treatment preferences of elderly patients. Patients were presented with hypothetical scenarios, and they were asked whether they would want various possible interventions (e.g., tube feeding, dialysis, mechanical ventilation). Several years later, the authors analyzed hospital records to ascertain whether any of these interventions had been accepted or refused and whether these interventions occurred in the context of any of the hypothetical conditions previously described. Decisions were consistent in the majority of cases when the patients made the decisions for themselves (vs. a surrogate decision-maker), but many patients changed their minds about the interventions they wanted. For example, of the 10 patients for whom mechanical ventilation was considered appropriate, 9 elected to have this intervention, but 5 of the 9 patients had previously indicated that they would not want this treatment if it became necessary. Not surprisingly, surrogate decision-makers were considerably worse at matching the advance preferences of the patients. Of the 28 cases in which surrogate decision makers made end-of-life care decisions, only 17 were consistent with the patient's previously expressed preferences. Seven of the 11 discrepant treatment decisions made by surrogates also involved accepting interventions that were not desired by the patient during the initial assessment. Thus, although many consistencies in decision making were noted, particularly among CPR decisions (e.g., most patients who had indicated that they would not want CPR performed ultimately signed DNR orders), a strong tendency to accept life-sustaining interventions (such as mechanical ventilation) was observed even among patients who had not anticipated wanting such interventions.

On the other hand, given the likelihood that patients themselves change their minds about what treatments are desired, discrepancies between earlier preferences and current treatment decisions are not necessarily negative. Rather, these findings suggest the importance of appointing a surrogate decision-maker who is well informed about the patient's goals and values.[13] By selecting a surrogate who is best able to determine what decisions the patient might have made, novel situations can be handled that cannot be antici-

---

[13]Even Smucker and colleagues (2000), who found that the accuracy of surrogate decisions was improved by simply substituting the most common, or "modal" preference, acknowledged that this "solution" was not feasible in actual clinical practice as the principle of autonomy mandates that one attempt to improve surrogate decision-making rather than simply eliminating surrogates and basing treatment decisions on the overall consensus of similar patients.

pated in a Living Will or other form of advance directive. Of course, no legal mechanisms can guarantee that patient autonomy will be preserved, and appointing a Health Care Proxy/Durable Power of Attorney simply enables the patient to select his or her preferred surrogate (who is often *not* a family member), not guarantee that the surrogate will perform the duties adequately (no matter how *adequacy* is defined). Moreover, the possibility that surrogate decisions might not coincide with patients' earlier preferences does not negate the psychological benefits of enabling terminally ill patients to continue to influence the course of their illness and treatment even after they are no longer competent to make decisions for themselves. Likewise, the benefits to surrogates from alleviating some of the pressure involved in making end-of-life decisions for an ill relative does not necessarily hinge on the concordance of these decisions with what the patient would have wanted.

SUMMARY

A number of mechanisms have been developed to preserve the autonomy of decision making by patients who are no longer competent to make decisions for themselves. These instruments have grown in both scope and complexity, from the relatively simple but highly specific DNR order to the broader but often ambiguous guidance provided by living wills and health care proxy designations. Although these instruments are not sufficient to guarantee that decisions made on behalf of an incompetent patient will be the same as those the patient would have made had he or she been able, they nevertheless offer substantial advantages over allowing available family members to make decisions without any formal guidance. Perhaps most important, however, is that advance directives have primarily been utilized to help expedite the dying process, typically among terminally ill individuals who fear living longer than they would like. Many commentators have even noted that such instruments might eventually be used as a means of seeking physician-assisted suicide directly, rather than simply allowing the dying process to proceed unhindered. This development has not yet occurred in the United States, but it has been accepted in the Netherlands.

Regardless of whether advance directives are used to expedite death or simply to control the course of treatment and choose from available options (e.g., advance directives for research, a practice that has recently grown in popularity), the impact of advance directives clearly extends beyond simply facilitating health care decision making. Enabling patients to feel in control of the dying process appears to meet a significant, and perhaps even growing, psychological need that has yet to be understood or even adequately studied. Understanding the importance of control as a means of coping with terminal illness represents a much-needed aspect of health psychology and may have substantial implications for understanding the appeal of more controversial end-of-life issues such as physician-assisted suicide and euthanasia. Finally, the relevance of policies and mechanisms for expediting the dying process has obvious implications for discussions of assisted suicide, particularly as a growing body of scientific research has studied "desire for hastened death," a construct that encompasses a wide array of issues such as suicide, assisted suicide, and decisions to expedite death by treatment refusal. These issues, and the factors that appear to influence each, are the focus of the next chapter.

4

RESEARCH ISSUES IN ASSISTED SUICIDE AND EUTHANASIA: METHODS AND OPPORTUNITIES FOR FUTURE RESEARCH

Any attempt to understand the rapidly growing empirical literature on assisted suicide and other end-of-life issues must be considered in terms of the research methods involved.[1] Like many areas of social science research, end-of-life research is greatly influenced by choices in research methodology, yet this source of influence has rarely been acknowledged. Given the potential importance of this research literature, both in terms of shaping legal and social policy as well as influencing health care decision making, it is necessary to clearly acknowledge any source of bias or influence on what otherwise might be an "objective" scientific process. In the case of assisted suicide and end-of-life research, these issues comprise the who, what, when, and how of research design. This chapter reviews the various problems and issues involved in operationalizing relevant dependent variables (what to study), sampling constraints and biases involved in studying sensitive issues

---

[1]An earlier version of this chapter appeared in *Psychology, Public Policy, and Law*, 6 (2000): 559–574.

among vulnerable populations (who to study and when and where to conduct the research), and influences that often confound the measurement of relevant variables (how to measure relevant variables). Although broader questions exist such as whether to use qualitative or quantitative methods, many of the issues outlined in this chapter pertain to both. Finally, although some criticism is necessary in order to highlight the methodological issues discussed, the purpose of this chapter is not simply to criticize the works of others. Rather, this chapter is intended to provide for a more accurate understanding of the existing research literature and hopefully contribute to increasing the sophistication of future research efforts.

WHAT TO STUDY (OPERATIONALIZING DEPENDENT VARIABLES)

Research on assisted suicide and related end-of-life issues has changed considerably over the past decade. This evolution is perhaps best exemplified by the changing conceptualization of what constitutes an appropriate dependent variable. Much of the early end-of-life research (and my early research was no exception) involved a single hypothetical question or vignette, typically asking whether an individual would "consider" assisted suicide at some future point (e.g., Breitbart, Rosenfeld, & Passik, 1996; Owen, Tennant, Levi, & Jones, 1992). Curiously, we often chose to analyze whether current psychological or physical status would influence these hypothetical future decisions. This choice of methods seemed logical, at that time, given the limited opportunity to assess current interest in assisted suicide or euthanasia (because asking people whether they actually want an option that is not legally sanctioned is ethically tenuous). Yet the interpretation of these studies was clearly dubious, particularly because the single-item dependent variable used often had unknown reliability (e.g., stability over time) and validity (e.g., correspondence to later, actual decisions). Although hypothetical vignette methods may be useful for determining what percentage of respondents might approve of assisted suicide or euthanasia under certain conditions, or agree in principal with the legalization of assisted suicide, most researchers interpreted these data as having more far-reaching implications than were warranted.

The limitations in these hypothetical questions are clear when data derived from this method are compared to current studies on assisted suicide or euthanasia. Several researchers have noted dramatic differences between the frequency with which patients indicate a willingness to "consider" assisted suicide in hypothetical vignettes and their actual interest in dying more rapidly (e.g., E. J. Emanuel, Fairclough, & Emanuel, 2000; Ganzini, Johnston, McFarland, Tolle, & Lee, 1998). For example, in their study of 100 patients with ALS, Ganzini et al. found that 55% of their sample would "consider" assisted suicide, yet only one individual was actually interested in hastening death at the time of study participation. My colleagues and I also found that 55% of ambulatory patients with AIDS were willing to consider assisted suicide if it were legalized, yet only 6% to 8% of a similar sample had a high desire for hastened death (compare Breitbart et al., 1996, with Rosenfeld et al., 1999). The sheer magnitude of these discrepancies should lead readers to question the meaningfulness of studies that are based on hypothetical interest.

One explanation for the marked discrepancy between how many individuals "consider" ending their lives and how many actually want their lives to end sooner is that patients become increasingly tolerant of unpleasant health states as their illness progresses. Data published by Emanuel and his colleagues support this explanation (E. J. Emanuel, Fairclough, Daniels, & Clarridge, 1996). They found that cancer patients who were in pain at the time of their study were less likely than patients without pain to consider euthanasia "acceptable" in a vignette describing uncontrolled pain as the reason for ending one's life. Likewise, the advance "preferences" of medically ill or terminally ill patients often differ from their later behavior (e.g., M. A. Lee et al., 1998), because many patients opt to accept life-extending interventions that they had previously anticipated rejecting. Such findings not only raise questions about the meaning of hypothetical advance preferences (as discussed in the preceding chapter), but they are also troubling for the advocates of advance directives (e.g., Living Wills, DNR orders, etc.) since many people may change their minds about the preferences they had previously expressed in an advance directive.

One response to the questionable relevance of hypothetical questions and future interest in assisted suicide has been to focus instead on measures of current interest in death. Two different methodologies have been used toward this end: studies of patients who have requested assisted suicide and studies of the desire for hastened death. It is not surprising that these two methodologies have produced somewhat different but largely complementary results.

Requests for (or Completed) Assisted Suicide

The first studies of patients who requested assisted suicide were the descriptive reports published by researchers from the Netherlands (this literature is described in more detail in chap. 8). Although the primary focus of these studies was to document the frequency of assisted suicide and euthanasia, they also reported data regarding the primary reasons behind patient requests for hastened death (e.g., van der Maas, van Delden, Pijnenborg, & Looman, 1991). After the 1997 enactment of the ODDA, researchers in the United States followed suit, publishing annual reports on the practice of assisted suicide in Oregon (described in chap. 9). In one study, Ganzini and colleagues (Ganzini, Nelson et al., 2000) described the results of a survey of Oregon physicians who were asked to provide details regarding patients who had requested assisted suicide. Responding physicians were asked to recall the reasons behind their patient's request as well as what, if any, interventions took place in response to this request. Without belaboring the limitations of relying on physician recollection or and the validity of patient's report as to why they requested assisted suicide, this methodology certainly has the potential to provide some indication of what reasons are offered by the patients who request assisted suicide. However, it is also quite likely that physicians would be more inclined to report the most salient or "legitimate" reasons for their patient's request (i.e., the reasons *they* felt were most valid or compelling) and neglect other, potentially important influences such as undetected depression or concerns about becoming a burden to family. On the other hand, critics might be reassured by the convergent findings reported from studies of other health care professionals who care for terminally ill individuals (e.g., nurses, social workers), because this research has largely supported the findings of physician surveys (Ganzini et al., 2002).

Although the problem of selective recall might be minimized by interviewing the patients themselves after they have requested assisted suicide (rather than relying on physician recall), such an approach faces substantial practical impediments. First, it is doubtful that physicians would (or should) be willing to refer their terminally ill (and likely physically or psychologically distressed) patients to a research study. Furthermore, in jurisdictions where assisted suicide is illegal (which includes most states in the United States and most developed countries), there may be substantial legal and ethical implications for both clinicians and researchers who even attempt to apply this sort of method. At the time of this writing, I am aware of only one unpublished study that has attempted to directly interview patients who requested assisted suicide. Back and Gordon (2001) described preliminary results from their interviews with patients planning to end their lives or with their family members. Whereas this innovative methodology has yielded interesting findings, the difficulties are equally evident. In many cases they were able to interview only family members, and their data suffers from the same possible confounds as physician recall. Also, because most of their participants resided outside of Oregon, all patients were illegally ending their lives (with a physician's assistance). At present, we simply do not know whether any differences exist between individuals who seek assisted suicide despite the illegality versus those who might request assisted suicide when it is legal. Related to the issue of legality was the investigators' decision not to interview physicians because their data could have adverse consequences for physicians if their actions were discovered. Thus, the accuracy of medical information reported (e.g., life expectancy, existing treatment options) is unknown. Despite these potential limitations, this methodology is likely to become increasingly popular, particularly in settings where assisted suicide has already been legalized.

Desire for Hastened Death

Another approach that has grown in popularity, particularly in settings where assisted suicide is illegal, involves studying the desire for hastened death. The term *desire for death* was first coined by Harvey Chochinov and his colleagues in their seminal study of terminally ill cancer patients (Chochinov et al., 1995).[2] Several years later, my colleagues and I developed a self-report inventory to measure this construct, the Schedule of Attitudes toward Hastened Death (SAHD; Rosenfeld et al., 1999). Our goal in developing this measure was primarily to facilitate our own planned research studies as well as to offer an alternative methodology to more commonly used hypothetical questions that had been used in much of the research to date.

We have conceptualized the construct of desire for hastened death broadly, as a phenomenon underlying a number of related end-of-life behaviors including requests for assisted suicide, suicidal ideation that does not involve a physician, hopes or efforts to speed one's death that do not involve active steps (i.e., refusal of treatment other than palliative care), and perhaps even some decisions regarding advance directives (e.g., DNR orders). By studying the desire for hastened death, researchers can presumably identify individuals who might consider assisted suicide as well as those who might wish for a more rapid death but have personal reasons for not actually acting on this desire (e.g., religion, family obligations, fear of legal repercussions). Although distinguishing between those patients who do and do not actually seek to hasten their death is crucial for many research questions, other important issues are better studied by including patients with a high desire for death regardless of whether they would actually act on their desire.

Chochinov and his colleagues (1995) developed the first measure of desire for hastened death, the Desire for Death Rating Scale (DDRS). This measure consists of a series of semi-structured questions and prompts to guide clinicians in rating patients along a single scale. Low scores on this scale (1–2) reflect little or no interest in a hastened death, moderate scores (3–4) reflect thoughts of a more rapid death without any preoccupation or intent, and high scores (5–6) are assigned to patients who reveal a marked fixation or active plan to end their lives. Although Chochinov et al.'s study represented a significant advance in assisted suicide research, both by exploring the construct of desire for hastened death as well as providing a method for

---

[2]Brown and colleagues (1986) used an analogous question in their study: "Is it normal for terminally ill patients to desire death?" Their use of this question, however, was more limited than Chochinov's and our phrase, referring essentially to expressions of suicidal ideation in terminally ill individuals.

its measurement, the DDRS has a number of limitations as a research tool. First, because the DDRS is rated by clinicians or interviewers, training raters and establishing interrater reliability is crucial and adds an additional burden to potential investigators (particularly those who might want to use lay interviewers rather than trained clinicians). Similarly, whether accurate and reliable ratings can be obtained by research assistants who do not have a mental health background is unknown. The narrow range of possible scores (1–6) along a single scale substantially limits the data analytic methods available. (Chochinov and his colleagues resolved this problem by dividing respondents into those who had a "significant and pervasive" desire for death and those who did not.)

In response to the limitations of the DDRS, my colleagues and I developed the SAHD, a 20-item self-report scale to measure desire for hastened death (Rosenfeld et al., 1999, 2000). This true–false questionnaire, which we have administered to samples of patients with AIDS and cancer, has been used as the primary dependent variable in several recent and ongoing research studies (e.g., Breitbart et al., 2000). Other research groups have used this questionnaire with different terminally ill populations (see e.g., Rabkin, Wagner, & Del Bene, 2000). We deliberately avoided questions regarding actual behaviors that may be illegal in order to circumvent the legal and ethical issues noted above (i.e., potential liability if a researcher knew in advance that a patient intended to commit suicide but did not intervene).[3] In addition, the self-report format has obvious appeal for large-scale research studies.

However, studying desire for hastened death has also raised questions about precisely what behaviors or cognitive processes are being studied. For example, there is no evidence that desire for hastened death (as measured by either the SAHD or DDRS) actually corresponds to requests for assisted suicide or suicide attempts. One can easily imagine a patient with a high desire for hastened death yet no interest in actually ending his or her life, perhaps because of religious prohibitions or family obligations. Conversely, it is often suggested that some requests for assisted suicide or suicide attempts are not necessarily an indication of a true desire to die. Patients may use discussions of assisted suicide as a way to express their physical discomfort or psychological distress to their physicians or family members. Others may seek to exert some control over their illnesses and the dying process rather than genuinely desire a more rapid death. Thus, although studying desire for hastened death is often preferable to the hypothetical questions used in early research investigations and offers an important alternative to studying actual requests for assisted suicide, substantial differences are likely to emerge between these alternative approaches.

---

[3]Although the likelihood of legal liability is probably low, this possibility might nevertheless influence some researchers, funding agencies, and institutional review boards.

WHOM TO STUDY AND WHEN (SAMPLING ISSUES)

Another common dilemma in assisted suicide and end-of-life research is determining whom to study. Unlike much of the research that fills psychology textbooks, the assisted suicide literature has been almost devoid of studies investigating the preferences or beliefs of undergraduate students. Instead, most researchers have selected patient populations that are most clearly relevant for the various legal and clinical issues of interest such as elderly adults, medically ill or terminally ill patients, and health care providers. Nevertheless, many empirical studies have utilized "convenience samples," which have at times limited the significance or generalizability of the research findings.

Sample Representativeness

Many areas of medical and mental health research suffer from inadequate attention to the generalizability of samples, and the assisted suicide literature is certainly no exception. Researchers are inclined to give short shrift to sampling methods for several reasons, including the seemingly sensitive nature of end-of-life research. Researchers are no doubt inclined to exclude patients whom they perceive to be emotionally fragile, even though these patients may be the most relevant to the clinical and policy questions at issue. Although hospital institutional review boards may even encourage researchers to exclude emotionally vulnerable participants, this type of pre-screening has negative implications for interpreting the results. For example, my colleagues and I conducted a pilot study of desire for death among terminally ill cancer patients (Breitbart et al., 2000), in which attending physicians were asked to exclude patients whom they believed to be especially vulnerable to become upset by the study questions. Although such exclusions were few, we found somewhat higher rates of both depression and desire for hastened death in a subsequent (ongoing) study in the same facility in which this pre-screening did not occur. More important, by eliminating the most psychologically distressed participants, associations between psychological distress and desire for death may be attenuated. Although some biased sampling may be inevitable, because the most distressed patients are probably less likely to consent to participate in a research study regardless of the sensitivity of the topic, efforts to minimize this source of bias are clearly desirable. Perhaps most important, our group's observations, as well as those of other end-of-life researchers, have suggested that adverse reactions to end-of-life research are relatively uncommon. In fact, our research team has found that most terminally ill patients respond positively to participating in studies of end-of-life issues (even after extensive interviews and a lengthy questionnaire battery focusing on seemingly sensitive topics), and they express appreciation for the opportunity to discuss these issues in an open and forthright manner (Pessin, Galietta, & Rosenfeld, 2002).

A second issue pertaining to sample generalizability concerns the potential differences that might exist among different populations of medically ill individuals. Not only are differences likely to occur between individuals depending on their particular disease stage, but the type of illness itself may influence the research questions asked. For example, interest in assisted suicide may be driven by different factors among patients with ALS versus cancer or AIDS. Patients with ALS may be primarily concerned about their impending loss of control over their behavior and fear becoming a burden to others, whereas patients with cancer may be more concerned about the potential for pain, which often accompanies their disease. Thus, pain may be more likely to emerge as a significant predictor of interest in assisted suicide among patients with cancer whereas this variable may be insignificant in patients with ALS. Patients with AIDS, on the other hand, may anticipate further treatment advances and therefore have much higher expectations about their potential for improvement compared to cancer patients and therefore may be much less likely to desire hastened death or consider assisted suicide as a future option. Because differences among study populations have significant implications for the results achieved, researchers may want to select patient populations and study methods which best fit their research purposes rather than to rely on the most readily accessible samples. Moreover, investigators must consider how their results might vary with different populations.

Study Timing

The potential difficulties involved in studying medically ill or terminally ill individuals are well-known to most researchers who work in medical settings but have particular salience for assisted suicide researchers. Although many of the questions most central to the assisted suicide debate pertain to dying individuals, the research process is complicated when study participants are dealing with the final stages of their disease. Cognitive dysfunctions that cause confusion such as delirium and dementia are common, and these complicate researchers' ability to gather accurate research data. Our research group has addressed this difficulty in longitudinal studies by using a brief cognitive screening battery before each data collection point in order to ensure that participants have not deteriorated since the last assessment. Although excluding cognitively impaired patients may adversely affect sample representativeness (especially if cognitive functioning is one of the issues to be studied), this source of bias is less problematic for some types of assisted suicide research. Because existing legislation such as the ODDA requires that individuals be competent to make treatment decisions before assisted suicide can be considered, the subset of patients who are cognitively intact enough to participate in research is also the same group of patients for whom assisted suicide legislation is relevant.

The potential for cognitive deterioration among terminally ill research participants also has significant implications for longitudinal or prospective research. Because many important end-of-life research questions are best addressed with longitudinal investigations (e.g., the impact of medical interventions on requests for assisted suicide or the stability of preferences expressed in advance directives), this type of research is likely to become increasingly common. However, many participants who are cognitively intact at the beginning of a research study are likely to deteriorate before follow-up assessments are completed. Statistical techniques have been developed to help deal with this problem of attrition (e.g., Schafer & Olsen, 1998), but the proportion of patients who are unable to participate at follow-up can be high. In an ongoing study conducted by our research group, only 50% of the terminally ill cancer patients who participated in the baseline data collection (shortly after admission to a palliative care hospital) were sufficiently intact and medically stable enough to complete the second data collection point 2 weeks later. This rate of attrition necessitates recruitment of large initial samples in order to insure adequate statistical power for longitudinal analyses. Attrition is lessened when the interval between assessment points is brief, but the chance of observing meaningful changes in a patient's psychological well-being or medical condition decreases with the shrinking time interval. Balancing the trade-off between attrition and interval length is a difficult task and is likely to differ depending on the study goals.

In summary, the impact of sample selection and study timing has substantial implications for the interpretation of data regarding interest in or requests for assisted suicide. Although obtaining large, representative samples is a difficult task, efforts to maximize the generalizability of one's data are needed. As in any area of research, there is a potential for erroneous conclusions drawn from misleading data. In particular, when research findings have the potential to influence important policy decisions, it is necessary to honestly acknowledge the limitations of the data and the influence of sampling biases on the results.

CONFOUNDING FACTORS IN VARIABLE MEASUREMENT

Another set of methodological issues in assisted suicide research concerns the influence of confounding factors on variable measurement. One example of a confounding influence described above is the cognitive deterioration that often accompanies terminal illness. In severe cases, cognitive impairment can render data collection completely meaningless. However, many more subtle factors can substantially affect the accuracy of assisted suicide research. Some of these influences are relatively easy to address or resolve, but others are much more problematic.

Depression and Psychological Distress

One of the most hotly debated issues in assisted suicide research, which is addressed in considerable detail in the next chapter, concerns the role of depression. Whereas many studies have investigated the relationship between depression and desire for death or interest in assisted suicide, few have acknowledged the difficulties in studying depression in the medically ill. Clinicians who work in medical settings are intimately familiar with the overlap between symptoms of a medical illness, side effects of treatment, and symptoms of depression. A number of guidelines have been offered to improve assessment of depression in patients with cancer and other medical illnesses (e.g., Endicott, 1984; Lynch, 1995; Massie, Gagnon, & Holland, 1994). Yet these recommendations have not been translated into valid measurement techniques that are free of these influences.[4] Instead, most researchers (our group included) have used standard measures such as the Beck Depression Inventory (Beck, Ward, Mendelson, & Erbaugh, 1961) or Brief Symptom Inventory (Derogatis & Melisaratos, 1983) without regard to this potential confound. Others modify these scales by omitting items that might be the result of a medical illness (i.e., somatic symptoms), but the validity of these abbreviated measures is unknown. In one such study, my colleagues and I found that the typical distinction made between somatic and cognitive or affective symptoms of depression was a questionable one, because the factor structure of a standardized depression scale did not fit this model in a large sample of cancer patients (Passik et al., 2000). On the other hand, studies that have compared results based on both complete depression inventories (i.e., those "contaminated" by somatic items) and modified versions of the same scale with somatic items omitted have reported comparable findings for each (e.g., Rosenfeld et al., 1996). These findings raise the question as to whether removing the somatic items from depression inventories does not actually resolve this confound or whether the potential for overlapping symptoms is less problematic than it might seem.

An alternative to the traditional self-report inventories, where distinguishing between a medical versus psychological etiology for a particular symptom is not possible, is to ask well-trained clinicians to make such judgments. Clinician-rated scales are available for measuring depression, anxiety, and virtually any other psychological construct that might be of interest in a study of patients at the end of life. In addition, a number of structured interview schedules exist to establish whether a particular clinical diagnosis is warranted (e.g., major depressive episode), and these have occasionally been modified to avoid the confound of somatic symptoms (e.g., Chochinov, Wil-

---

[4]Measures such as the Hospital Anxiety and Depression Scale (Zigmund & Snaith, 1983) have been developed specifically to avoid confounding physical and psychological symptoms but the extent to which they accomplish these goals is far from clear (i.e., quantifying depression without the influence of organic or iatrogenic factors).

son, Enns, & Lander, 1994). The added research burden of using trained clinicians to rate depression or anxiety rather than simply relying on self-report inventories is probably obvious (issues of rater training, establishing reliability, etc.). Nevertheless, given the treatment implications of a clinical diagnosis of depression (or any other mental disorder), studies that establish specific diagnoses offer many advantages from both clinical research and public policy perspectives.

Perhaps the most difficult confound in assisted suicide research concerns the interpretation of "suicidal ideation." Although thoughts of death or suicide are typically considered indicative of depression, this assumption is problematic for researchers attempting to disentangle the two constructs, particularly if one accepts the premise that some medically ill individuals who have thoughts of death and suicide are not depressed. This confound is perhaps best exemplified by Brown and colleagues' (Brown, Henteleff, Barakat, & Rowe, 1986) study of depression and desire for death in hospitalized terminally ill patients. In this study, Brown et al. found that 10 of the 44 patients interviewed had a desire for death and that all 10 were diagnosed with major depression. However, not only did they consider suicidal ideation and desire for death to be essentially equivalent, but the same clinical data were used to assess both depression and desire for death and suicidal ideation. Because the expression of thoughts of death or suicide was probably influential in forming clinician opinions regarding depression, particularly in the absence of a structured diagnostic interview, the overlap they observed is hardly surprising. Without independent ratings of depression and desire for death, finding a high concordance between the two is of limited significance. Self-report measures may actually help resolve this issue, because items reflecting suicidal ideation can (and in this context should) be omitted when summing scores on a depression measure. Although this might minimize the overlap between desire for death and depression (i.e., items reflecting thoughts of death or suicide which may be present in both rating scales), the conceptual overlap between thoughts of death and interest in hastened death is not so easily resolved. Future research investigating the interrelationships between thoughts of death, suicidal ideation, desire for hastened death, and requests for assisted suicide might help clarify these distinct but overlapping constructs.

"Demographic" Variables

Among the numerous demographic variables frequently studied in assisted suicide research, two have emerged as significant correlates in most studies: racial background and religious affiliation or strength of religious conviction (e.g., Blendon et al., 1992; Breitbart et al., 1996). Although these variables are included in nearly every empirical study, most researchers have used relatively simple classification schemes such as grouping individuals by race or religious affiliation. Yet important differences might exist among members of any particular religion depending on the degree of conservatism (e.g., Fundamentalist Baptist vs. Protestant, Orthodox vs. Reformed Jewish) or among members of broad racial designations (e.g., Mexican vs. Puerto Rican or Colombian).

Although comprehensive measures of religiosity and spirituality exist and have been occasionally integrated into medical or psychological research they have rarely been incorporated into studies of assisted suicide or desire for death. Yet, when measures of religiosity and spirituality have been included, they have increased our understanding of end-of-life decision making. My colleagues and I found a significant negative association between spiritual well-being and desire for hastened death that is independent of depression (McClain, Rosenfeld, & Breitbart, 2003) and have since developed a "meaning-centered" psychotherapy intervention to help bolster spiritual well-being in the terminally ill in hopes of lessening desire for hastened death.

Similarly, simple racial or ethnic classifications (e.g., Caucasian, Black Hispanic, Asian) ignore the differences within these broad categories. Instead, all members of a given "race" are assumed to be ethnically similar. More meaningful data might be obtained by using measures of acculturation and ethnic identity (e.g., Helms & Parham, 1996; Landrine & Klonoff, 1994), but these measures have also been absent from the literature on end-of-life care. Nevertheless, the importance of racial differences in attitude toward assisted suicide highlights the need for more careful attention to these "demographic" variables if researchers are to better understand the influence of ethnicity and culture on end-of-life attitudes and behaviors.

STATISTICAL CONSIDERATIONS

Few experienced researchers would dispute the truism that statistical concerns are inherent in all social science research, and this truism certainly applies to studies of assisted suicide. Nevertheless, a number of issues that have arisen with some frequency in the assisted suicide literature warrant a brief review. Among the most obvious problems in statistical analysis is the lack of adequate sample size. Particularly in assisted suicide research, where the relatively low frequency of requests for assisted suicide or desire for hastened death exists, the need to conduct large-scale investigations has become increasingly apparent. Empirical studies of terminally ill cancer and AIDS patients have typically found rates of interest in assisted suicide or desire for hastened death ranging from 8–15% (Chochinov et al., 1995; E. J. Emanuel et al., 2000; Rosenfeld et al., 1999; Rosenfeld et al., 2000). Rates of actual suicides in Oregon are even lower, with fewer than 1 completed assisted suicide per 1,000 deaths. Of course, studies relying on less rigorous dependent variables (e.g., hypothetical interest in assisted suicide in the future) often report substantially higher proportions of interested participants, but the large proportion who respond positively to these hypothetical questions highlights the inadequacy of the dependent variable rather than offering a plausible alternative to obtaining a sample of adequate size. In fact, very large samples are likely necessary in order to obtain a large sample of patients who are genuinely interested in hastened death, and multicenter studies are probably necessary in order to obtain sufficient subject pools. In addition, without large samples, investigators have been forced to rely on simple univariate analyses, and thus potentially interesting and important results that might emerge from studies utilizing more sophisticated methods (e.g., structural equation modeling, cluster analysis, or other multivariate methods) have been ignored.

Because only a small proportion of patients screened are likely to report a high desire for hastened death or express a desire for assisted suicide, variables measuring these constructs (whether dichotomous or continuous) are likely to have highly skewed distributions. Skewed distributions are particularly relevant because of the marked impact they can have on results when standard parametric analyses are used. Instead, nonparametric statistical procedures or data transformations should be considered whenever significant deviations from normality exist in the distributions of relevant variables. Unfortunately, because many novice researchers are unfamiliar with these techniques and instead use standard parametric analyses (e.g., Pearson correlation coefficients, t tests, and analyses of variance), the probability of misleading and even erroneous results is increased.

Another limitation in much of the assisted suicide literature, as in many empirical studies, is the difficulty in establishing causal relationships from cross-sectional or correlational data. There is little doubt that a correlation between depression and interest in assisted suicide does not necessarily mean that depression is the reason behind a particular individual's interest, yet researchers often ignore the well-known adage that correlation does not imply causality. What does help establish causality is the use of longitudinal or prospective designs, which can help disentangle the relationship between relevant variables at baseline and later (i.e., follow-up) attitudes toward assisted suicide or desire for death. Yet longitudinal studies have been rare in the assisted suicide literature and, perhaps not surprisingly, those that have been published have typically focused on relatively healthy participants. Longitudinal designs are obviously difficult to carry out with terminally ill patients because many die or become increasingly cognitively impaired during the course of the study. Nevertheless, important findings have emerged from the limited research that does exist applying longitudinal designs to analyze end-of-life issues. Linda Ganzini and her colleagues (Ganzini, Lee, Heintz, Bloom, & Fenn, 1994) reported that end-of-life decisions of severely depressed elderly patients changed substantially after they were treated for their depression.[5] With sufficiently large samples to compensate for the high rate of attrition that may occur, and cognitive assessments prior to data collection at each assessment point, short-term longitudinal studies of assisted suicide may be feasible even with terminally ill populations or in palliative care institutions. In addition, long-term longitudinal studies focusing on medically ill, but relatively healthy individuals (e.g., shortly after diagnosis) are crucial to understanding how attitudes toward assisted suicide or interest in hastened death may evolve over the course of illness. This clearly involves recruiting and following extremely large samples of patients in order to accrue even a modest sample of individuals who ultimately seek assisted suicide, given the infrequency with which this occurs.

A CALL FOR QUALITATIVE RESEARCH?

Despite the infrequency of assisted suicide requests and the complexity of individual cases, few qualitative researchers have attempted to disentangle the myriad factors that are involved in these decisions. Most studies, such as those described in this volume, have applied relatively simplistic empirical or descriptive approaches to studying end-of-life decisions. In fact, few studies have applied a truly qualitative method to studying interest in assisted suicide or desire for hastened death. Some of this literature has supported the findings from more empirical analyses (e.g., Wilson et al., 2000) but others have revealed important variables that may have been obscured in large empirical studies (e.g., Lavery, Boyle, Dickens, Maclean, & Singer, 2001). Continued application of such "multimethod" approaches to the assessment of assisted suicide may reveal important influences on assisted suicide decisions that researchers have not yet identified.

SUMMARY

The challenges to assisted suicide research highlighted above are numerous but hardly insurmountable. Specialized instruments developed to assess desire for hastened death should facilitate research in this area, as has the legalization of assisted suicide in Oregon. Legalization offers unique opportunities for researchers to study patients who actually seek assisted suicide instead of relying on the hypothetical preferences typically studied. These developments have greatly facilitated the growing empirical literature, although conceptual developments, as might be obtained through rigorous

---

[5]The details of this study are described further in chapter 7. Although end-of-life decisions changed substantially, there was no clear pattern to these changes (i.e., less depressed patients were not necessarily more likely to desire life-sustaining interventions).

qualitative studies of terminally ill individuals, have lagged farther behind. The opportunities to improve assisted suicide research, however, will not be fully realized until researchers begin to incorporate more rigorous research methods that are designed to address the relevant clinical and policy issues. Clearly, the choice of appropriate dependent variables, research methods, and data analysis (whether quantitative or qualitative) is necessary in order to further understand these important issues. Although there is no "prescription" for the optimal study methodology, there are certainly better and worse approaches for the many different research questions that exist. Applying a method that may be appropriate for one research question to another, altogether different question will inevitably be of less benefit than choosing the method that best fits the question at hand.

5

INFLUENCE OF DEPRESSION AND PSYCHOSOCIAL FACTORS ON PHYSICIAN-ASSISTED SUICIDE

Proposing a relationship between depression and physician-assisted suicide seems a bit like suggesting that there is a relationship between health concerns and visits to the doctor.[1] How could the two not be related? Most people would probably assume that anyone seeking to end his or her life, whatever the circumstances, must be quite depressed. Yet common sense and empirical data do not always agree. In fact, although the research on depression and interest in physician-assisted suicide or desire for death is far more consistent than the research on pain and physical symptoms (described in the next chapter), discrepancies exist in this literature that are only partially attributable to research methodology. Like much of the research discussed in this book, research addressing psychosocial influences on end-of-life issues can be broken down in terms of the outcome variables used. What's more, important differences have emerged between studies of hypothetical interest in assisted suicide, current desire for death in medically ill individuals, and reasons behind patient requests for assisted suicide or euthanasia.

---

[1]An earlier verion of this chapter appeared in Rosenfeld, "Assisted Suicide, Depression, and the Right to Die," *Psychology, Public Policy, and Law*, 6 (2000): 529–549.

Beginning in the mid 1990s, several studies were conducted on the association between depression and "interest" in assisted suicide.[2] Although the limitations of these studies of hypothetical interest in assisted suicide have been well-documented (see chap. 4), these studies have served as a catalyst for the more sophisticated research that has recently begun to emerge. Yet, several additional limitations must be noted in these studies of hypothetical interest in physician-assisted suicide beyond concerns about the appropriateness of the dependent variable described in the preceding chapter. First, measures of depression have varied in their adequacy, ranging from well-designed self-report questionnaires (e.g., the Beck Depression Inventory; Beck, Ward, Mendelson, Mock, & Erbaugh, 1961) and structured diagnostic interviews (e.g., the Structured Clinical Interview for DSM–IV [SCID]; First, Spitzer, Gibbon, & Williams, 2001) to abbreviated questionnaires of unknown or questionable utility. Although measures of depressive symptom severity are a useful method for quantifying depression, they do not permit a determination of which patients meet criteria for a depressive disorder diagnosis. A clinical diagnosis, whether for Major Depressive Disorder or any other disorder, is often more clinically useful and intuitively appealing for both practitioners and research scientists. In addition, other psychosocial measures (e.g., social support, quality of life) that are often used in end-of-life research have varied tremendously in terms of psychometric adequacy (Bowling, 1997). Some studies have relied on single questions to tap potentially relevant constructs, others have used well-conceived questionnaires, and still others have not measured potentially relevant constructs at all. Given the tremendous differences in research methods and sample composition, the consistency of some of the findings is all the more remarkable.

Of the studies that have addressed depression and interest in assisted suicide, five stand out as the most comprehensive, and four of these have identified a significant role for depression (see Table 5.1). The only study that did not observe a significant relationship between depression and interest in assisted suicide (Ganzini et al., 1998), nevertheless observed a strong relationship between hopelessness and interest in assisted suicide and has some limitations in terms of their measurement of depression. The specific role of hopelessness, both as a facet of depression as well as an independent construct, is discussed later.

One of the first studies to address correlates of interest in assisted suicide was conducted by my colleagues William Breitbart and Steven Passik and myself (Breitbart et al., 1996). We studied 378 patients with HIV and

---

[2]In many of the early studies, patients were asked whether they might consider assisted suicide at some future time. These studies often used the term "interest" in assisted suicide to refer to the willingness to consider physician-assisted suicide.

TABLE 5.1
Depression and Interest in Assisted Suicide

	Study characteristics			Correlation–effect size		
Author	Participants	Method	Dep	BHS	Anx	SS
Brietbart et al., 1996	378 AIDS outpts	Interview	.27[a]			25[a]
Emanuel et al., 1996	155 cancer pts	Survey		data not reported		
Ganzini, et al., 1998	100 ALS pts	Interview	ns[b]	2.5[a]		ns[b]
Berkman et al., 1999	505 MS outpts	Survey	.28			.52[a]
Emanuel et al., 2000	988 cancer outpts	Survey	.18			

Note. Dep = depression; BHS = Beck Hopelessness Scale; Anx = anxiety; SS = social support; outpts = outpatients; pts = patients; ALS = amyotrophic lateral sclerosis; MS = multiple sclerosis.
[a]Numbers reflect Cohen's *d*; other numbers reflect correlation coefficients.
[b]Data were not reported, but the association was not statistically significant.

AIDS drawn from the metropolitan New York City area and, in addition to an extensive battery of self-report instruments, we asked whether participants "would consider physician-assisted suicide if it were legal." More than half of these patients (55%) affirmed that they would consider physician-assisted suicide if it were legal, and these individuals scored significantly higher on self-report measures of depression (the Beck Depression Inventory) and overall psychological distress (the Brief Symptom Inventory; Derogotis & Melisaratos, 1983). Patients who indicated a willingness to "consider" physician-assisted suicide at some future time also reported significantly lower levels of social support than did patients who would not consider this option and were more likely to acknowledge concerns about becoming a burden to their family or friends and more likely to have experienced the death of a close friend or family member from AIDS. Although these findings were consistent with our expectations, the magnitude of the correlation was relatively small, accounting for only a modest portion of the variance in patient interest in physician-assisted suicide. What remains unclear is whether this modest association was the result of our imperfect approach (e.g., using a single hypothetical question as the dependent variable) or in fact provide an accurate estimate of the magnitude of the depression–desire for death relationship.

E. J. Emanuel et al. (1996) used a very different method but reached a number of similar conclusions. They surveyed cancer patients, their physicians, and the general public, and they asked whether the respondent considered euthanasia "acceptable" in each of four different hypothetical scenarios (one described a cancer patient with unremitting pain, one pertained to functional disability, one to excessive family burden, and one described a patient who viewed life as meaningless). They found no relationship between depression or psychological distress (based on questions extracted from a quality-of-life measure) and approval of euthanasia in any of the four vignettes, although their analysis of the sample drawn from the general public apparently approached significance; they stated that "members of the general public with depression and psychological distress were slightly, but not significantly, more likely to find euthanasia and physician-assisted suicide acceptable in the vignettes" (p. 1808). However, behaviors thought to be related to interest in assisted suicide and euthanasia (i.e., having discussions regarding these issues with their physicians, having read the book *Final Exit*, or having hoarded medications for a possible suicide attempt) were significantly more common among cancer patients who were classified as depressed or distressed compared to those who were not.[3]

Linda Ganzini and colleagues (Ganzini et al., 1998) studied attitudes toward physician-assisted suicide among patients with ALS. They asked whether patients would "consider taking a prescription for a medication whose sole purpose was to end my life" and compared those who responded affirmatively (56%) to those who did not (44%). Although they found a significant association between interest in physician-assisted suicide and scores on the Beck Hopelessness Scale (BHS; Beck, Weissman, Lester, & Trexel, 1974), there was no association with either the presence of a depressive disorder or perceived social support. However, because Ganzini et al. relied on a measure of depression that has significant limitations in the context of severe medical illness (the Diagnostic Interview Schedule; Robins, Helzer, Croughan, & Ratcliff, 1981), the accuracy of these depression diagnoses is questionable. Not only is the Diagnostic Interview Schedule designed to be administered by lay raters, but no data regarding rater training or interrater reliability were reported in this article, raising concerns regarding the accuracy of their depression diagnoses. Whether an association would have been found between interest in assisted suicide and depression diagnoses established by trained mental health clinicians or depressive symptom severity is unknown.[4]

---

[3]Common sense would certainly suggest that reading a book detailing ways to commit suicide (*Final Exit*; Humphry, 1991), discussing assisted suicide with one's doctor, or hoarding medications would reflect interest in physician-assisted suicide or elevated desire for death. However, our research conducted in the development of the SAHD contradicted this assumption (Rosenfeld et al., 1999). Behaviors such as discussing suicide with one's physician, signing DNR orders, making or revising a will, and so on were included in an earlier version of this measure but were eventually deleted, largely because of the low correspondence between these behaviors and desire for hastened death.

[4]Some writers have suggested that clinical depression is uncommon among ALS patients, which would be consistent with Ganzini et al.'s data. However, this hypothesis, if true, would indicate that studies of ALS patients have little generalizability to other medically ill or terminally ill populations. Nevertheless, given the nature of ALS, in which virtually no treatment options are available (unlike cancer or AIDS), hopelessness may be a better marker of patient distress than depression per se. Indeed, because of the nature of this disease, patients with ALS may label their depression in terms of hopelessness rather than sadness or dysphoria, further confounding the distinction between these two constructs. Future research attempting to understand the relationship between hopelessness and depression, both in patients with ALS as well as in other terminal illnesses, is clearly needed.

Berkman, Cavallo, Chesnut, and Holland (1999) also studied interest in assisted suicide. They too utilized a hypothetical question method to study attitudes toward assisted suicide among persons with multiple sclerosis (MS), mailing questionnaires to 750 individuals with MS from Oregon and Michigan; roughly 2/3 of them responded. Respondents were asked whether they would consider assisted suicide under several hypothetical conditions: unbearable pain, causing a financial burden to family or caregivers, feeling extreme emotional distress, inability to do things that make one happy, and lack of enjoyment in life. Most analyses, however, were based on comparisons of responses of people who indicated a willingness to consider assisted suicide in any of these five conditions with the responses of those who would not consider assisted suicide at all. They found that willingness to consider assisted suicide in at least one vignette, roughly 1/3 of their sample, was significantly associated with severity of depressive symptoms based on a self-report scale frequently used in medical settings (the Center for Epidemiological Studies, Depression Scale; CES-D; Radloff, 1977). When they divided respondents into "depressed" and "nondepressed" groups, they found that nearly half of the depressed patients were willing to consider assisted suicide under some circumstances compared to only 20% of the nondepressed patients. Social support was also significantly stronger among those who would not consider assisted suicide compared to those who would. Interestingly, in a multivariate logistic regression model, lack of support derived from religion was the single strongest predictor of willingness to consider physician-assisted suicide, dwarfing the effects of both depression and poor social support in general.

E. J. Emanuel et al. (2000) addressed the relationship between depression and interest in assisted suicide. Their method was similar to the one used in their earlier study, but this time they focused more specifically on the factors that predicted consideration of assisted suicide. They surveyed nearly 1,000 terminally ill outpatients using a battery of specific questions and self-report measures. Patients were classified as having "personal interest in euthanasia or PAS" if they answered affirmatively to the question "have you ever seriously discussed taking your life or asking your doctor to end your life?" (endorsed by 10.6% of the total sample). Patients who "had depressive symptoms" (no further details were provided regarding the basis for this classification) were significantly more likely to have "personal interest in euthanasia or PAS" (19.5% vs. 8.7%) as were patients who reported "feeling unappreciated" (22.0% vs. 8.4%) and both of these variables remained significant in a multivariate logistic regression model that also included age, race, the presence of moderate or severe pain, and needing moderate or significant assistance with daily care needs.

In summary, all three of the studies that have used standardized measures of depressive symptom severity have observed a significant association between interest in assisted suicide and severity of depression. Even the exception to this trend, Ganzini's study of ALS patients (1998), noted a strong association between hopelessness (which clearly bears some similarities to depression) and interest in physician-assisted suicide. However, the relationship between social support and hypothetical interest in physician-assisted suicide is somewhat less clear in the studies described above. Although our research group and Berkman's study found significant associations between social support and interest in physician-assisted suicide, Ganzini et al.'s did not. In Emanuel's first study (E. J. Emanuel et al., 1996), social support was not addressed, but in their more recent study (2000) they found a significant association between interest in physician-assisted suicide and "feeling unappreciated," a variable that likely overlaps with the construct of social support even if this connection is ill-defined. Thus, although firm conclusions about the role of social support in interest in physician-assisted suicide are perhaps premature, there is certainly reason to believe that this variable will continue to be an important one in future, more sophisticated research efforts as well as in clinical practice.

DEPRESSION AND DESIRE FOR HASTENED DEATH

In part because of the methodological shortcomings inherent in studies of hypothetical interest in physician-assisted suicide, a growing body of literature has focused on the construct *desire for hastened death*. Desire for hastened death is construed as an umbrella concept encompassing interest in physician-assisted suicide, suicidal ideation that does not involve a physician, and decisions regarding terminal sedation or the termination or withholding of life-sustaining interventions (Rosenfeld, 2000b). Almost without exception, studies of desire for hastened death have found a strong role for depression, regardless of whether depression is conceived as symptom severity or the presence or absence of a depressive disorder diagnosis.

Although the construct of desire for hastened death has been primarily linked to the assisted suicide debate, the first research addressing the relationship between desire for death and depression was published several years before Drs. Kevorkian and Quill brought the issue of assisted suicide into the public spotlight. Brown et al. (1986) conducted clinical interviews with terminally ill patients residing in a hospital-based palliative care facility. Of the 44 patients studied, 10 acknowledged some desire for hastened death or suicidal ideation, and each of these individuals was subsequently diagnosed with a major depressive disorder in accordance with the third edition of the *Diagnostic and Statistical Manual of Mental Disorders* (*DSM–III*; American Psychiatric Association, 1980) diagnostic criteria. Not surprisingly, the authors concluded that desire for death among terminally ill patients was likely due to depression rather than a "rational" response to terminal illness. Unfortunately, like most initial forays into uncharted research territory, this study contained a number of methodological limitations that affect the validity of their conclusions. Foremost among these limitations is the lack of independent assessments of depression and the desire for death (which included expressions of suicidal ideation). Because all data appear to have been derived from a single clinical interview, depression diagnoses were likely confounded by the investigator's knowledge of the patient's thoughts of death or suicidal ideation (i.e., patients who expressed a desire to die or expressed suicidal thoughts would likely have been perceived as "depressed" by the clinician). Similarly, because diagnoses were based on unstructured clinical interviews (as opposed to structured or systematic diagnostic interviews), the reliability and validity of these diagnoses are unclear. Some depressed individuals who did not express overt symptoms (e.g., suicidal ideation) might have been classified as nondepressed because of their atypical presentation. Nonetheless, although depression and desire for death might not be as closely linked as Brown et al.'s results would suggest, some concordance no doubt exists and has been increasingly clarified in subsequent studies.

Perhaps the seminal study (to date) of desire for death and depression in terminally ill individuals was conducted by a group of Canadian researchers led by Harvey Chochinov (Chochinov et al., 1995). They studied 200 terminally ill cancer patients admitted to a palliative care hospital in Winnipeg, Canada, a sample size nearly five times that studied by Brown et al. They also improved upon the assessment of depression by interviewing patients with a structured interview schedule designed to yield *DSM–III* diagnoses, the Schedule for Affective Disorders and Schizophrenia (Endicott & Spitzer, 1978). The most significant innovation in Chochinov et al.'s method was the development of a systematic measure for rating desire for hastened death. Following a series of relatively standardized prompts, they used a 6-point rating scale, the DDRS, to rate each patient's desire for death (Chochinov et al., 1995). Patients for whom desire for death was rated at least "moderate" (scores of 4 or greater) were classified as having a "serious and pervasive" desire for death and contrasted with patients with "none," "minimal," or "mild" desire for death (scores of 1, 2, and 3, respectively). Of the 200 patients studied, 17 (8.5%) were considered to have a "serious and pervasive" desire for death, and 10 of these (58%) were diagnosed with a current major depressive episode. Scores on the Beck Depression Inventory also differed substantially (and significantly) between these two groups; patients with a high desire for hastened death obtained scores that were more than double those obtained by patients with low desire ($d = 1.7$). In addition, desire for death was modestly associated with perceived social support ($d = .65$).[5] Thus, although still demonstrating a strong relationship between de-

---

[5] This significant effect was found for the analysis of perceived family support; no significant effects were found for staff or friend support or for frequency of visits from family or friends.

pression and desire for death, the degree of association between them observed by Chochinov et al. was far more modest than the findings of Brown et al. a decade earlier.

In an effort to expand upon Chochinov's measure, William Breitbart and I, in collaboration with colleagues at the Memorial Sloan-Kettering Cancer Center, developed a self-report measure of desire for hastened death, the SAHD. In our initial studies of patients with AIDS and cancer (Rosenfeld et al., 1999; Rosenfeld et al., 2000), we observed somewhat higher rates of desire for hastened death than those reported by Chochinov et al. (1995); between 10% and 15% of terminally ill patients were classified as having "high" desire for death with this instrument depending on the cut-off score used. Scores on the SAHD were highly correlated with measures of depressive symptom severity in both samples ($r = .59$ in patients with HIV/AIDS and $r = .52$ in cancer patients). As in Chochinov's study, we found that roughly half of those patients with high desire for death also met diagnostic criteria for a major depressive episode. Conversely, of patients with a major depression, roughly half had a high desire for death. In addition to studying the relationship between depression and desire for hastened death, we also included a measure of hopelessness in our study of terminally ill cancer patients, the Beck Hopelessness Scale (BHS; Beck, Weissman, Lester, & Trexel, 1974). Despite the conceptual overlap between depression and hopelessness, we found that both provided significant, unique, and roughly comparable contributions to the prediction of desire for hastened death (see Figure 5.1). Of the patients who were neither depressed nor hopeless (i.e., endorsed eight or fewer BHS items), none had a high desire for hastened death whereas 5 of 8 patients who were both depressed and hopeless did. Roughly 25% had high desire for hastened death when one of these two risk factors (either depression or hopelessness but not both) was present.

The role of social support and other psychosocial factors in our initial SAHD studies was somewhat more complex than that of depression. In our initial study of patients with HIV/AIDS, we observed a significant correlation between desire for hastened death (SAHD total scores) and a measure of perceived social support ($r = -.39$). However, in our sample of terminally ill cancer patients we found no direct association between desire for death and social support ($r = -.06$). Yet when social support was entered into a multiple regression model, this variable was a significant predictor of SAHD scores in the cancer study (Breitbart et al., 2000). Thus, the most cautious conclusion regarding the role of social support and desire for hastened death is that this relationship, although partially supported, is perhaps more complex than is often assumed.

In another study of patients with ALS, Judith Rabkin and her colleagues (Rabkin et al., 2000) investigated both interest in assisted suicide as well as desire for hastened death (using the SAHD) in 51 outpatients attending a specialty clinic. They found comparable levels of desire for hastened death to

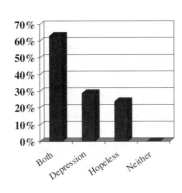

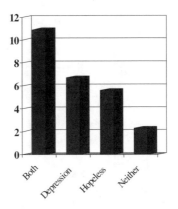

% High Desire for Death (SAHD > 10)

Mean SAHD Scores

Figure 5.1. Depression, hopelessness, and desire for hastened death. SAHD = Schedule of Attitudes Toward Hastened Death. Data from "Depression, Hopelessness, and Desire for Hastened Death in Terminally Ill Patients With Cancer," by W. Breitbart et al., 2000, *Journal of the American Medical Association*, *284*, p. 2909.

those observed in our studies of cancer and AIDS patients (based on the SAHD). Moreover, scores on the SAHD were highly correlated with scores on the Beck Depression Inventory (r = .46), the Beck Hopelessness Scale (r = .61), and measures of anxiety (r = .51) and social support (r = −.38). Although they did not report on the association between a diagnosis of depression (based on the SCID), only one patient in their sample met criteria for a major depressive disorder. Interestingly, patients who responded affirmatively to the question "Are there circumstances in which you would consider asking for a prescription for medicine whose sole purpose was to end your life?" obtained significantly higher scores on the SAHD than patients who responded negatively to this question (supporting the validity of the instrument), although they did not differ in terms of level of depression, hopelessness, or pain.

Keith Wilson and his colleagues (2000) applied a qualitative methodology to the study of desire for hastened death; they used semi-structured interviews to rate patient depression, hopelessness, anxiety, and a number of other theoretically relevant constructs. They interviewed 70 terminally ill cancer patients about both interest in assisted suicide and desire for hastened death. They compared patients who (a) would never consider euthanasia or physician-assisted suicide (n = 19), (b) would consider these options in the future but had no current desire for hastened death (n = 32), and (c) would request physician-assisted suicide or euthanasia in their current circumstances if possible (n = 8). The variables that most strongly differentiated these groups were hopelessness, desire for hastened death, and loss of interest or pleasure in activities (i.e., anhedonia). Post-hoc analyses revealed that these differences were primarily related to differences between the 8 patients who indicated a current desire to request physician-assisted suicide or euthanasia and the other 51 patients; no differences were found between patients who would consider physician-assisted suicide in the future and those who would not.

Chochinov and his colleagues studied the "will to live" in terminally ill cancer patients with particular emphasis on the factors that influence changes in will to live (Chochinov et al., 1999). Arguably, the will to live reflects the opposite end of the spectrum from desire for hastened death, although neither this report nor any other has thoroughly explored the meaning of this construct.[6] Chochinov and his colleagues studied 168 cancer patients in a Canadian palliative care facility, periodically asking each patient to rate his or her will to live on a visual analog scale over a period of several weeks. Multiple regression models were used to predict will to live on the basis of psychological and symptom variables, including depression, anxiety, pain, shortness of breath, and "sense of well-being." Unfortunately, neither social support nor any other social factor was studied. Also, the vast amount of data accumulated and analyzed generated a somewhat confusing set of results despite the emergence of some general trends in the findings. Will to live was most strongly influenced by psychological factors during the first few weeks after admission. Anxiety was the strongest predictor of will to live during the first days after admission, but depression emerged as a more powerful factor by the first and second weeks. Later assessments, at weeks 3 and 4, did not reveal any psychological factors influencing will to live; only dyspnea (shortness of breath) was significantly associated with will to live in these models. Although the results are intriguing, the use of stepwise multiple regression models might lead one to question how much of the results were due to chance rather than reflecting genuine patterns of influence. Nevertheless, Chochinov's results identifying depression and psychological distress as significant influences on will to live relatively early in the dying process clearly echo those of his earlier research as well as my group's studies of desire for hastened death.

Taken together, all of these studies reveal an emerging consensus that depression, and to a lesser extent social support, are significant contributing factors to desire for hastened death among terminally ill patients (see Table 5.2). Regardless of whether depression has been operationalized in terms of symptom severity or clinical diagnosis, all of the studies that have identified predictors of desire for hastened death (or the will to live) have concluded that depression is the single strongest predictor. The only exception to this statement pertains to the influence of hopelessness, which has been found to be more highly associated with desire for hastened death in several recent studies (Breitbart et al., 2000, Rabkin et al., 2000, Wilson et al., 2000).[7]

---

[6]Some theorists have disputed the conceptualization of "will to live" as the opposite of a desire for hastened death (e.g., Preston, 1995).

[7]Similar results were found in a study (Chochinov, Wilson, Enns, & Lander, 1998) focusing on the relative influence of depression and hopelessness in predicting suicidal ideation among terminally ill

TABLE 5.2
Depression and Desire for Hastened Death

	Study characteristics			Correlation–effect size		
Author	Participants	Criterion	Dep	BHS	Anx	SS
Chochinov et al., 1995	200 terminally ill cancer pts	DDRS	1.71[a]			.01[a]
Chochinov et al., 1999	168 terminally ill cancer pts	"Will to live"	.37–.49*		.30–.40*	
Rosenfeld et al., 1999	195 AIDS pts	SAHD	.43	2.5[a]		−.39
Breitbart et al., 2000	92 terminally ill cancer pts	SAHD	.49	.55		−.06
Rabkin et al., 2000	51 ALS pts	SAHD	.46	.61	.51	−.38
Wilson et al., 2000	70 cancer pts	Interview	.24	.56[b]	.19	

Note. DDRS = Desire for Death Rating Scale; SAHD = Schedule of Attitudes Toward Hastened Death; Dep = depression; BHS = Beck Hopelessness Scale; Anx = anxiety; SS = social support; pts = patients; ALS = amyotrophic lateral sclerosis.
[a]Numbers reflect Cohen's D; other numbers reflect correlation coefficients.
[b]Hopelessness scores are based on clinical rating.
*Data refer to models in which this variable provided a significant contribution; in some models the correlation was lower but was not reported.

Understanding the meaning and implications of hopelessness in patients with a terminal illness is, unfortunately, far from simple. Although measures of hopelessness (e.g., the Beck Hopelessness Scale) typically consider hopelessness to be more closely aligned with pessimism rather than an assessment of one's prognosis, future expectations are nevertheless an integral part of this construct (e.g., Rosenfeld, Gibson, Kramer, & Breitbart, 2002). Terminally ill individuals clearly have good reasons to feel pessimistic, but this outlook is far from universal. Indeed, many terminally ill individuals maintain a high degree of hope and optimism about a number of important aspects of their lives, consequently obtaining relatively low scores on the BHS. Yet, high levels of pessimism and hopelessness appear to occur more often than does clinical depression and, more importantly, the two often occur independently of one another. Further research exploring the construct of hopelessness in terminally ill populations and the implications of hopelessness for end-of-life decision making clearly is needed to more fully understand this phenomenon.

---

cancer patients. Hopelessness emerged as the strongest predictor of suicidal ideation in a multiple regression model. Although depression was significantly correlated with suicidal ideation (and highly correlated with hopelessness), it did not contribute significantly to this model when hopelessness was entered into the prediction model first (see also Ganzini et al., 1998).

REASONS BEHIND REQUESTS FOR
ASSISTED SUICIDE AND EUTHANASIA

Perhaps the most intuitively appealing avenue for research into the reasons behind requests for physician-assisted suicide or euthanasia entails no more than simply asking people why they make them. Several studies have typically asked physicians to recall the reasons behind their patient requests (rather than asking patients themselves). In fact, only one study has focused on information elicited directly from terminally ill individuals who sought assisted suicide; all other studies have instead relied on information contained in the case files of these individuals (B. C. Lee & Werth, 2000). Despite the potential for biased or selective recall, these studies have yielded useful data about the factors that drive requests for physician-assisted suicide.

The first study that described reasons behind patient requests for assisted suicide or euthanasia was published by a group of Dutch physicians and is described in more detail in chapter 8 (van der Maas et al., 1991). Included in this report were estimates of the most common reasons and were based on physician's recollection of the patients they had helped to die.[8] Of the five most common reasons, four fall within the general domain of "psychosocial factors." The most common reason for patient requests, cited by 57% of patients, was a "loss of dignity." Other commonly cited reasons included "unworthy dying" (which was not elaborated further in this report, but was given by 46% of patients), being dependent on others (33% of patients), and tiredness of life (23%). The only physical symptom that broke the list of top five reasons was pain, which was cited as a reason by 46% of patients.[9]

In another study of factors influencing patient requests for euthanasia, Seale and Addington-Hall (1994) surveyed 2,000 British individuals whose family members had died during 1990. Family members were asked to recall whether their relative had expressed a desire for hastened death at any time prior to their actual death (reported in 24% of cases) and whether a specific request for euthanasia had been made (reported in 3.6% of cases). Both expressions of a desire for hastened death and requests for euthanasia were significantly associated with a measure of quality of life, but the magnitude of these correlations was relatively small. (Quality of life had a .13 correlation with reported requests for euthanasia and a .23 correlation with expressions of a desire for hastened death.) Although this ambitious study utilized a unique

---

[8] Euthanasia is much more commonly applied in the Netherlands whereas physician-assisted suicide has more often been the subject of debate in the United States.

[9] Although some overlap clearly exists between terms like *loss of dignity*, *being dependent on others*, and *unworthy dying*, important distinctions also exist. For example, many individuals maintain a sense of dignity despite increased dependency on others. Unfortunately, researchers have often spent far too little time defining the variables they measure to enable a full understanding of these constructs. Nevertheless, patients are often aware of the differences between these seemingly overlapping terms as evidenced by differential responses to such questions.

methodology, relying on family members to recall expressions of desire for hastened death is almost as suspect as asking them to rate the quality of life of their deceased relative (a rating that appears to have been based primarily on their estimates of their relative's physical and psychological symptom severity). Also, because none of the deceased individuals were known to have made an actual request for assisted suicide or euthanasia, the validity of the dependent variable (family recollection regarding whether the patient expressed any desire to die sooner or interest in euthanasia) is clearly questionable.

Several physician surveys regarding the practice of assisted suicide and the reasons behind patient requests have also appeared in the literature. For example, Anthony Back and his colleagues (1996) conducted a survey of Washington physicians, asking whether they had received requests for assisted suicide and if so, to describe the circumstances of the cases (i.e., why the patient had made the request and how they responded). A full 26% of respondents reported having received at least one request for physician-assisted suicide, and 12% reported having received such requests within the preceding year. Of the physicians who received a request, 24% of the requests were fulfilled, typically by providing a prescription for a lethal medication. The most commonly cited reasons for patient requests were social factors, including concerns about a future loss of control (cited in 77% of cases), being a burden (75%), being dependent on others for some or all personal care (74%), and loss of dignity (72%).[10] Depression was listed as a factor in 55% of these cases. One of the most frequent responses to physician-assisted suicide requests reported by physicians was to prescribe medications for depression or anxiety (65% of cases) and/or refer the patient to a psychiatrist or psychologist (24%), indicating that physicians perceived many of these patients as depressed and believed that treatment might be appropriate or beneficial.

Diane Meier and her colleagues (1998) conducted a national survey of nearly 2,000 physicians whose areas of specialization made them likely to receive requests for assisted suicide or euthanasia (e.g., oncology, infectious disease, geriatrics). The rate of requests for physician-assisted suicide in this sample was slightly lower than that reported by Back et al.'s sample of Washington physicians, with 18.3% of responding physicians having received at least one request for assisted suicide and 11.1% having received requests for "lethal injection" (although the majority of the requests for lethal injection were made by family members). Of the subset of physicians who reported having received requests for physician-assisted suicide or euthanasia, a small proportion reported acceding to these requests. Only 3.3% of responding physicians acknowledged having written a prescription for a lethal medication, and 4.7% provided a lethal injection. The most common reasons cited

---

[10]Total percentage exceeds 100 because respondents were allowed to give more than one reason.

in these requests for hastened death included "discomfort other than pain" (present in 79% of requests), "loss of dignity" (53%), "fear of uncontrollable symptoms" (52%), pain (50%), and "loss of meaning in their lives" (47%). Depression was noted in only 19% of patients who requested assisted suicide but 39% of cases in which a lethal injection was sought. Although most physicians responded to requests for hastened death with more aggressive palliative care (i.e., increased analgesic medications, 68%) or less aggressive life-prolonging treatments (30%), 25% of physicians reported having prescribed antidepressant medications in response to such requests. Despite this seeming acknowledgment of the impact of depression on patient requests for hastened death, only 2% of the responding physicians referred their patients for a psychiatric consultation in response to a request for assistance in dying.

More current data on requests for assisted suicide have emerged in Oregon as a result of the ODDA. These studies are discussed in more detail in chapter 9; here, the elements relevant to this chapter are summarized briefly. The most detailed study of reasons for patient requests for assisted suicide was published by Ganzini and her colleagues (Ganzini, Nelson et al., 2000). They surveyed all Oregon physicians who were eligible to provide assistance in dying under the ODDA. More than 4,000 questionnaires were mailed, and 2,649 physicians responded; of them, 144 reported having received a total of 221 requests for assisted suicide under the new law (a substantially greater number than actually received lethal medications).[11] The most commonly cited factors driving patient requests for physician-assisted suicide included a loss of independence (noted in 57% of cases), poor quality of life (55%), and a desire to control the circumstances of one's death (53%). Inadequate social support was cited in only 6% of cases and financial considerations (i.e., being a financial burden to others) in 11%. Depression was considered present in 20% of the cases but not cited as a factor in decision making by any of the respondents. The authors concluded that concerns regarding the implementation of assisted suicide legislation were not supported. That is, depressed or otherwise vulnerable populations did not appear to be at substantially greater risk of requesting physician-assisted suicide. Of course, other possible explanations have been suggested such as the possibility that many patients who request physician-assisted suicide are in fact depressed but their depression is simply not recognized by the physicians responding to their requests (Rosenfeld & Breitbart, 2000). One would hope that physicians would be adequately trained to recognize depression in their patients, but research studies have consistently shown otherwise (e.g., Garrad et al., 1998; Passik et al., 1998).

Indeed, one study of oncologists found that their ability to recognize depression in their patients was startlingly poor (Passik et al., 1998). Of pa-

---

[11] A subsequent survey of nurses and social workers who work in palliative care settings generated largely comparable results (Ganzini et al., 2002).

tients with "moderate" to "severe" levels of depression, 49% were rated by their physicians as not at all depressed, and another 38% of patients were rated as having only "mild" depression. Physicians accurately recognized the extent of their patient's depression (when it was moderate to severe) in only one of eight cases. Although many writers have speculated on the reasons for this state of affairs (and other studies have demonstrated similarly poor levels of recognition), frequently cited barriers include the relatively limited training most physicians (other than psychiatrists) receive in mental health issues and the discomfort many physicians feel when discussing emotional or psychological issues with their patients. Physicians, like the general public, are also prone to assume that sadness and depression are an inherent part of the dying process and therefore might normalize the symptoms that they observe (frequent crying, expressions of hopelessness, feelings of guilt, etc.). By not recognizing depression when present, physicians may assume that depression is simply not a factor in many physician-assisted suicide requests when it is in fact both present and important. It also is certainly possible that physicians would be more likely to suspect, or even inquire about, depression when a patient has requested assisted suicide (as opposed to a routine oncology setting), but no research has addressed this possibility.

However, the failure to detect a role for depression in requests for assisted suicide may not reflect a simple lack of recognition on the part of physicians. Physicians may realize that their patients are depressed yet not mention this symptom because they perceive other symptoms, such as pain or functional decline, to be more important or legitimate. Also, responsibility for the failure of physicians to detect depression in their patients, regardless of whether they have requested assisted suicide, may not lie solely with physicians. Patients, too, may not realize the influence their depressed mood has on their interest in physician-assisted suicide. The presence of cognitive distortions in the course of depression is well known and may interfere with a patient's ability to perceive the role depression plays in his or her decision making. Even when patients are aware of their depression and its impact on their decision making, they may simply neglect to mention it to their physicians. They may prefer to focus on what they perceive to be more "legitimate" reasons for ending their life (such as physical symptoms or deteriorating physical abilities) or be justifiably concerned that their doctor will demand they seek mental health treatment instead of providing a prescription to hasten death (as may be required under Oregon law; see chap. 9). Both patients and physicians may also be reluctant to invite the additional scrutiny, and intrusion, that a label of depression might entail, leading both parties to avoid discussing, acknowledging, or addressing possible depressive symptoms. Finally, the same predictors that emerge in studies using standardized measures of depression (e.g., depression, hopelessness, social support) might simply be articulated differently when patients discuss their reasoning with their doctor and are therefore not perceived as analogous. In any case, it is clear that without more systematic research on the role of depression in requests for assisted suicide, understanding the factors that drive patient requests will remain elusive.

SUMMARY

Studies of depression at the end of life have revealed an interesting pattern of differences depending on the study methodology that has been used. Research focusing on interest in physician-assisted suicide or desire for hastened death has consistently identified depression as the leading influence, although hopelessness has recently emerged as a strong contender for that position. Social support has also emerged as a significant factor in many of these studies, but its influence has been varied and far weaker. However, studies of patient requests for physician-assisted suicide have been nearly universal in not finding a role for depression in patient requests. Instead, a range of other psychosocial influences has been described. These influences center primarily on feelings of dependence on others, perception of oneself as a burden, a desire to retain some control during the last days or weeks of life, and a sense of diminished dignity or quality of life in general. How these factors relate to the more commonly studied psychosocial variables such as depression and social support is unknown, but some conceptual overlap may exist.

Resolving the discrepancies across these studies is hindered by the methodological differences. It may be that the failure to observe the important role of depression in studies of actual requests for physician-assisted suicide is largely due to the failure of physicians to identify or acknowledge this issue. However, a similar criticism, lack of sensitivity, can also be levied against the literature on interest in physician-assisted suicide and desire for death. Although most of these studies have included a measure of social support, few have included systematic measures of other psychosocial variables. For example, Breitbart and I included a single question regarding whether patients considered themselves to be a burden to others, and responses to this question were significantly associated with desire for death (although this "variable" was not included in multivariate analyses because of excessive missing data; Breitbart et al., 2000). Other variables, such as dependency on others, the desire (or need) to control the circumstances one's death, and perhaps most important, level of dignity and self-respect, have never been systematically studied in the context of terminal illness. Had such variables been included in studies of interest in assisted suicide or desire for hastened death, the influence of depression per se may have receded into the background with other psychosocial factors emerging as more important predictors.

Another variable that has only recently begun to be explored is the construct of hopelessness. The handful of studies that have included measures of hopelessness have found this variable to be the strongest predictor of desire for death and interest in physician-assisted suicide. However, the construct of hopelessness has also generated considerable confusion in the context of terminal illness, with researchers (and journal reviewers) often questioning whether hopelessness pertains to a cognitive style (e.g., pessimism), an emotional of affective state, or a prognostic assessment (i.e., that no *hope* for a cure exists). The possibility that hopelessness conveys a cognitive or affective state in which one feels unable to accomplish the goals they have set has much more important implications for understanding the desire for hastened death and requests for assisted suicide than does a simple prognostic assessment. Researchers will no doubt benefit from studying the construct of hopelessness in the context of terminal illness, and this research will likely help further our understanding of these important end-of-life issues. Moreover, understanding what factors help patients retain hope in the context of terminal illness has important implications for end-of-life care.

Finally, a discussion of the role of depression and other psychosocial influences on desire for hastened death or requests for assisted suicide might lead one to presume that the depression automatically "invalidates" a request for assisted suicide. However, depression does not necessarily preclude rational decision making regarding assisted suicide or any other end-of-life issue. In fact, a depressed mood or social difficulties in addition to a terminal illness might constitute yet another "rational" reason why one would consider assisted suicide. Studies of depression and decision making have occasionally concluded that depressed individuals are *more* rational decision makers than non-depressed individuals (Costello, 1983), although whether such findings apply to end-of-life decisions is unknown. The influence of depression on decision making is explored in more depth in chapter 7.

There is little doubt that depression might lead a medically ill or terminally ill patient to consider physician-assisted suicide, but the precise role of depression in such requests is less clear. The dramatic differences observed across studies shows just how profound an impact study method can have on the results obtained. Yet researchers and policymakers seem quick to accept those results that fit their expectations and ignore those that do not. Given this complexity, perhaps the only reasonable conclusion that can be offered is that although depression and psychosocial factors are clearly among the most important influences on end-of-life decisions such as physician-assisted suicide, the precise nature of these influences is still largely unclear. Answers to these important questions must await the more sophisticated research efforts that will inevitably follow.

6

THE ROLE OF PAIN AND OTHER PHYSICAL SYMPTOMS IN THE DESIRE FOR HASTENED DEATH

Since interest in physician-assisted suicide and euthanasia resurfaced in the late 20th century, pain and physical disability have been perhaps the most frequently cited justifications for legalization of assisted suicide (K. M. Foley, 1991, 1995; M. Sullivan, Rapp, Fitzgibbon, & Chapman, 1997). Palliative care specialists have often claimed that adequate pain control would virtually eliminate requests for assisted suicide, although the evidence to support these assertions has never been clear (K. M. Foley, 1995). Nevertheless, there is little dispute that pain often accompanies terminal illnesses such as cancer and AIDS and that the incidence of severe pain is both well-known and intensely feared by many medically ill patients (Passik, Kirsch, Rosenfeld, McDonald, & Theobold, 2001). Unfortunately, patient fears are often justified, because research has documented not only high rates of pain but disturbingly high rates of inadequate treatment for patients with pain (Breitbart et al., 1996; Cleeland et al., 1994). Therefore, not only is there a legitimate basis for patient concerns that they might suffer from pain at some point in their illness, there also is ample justification for patients to believe that their pain will not be adequately managed.

Against this backdrop, the belief that pain is a primary reason for assisted suicide requests is not particularly surprising. Much of the early, anecdotal writings on euthanasia and physician-assisted suicide focused on pain as the primary reason for the "rational" desire for suicide. Indeed, the authors of the early articles that fueled the assisted suicide debate, like the case reports published in the *Journal of the American Medical Association* (e.g., Anonymous, 1988; Quill, 1993), focused on uncontrolled or uncontrollable symptoms (including but not limited to pain) in justifying their decisions either to provide a prescription for, or to inject, people with a lethal medication. The belief that pain is perhaps the most legitimate justification for assisted suicide and euthanasia is echoed by the general public. In a survey of the responses of cancer patients, oncologists, and the public to various vignettes, E. J. Emanuel and his colleagues (1996) found that euthanasia was much more likely to be considered "acceptable" as a resolution for unremitting pain than it was for functional disability, perceiving oneself as a burden to family, or the view that life was meaningless.[1] It is interesting that patients who reported experiencing pain at the time of study participation were actually less likely to approve of euthanasia in the vignette describing unremitting pain than were patients who were not in pain.

Yet the legitimacy of this justification for assisted suicide or euthanasia, that pain associated with terminal illness is inevitable and intolerable, has been increasingly questioned. Unlike the research on depression and psychosocial influences on interest in, or requests for, physician-assisted suicide, studies focusing on the role of pain have been more equivocal in their results. Although some studies have shown that pain plays a role in end-of-life decisions, others have not. However, where these two literatures converge is the consistency with which study methods influence research findings; the relationship between pain and physician-assisted suicide has varied dramatically and systematically depending on how the research was conducted.

RESEARCH ON THE ROLE OF PAIN IN PHYSICIAN-ASSISTED SUICIDE

To date, virtually no researcher has found a significant relationship between pain and interest in physician-assisted suicide. My colleagues and I, in our study of ambulatory HIV/AIDS patients, found no relationship between interest in physician-assisted suicide and either the presence or severity of pain (Breitbart et al., 1996); nor did Ganzini et al. (1998) and Berkman

---

[1]These findings were consistent across samples of cancer patients, oncologists, and the general public.

et al. (1999) in their studies of patients with ALS and MS respectively. Ganzini and her colleagues found no relationship between "willingness to consider assisted suicide" and either pain or the extent of symptom-related physical disability; Berkman et al. (1999) found no relationship between considering assisted suicide as an option and severity of functional disability resulting from MS. (They did not study pain.) However, the Ganzini and Berkman studies share an important feature in that they have focused on populations (ALS and MS) in which pain may not be either widely anticipated (i.e., feared) or particularly common. Even our study of patients with AIDS, where the prevalence of pain is roughly comparable to that found in cancer patients (greater than 60%), pain has rarely been identified as a primary consequence of HIV or AIDS (Brietbart et al., 1998). Thus, although these studies are far from conclusive, the fact that studies of interest in assisted suicide have not focused on a population in which pain is a major factor (e.g., cancer) may have influenced the null results.

This criticism, however, cannot be applied to the study conducted by Mark Sullivan and his colleagues (M. Sullivan et al., 1997). Unlike the research described above, which typically included pain as one of many predictor variables, Sullivan and his colleagues focused squarely on the role of pain and its influence on end-of-life preferences. They studied 48 cancer patients with advanced or metastatic disease, all of whom had persistent pain, using a detailed measure of cancer pain as well as several questions regarding end-of-life preferences. Unfortunately, their unique approach did not necessarily improve on the single hypothetical questions used by other researchers. Sullivan et al. measured interest in hastened death by summing patient responses to several questions regarding active euthanasia, passive euthanasia, and "total means of hastening death." Although the nature of these questions was not clearly described, the authors referred to attitudes toward euthanasia "in the case of severe unrelieved pain" as a focus of many cases. Sullivan et al. found no demographic or medical variables that were significantly associated with these outcome variables, nor were any of the measures of current pain intensity or pain relief significantly associated with overall interest in a hastened death. However, specific physical symptoms were significantly correlated with this interest in hastened death, including a measure of overall symptom burden as well as several specific symptoms such as fatigue, sedation ("sleeping too much"), and lack of interest in sex. Despite the absence of a correlation between current pain and interest in hastened death among patients with chronic pain and advanced cancer, the authors concluded that "a person's need to get relief from pain and suffering" was the second most frequently cited reason in support of legalization of assisted suicide, endorsed by 27% of their sample.[2]

---

[2]The most frequently cited rationale for legalization in this study was "a person's right to choose what to do with his or her own life," endorsed by 50% as the most important reason for legalization.

The authors also described a logistic regression model predicting scores on the "active euthanasia" variable, but this model included only one statistically significant predictor variable: a summary score measuring the extent to which various pain consequences were perceived as "intolerable." Unfortunately, their study description did not detail what other variables were considered for inclusion in this analysis or how this dependent variable differed from the summary variables used earlier in their report. Nevertheless, the authors interpreted their data as evidence that "pain expectancies" (i.e., the expectation that the pain would be intolerable) were more important than either current pain or depression. However, given their use of an idiosyncratic and untested rating scale as the primary dependent variable, it is clearly premature to draw firm conclusions on these data. Despite these limitations, this study offers an alternative explanation as to how pain might influence end-of-life decision making—by emphasizing pain expectancies rather than current pain.

To date, only one study has observed a clear and statistically significant relationship between interest in assisted suicide and pain. E. J. Emanuel and his colleagues (2000), in their study of nearly 1,000 terminally ill patients (most of whom had cancer) became the first group to observe the pain–interest in assisted suicide relationship that has been so frequently assumed. By collapsing their sample into two groups, those with moderate or severe pain and those with no pain or only mild pain, they found that patients with moderate to severe pain were significantly more likely to express "personal interest in PAS." They also noted that patients who had "moderate or significant care needs" (reflecting limited physical functioning abilities) were significantly more likely to express an interest in physician-assisted suicide than were patients with less severe care needs. Moreover, both variables, pain and functional limitations, remained significant in a multivariate model in which depressive symptoms, age, and race were also included, indicating that these variables might provide a unique contribution to understanding interest in assisted suicide in terminally ill patients.

Although a superficial reading of this literature might lead one to conclude that pain is not a significant predictor of interest in assisted suicide (because the two were significantly associated in only one of five published studies), several alternative explanations also exist. First, as noted earlier in this volume (chap. 4), there is ample reason to believe that pain would be more relevant as a predictor of interest in assisted suicide in some medically ill populations than in others. Pain may be a less salient factor in patients with HIV/AIDS, MS, or ALS, compared to patients with cancer.[3] Thus, the failure to observe a relationship between pain and interest in assisted suicide

[3]Although pain often accompanies HIV/AIDS, this symptom has received far less attention than in diseases such as cancer. Therefore, pain might be less likely to influence decision making for patients with HIV/AIDS if they are unaware of the potential severity or frequency of this symptom.

might reflect the populations studied, not the importance of pain as a trigger. Only one of the studies described above focused squarely on cancer-related pain (M. Sullivan et al., 1997), although most of the patients studied by E. J. Emanuel et al. (2000) also had a primary diagnosis of cancer. Thus, in both studies of cancer patients, some relationship between pain (either expectancies or severity) has been noted, and the strongest relationship by far was observed in Emanuel et al.'s much larger, and far more methodologically sound study. Another explanation for this pattern of results is that most studies of pain (including our own) have analyzed pain as either present or absent or as a continuous variable, typically including only those patients who actually had pain. In Emanuel et al.'s study, on the other hand, patients were divided into those with moderate to severe pain, and they compared this subgroup to patients with either no pain or mild pain. If pain has a nonlinear relationship with interest in assisted suicide (a hypothesis that has often been suggested, with pain exerting little or no affect on interest in assisted suicide until a severity threshold has been passed), Emanuel et al.'s method of dichotomizing the sample might elucidate a relationship that is obscured in simple correlational analyses or linear models. Moreover, this method of dichotomizing pain into moderate–high versus none–mild has been used in some of the studies focusing on desire for hastened death, often with similar results.

Pain and the Desire for Hastened Death

Like the literature on interest in assisted suicide, studies of desire for hastened death have also varied in the extent to which pain has emerged as a significant predictor. Unfortunately, these inconsistent results are even more difficult to interpret than in studies of interest in assisted suicide. Take, for example, Chochinov et al.'s (1995) seminal study of desire for hastened death. The authors observed a significant, albeit modest, correlation between ratings of pain intensity and desire for death ($r = .20$). Like E. J. Emanual et al. (2000), they observed a significant difference in desire for death between patients with moderate or severe pain versus those with no pain or mild pain. However, when they used a multivariate model to predict desire for hastened death, pain did not account for a significant increase in explained variance after depression was entered into the prediction model. Thus, although this study supports the supposition that pain plays some role in desire for hastened death, the role may be less powerful (or less direct) than often assumed.

Our research group found a similar pattern in our first study of desire for hastened death among patients with advanced AIDS (Rosenfeld et al., 1999). Average pain intensity was significantly correlated (.30) with desire for hastened death (based on our self-report rating scale, the SAHD) for the subset of patients experiencing pain. This relationship was even stronger for the subset of patients who were classified as terminally ill ($r = .54$). Moreover, when pain intensity was entered into a multiple regression model predicting desire for hastened death for only the subset of patients who reported pain, this variable (pain intensity) accounted for a significant proportion of explained variance. However, the presence of pain itself (comparing those patients with and without pain) was not associated with desire for hastened death in any analysis, whether univariate or multivariate.

Yet in our subsequent study of terminally ill cancer patients, similar associations between pain and desire for hastened death were not observed (Breitbart et al., 2000; Rosenfeld et al., 2000). We found no relationship between desire for death and either pain (for the entire sample) or pain intensity (for those patients with pain), nor did any difference emerge when we divided patients into no pain or mild pain versus moderate to severe pain groups. However, our study of terminally ill patients with cancer was conducted in a state-of-the-art palliative care facility in which pain management was generally optimal. Thus, the impact of pain on desire for hastened death may have been masked by the high-quality pain management these patients received. This explanation is consistent, at least in part, with the claims of palliative care advocates who assert that adequate pain management would eliminate requests for assisted suicide. That is, our study suggested that optimal pain management might minimize or eliminate the role of pain in desire for hastened death, but it does not necessarily eliminate the role of other psychological or physiological factors or influences. For example, functional impairment remained a statistically significant predictor in this study of terminally ill cancer patients even after the effects of depression and hopelessness were considered (Breitbart et al., 2000).

On the other hand, pain was unrelated to "will to live" in Chochinov et al.'s study of terminally ill cancer patients (Chochinov et al., 1999). Their unusual method (described in the previous chapter) included twice daily ratings of will to live, pain, depression, anxiety, nausea, and dyspnea and revealed a number of interesting findings, but they found no relationship between pain and will to live in any of their analyses. This null finding is all the more striking in light of their statistical method, which relied on an extensive series of stepwise multiple regression analyses that markedly increased the possibility of Type I error (i.e., observing significant findings related to chance variation rather than a genuine association). Nevertheless, despite differences in research methodology and conceptualization of dependent variables, Chochinov et al.'s study of will to live did not support the pain–desire for hastened death relationship that they observed in their previous study.

In their first study of attitudes toward euthanasia, Emanuel and his colleagues described a number of findings relevant to the question of how, or whether, pain influences interest in a hastened death (E. J. Emanuel et al., 1996). One of their dependent variables in this study was the presence or absence of any behaviors they thought reflected an interest in hastened death.[4]

---

[4]The validity of this dependent variable is discussed in the previous chapter.

Specifically, they inquired whether their participants (outpatients with cancer) had discussed assisted suicide with their physician, hoarded drugs (presumably for a possible suicide attempt), or had bought the book *Final Exit* (describing methods for committing suicide; Humphry, 1991). However, the presence of pain was unrelated to these behaviors, and this report did not indicate whether pain severity was related to this dependent variable (although the failure to mention this analysis, if pain severity was indeed studied, presumably reflects a nonsignificant finding). Nevertheless, this questionable dependent variable and overly terse Results section precludes a strong interpretation of their findings.

Finally, in their analysis of 70 terminally ill cancer patients, Wilson et al. (2000) compared patients who would not consider assisted suicide under any circumstances to a group of patients who would consider it in the future but not the present, and a third group who were interested in physician-assisted suicide under their current circumstances. They found no significant differences in pain ratings (using a 7-point clinical rating scale based upon their in-depth interviews) across these three groups ($p > .05$). They did, however, observe a significant difference in the level of functional impairment concerns (described by the authors as "loss of control"), as well as significant differences in severity of "weakness" and "drowsiness."

In summary, six studies have addressed the relationship between pain and the desire for hastened death, and only two of these six have shown significant associations. Although a number of caveats have been offered with regard to the studies that produced these null results, the "conclusion" that no firm conclusions can be drawn from this literature seems inescapable. Furthermore, in the two studies that did note significant correlations between pain severity and desire for hastened death, only one (our study of patients with AIDS) found pain to offer a significant contribution to a multivariate model (i.e., independent of the impact of depression). Thus, despite any inclination to trust my own research group's findings, support for a unique role of pain in fueling desire for hastened death is at best questionable.

Requests for Assisted Suicide or Euthanasia

Whereas the empirical literature focusing on patients with terminal or chronic illnesses has not demonstrated a strong role for pain in driving interest in physician-assisted suicide or desire for hastened death, pain has consistently emerged as one of the foremost reasons offered by patients who actually request assisted suicide or euthanasia. Yet even these studies, which are often viewed as supporting the proposed relationship between pain and interest in assisted suicide, have revealed other, even more powerful psychosocial influences behind patient requests for a hastened death. Nevertheless, across a number of different studies, roughly half of all patients who request assisted suicide or euthanasia mention pain as one of the reasons for their request. Beginning with van der Maas et al.'s study of Dutch euthanasia cases (1991), researchers have routinely observed that pain is one of the most commonly cited reasons behind patient requests for assisted suicide or euthanasia. In their study of Dutch euthanasia requests, pain was the second most common reason offered for patient requests for euthanasia, present in 46% of cases. No other physical symptoms cracked the "top five" reasons for euthanasia requests and thus were not mentioned in van der Maas's report. Of course the potential for biased recall in their method, discussed previously, limits the conclusiveness of their findings, but these numbers nevertheless suggest that pain can play an important role in requests for physician-assisted suicide and euthanasia.

Terminally ill patients in England also cited pain as a primary reason for requests for euthanasia. In their survey of the family members of recently deceased Britons, Seale and Addington-Hall (1994) found that pain and physical symptom distress played a significant role in shaping patient and family members' attitudes. As noted in the previous chapter, family members were asked to recall whether their relative had expressed a desire to die sooner or requested euthanasia at any time prior to their actual death. In analyzing the role of pain, the authors found a significant association between pain severity (rated on a simple ordinal scale: *none, not very distressing, fairly distressing,* and *very distressing*) and expressions of a desire for hastened death. Specifically, in cases where the patient was described as experiencing "very distressing" pain, expressions that a more rapid death was desired and specific requests for euthanasia were substantially more likely (although the relationship between pain severity and requests for euthanasia was not statistically significant). The effect sizes for these associations were quite modest: .11 for the relationship between pain severity and interest in hastened death and .06 for the pain–euthanasia relationship. Substantially stronger results emerged for many other physical symptom variables (appetite disturbance, bowel or bladder control problems, cognitive dysfunction, and dependency on others); these symptoms were much more strongly associated with expressions of a desire for hastened death and requests for euthanasia. Nevertheless, the effect sizes for these relationships were still quite modest, ranging from .10 to .28 for most of the physical symptom variables. Finally, the authors noted that patients with cancer were significantly more likely to request euthanasia than were other patients and that cancer patients also had the highest level of symptom burden (e.g., pain, bowel and bladder control problems, diminished appetite, breathing difficulties). Thus, although pain appeared to exert some influence on expressions of a wish for euthanasia or a hastened death, other physical symptoms and overall symptom burden were much more influential in this study.

Meier et al. (1998) conducted a U.S. national survey and found that "discomfort other than pain" was more important than pain itself in fueling requests for assisted suicide. Physicians who had received requests for assisted suicide cited "discomfort other than pain" in 79% of cases in which patients sought assisted suicide or euthanasia. Pain, on the other hand, was cited as an important contributor among 50% of patients who sought physician-assisted suicide or euthanasia; 52% of patients cited "fear of uncontrollable symptoms."

Similar data regarding the reasons behind patient requests for assisted suicide have emerged from Oregon, where the 1997 Death with Dignity Act (ODDA) has facilitated a more detailed analysis of requests for assisted suicide in the U.S. than had previously been possible. In their survey of Oregon physicians, Ganzini, Nelson, et al. (2000) asked physicians why their patient requested assisted suicide and again found that overall quality of life and "existential" issues ("saw existence as pointless," "wanted to control circumstances of death") were the most prominent reasons given. Yet physical symptoms were also commonly cited, with pain leading the field. Pain was reported to be a factor in 43% of patient requests for physician-assisted suicide, whereas fatigue was noted in 31% and dyspnea in 27%. In addition, the most common physician interventions following a patient request for physician-assisted suicide were "pain control" and "control of other symptoms," each of which was reported in 30% of cases. The latter finding suggests that not only were pain and physical symptoms commonly seen as influential factors, but physicians perceived these symptoms as being potentially treatable.

In a subsequent study of nurses and social workers working in hospice settings, Ganzini and colleagues (Ganzini et al., 2002) found largely similar results. Hospice nurses perceived psychosocial variables such as a "desire to control circumstances of death," "readiness for death," "desire to die at home," and "continued existence viewed as pointless" as the most important reasons for patient requests for physician-assisted suicide. However, pain and physical symptoms were also seen as quite important, with "pain or fear of worsening pain" and "inability to care for self or fear of inability to do so" among the top 10 reasons for patient requests. Other physical symptoms, such as fatigue, dyspnea, loss of bowel or bladder function, and confusion, were perceived as moderately important. Interestingly, when these nurses were asked to compare patients they have known who requested physician-assisted suicide to other hospice patients, they reported that the vast majority of patients who requested assisted suicide had comparable or less pain than the typical hospice patient. However, concerns about a loss of control and loss of independence were viewed as more pronounced in the former group.

In sum, the relationship between pain and interest in or requests for assisted suicide depends on the research method used. Many of the early studies of interest in assisted suicide did not detect a significant relationship between pain and interest in physician-assisted suicide and in one study by E. J. Emanuel and his colleagues (1996), patients with pain were even *less* interested in such assistance than were patients without pain. Studies of desire for death have been somewhat more positive than the studies of "interest in" assisted suicide, but not nearly as much so as the studies of patient requests for physician-assisted suicide or euthanasia. Given this pattern, one might be tempted to conclude that pain is simply less relevant in hypothetical scenarios but that it emerges as a significant predictor when actual desire for hastened death is the focus of investigation. An alternative explanation is that the influence of pain is mediated by psychological factors such as depression or psychosocial variables. This hypothesis would explain why significant associations between pain and desire for hastened death have occasionally disappeared when multivariate models are used. It may be that unrelieved or severe pain leads to greater levels of depression and despair and that these psychological states lead patients to consider ending their lives. Yet when asked directly, patients themselves are unable to perceive the mediating role of depression and instead label pain and other symptoms as the reason for their request. Clearly, distinguishing between these alternative explanations will require additional and perhaps more creative research efforts.

OTHER ASPECTS OF PHYSICAL FUNCTIONING

The focus on pain as the physical symptom most likely to lead to interest in or requests for a hastened death may be intuitively appealing but is perhaps overly simplistic. A number of other physical symptoms (e.g., dyspnea or shortness of breath, fatigue, nausea) are frequently cited by terminally ill patients as either individually or collectively fueling a desire to end life. Overall physical functioning, or the ability to care for oneself, is frequently cited as a primary factor in quality of life and psychological well-being and may play a significant role in end-of-life decisions. However, whether these physical symptoms are mediated by depression or perhaps exert a more direct influence on interest in physician-assisted suicide or desire for hastened death has been much less often studied. Furthermore, unlike pain, where a standardized assessment method has been developed and widely used (Cleeland, 1989), the methods for assessing specific physical symptoms (such as intense fatigue, unremitting nausea, or long-term incontinence) and overall physical functioning are much less uniform. Thus, although a handful of studies have reported interesting and important findings, the consistency of this literature is even less so than the literature on pain and physician-assisted suicide.

Measures of physical functioning, such as the ordinal rating scale developed by Karnofsky and Burchenal (1949) or the five-category Eastern Cooperative Oncology Group rating scale (Cleeland et al., 1994), are typically simplistic. The Karnofsky Performance Rating Scale, perhaps the most widely used measure of physical functioning in medical settings, uses a 0 to

100 metric with anchors describing the patient's functioning abilities in 10-point increments. This scale has been used in countless empirical studies as a measure of overall physical functioning, but its simplistic rating system is clearly limited. Measures of specific physical symptoms, on the other hand, are even less uniform, in part because some investigators (and instruments) provide detailed assessment of specific symptoms and others focus on overall symptom burden. Thus, although some researchers have focused on selected symptoms that have been chosen a priori, others have used measures that tap overall symptom burden. In our studies of terminally ill patients with cancer and AIDS, we have typically adopted the latter strategy, utilizing the Memorial Symptom Assessment Scale, a self-report rating scale that inquires about the presence and distress associated with 32 common medical symptoms (Portenoy et al., 1994). This scale generates a number of summary scores, including the number of physical symptoms reported (regardless of severity or associated distress), as well as the Global Distress Index (GDI), which measures the distress associated with 10 common and particularly troubling symptoms, the Psychological Symptom Distress Index (five symptoms tapping depression–anxiety), and the Physical Symptom Distress Index (a subset of five physical symptoms that are most likely to be distressing). However, having used this multidimensional scale for nearly a decade, we have been unable to generate a consistent pattern of findings with regard to the relationship between physical symptoms and interest in assisted suicide or desire for hastened death.

For example, in our study of interest in assisted suicide among patients with advanced HIV/AIDS, we found no correlation between hypothetical interest in physician-assisted suicide and either the number of physical symptoms or the MSAS GDI (Breitbart et al., 1996). However, in our study of desire for hastened death in patients with HIV/AIDS we observed a significant correlation between SAHD scores and all of the MSAS indices (e.g., .30 between the MSAS GDI and SAHD scores; Rosenfeld et al., 1999). Furthermore, in a multivariate model for only the subset of patients who reported pain, the MSAS GDI remained a significant predictor of desire for hastened death along with depressive symptom severity, average pain intensity, and social support (Rosenfeld, Galietta, Breitbart, & Krivo, 1998). Yet the GDI was not associated with desire for hastened death in the analysis of the entire sample (including both patients with and without pain). In our most recent study of terminally ill cancer patients, both the number of symptoms endorsed on the MSAS and the MSAS GDI were even more highly correlated with desire for hastened death than they were in our studies of AIDS patients ($r = .38$ for each variable). Yet neither variable was retained in a multivariate model predicting SAHD scores that contained only depression, hopelessness, social support, and overall physical functioning ability (as measured by the Karnofsky Performance Rating Scale). Whether physical functioning ability overshadowed the influence of physical symptom distress is not clear from this analysis, but our studies have clearly documented a role for physical variables other than pain in predicting desire for hastened death.

This relationship between physical functioning and desire for hastened death was echoed in E. J. Emanuel et al.'s study of interest in assisted suicide among terminally ill individuals (E. J. Emanuel et al., 2000). As noted above, they found that patients with "significant care needs" (e.g., bedridden and needing assistance with daily self-care) were significantly more likely to have a "personal interest" in assisted suicide compared to patients without significant care needs. Although no definition of this variable was provided, it appears reasonable to interpret this variable as a rough indicator of physical functioning ability. Moreover, "significant care needs" remained one of five significant predictors in the multivariate analysis (in addition to depression, pain, age, and race).

Wilson and colleagues (2000) also found several physical symptoms that differentiated terminally ill cancer patients with no interest in assisted suicide (n = 19) from those who might consider physician-assisted suicide in the future (n = 32) and patients currently interested in a hastened death (n = 8). Specifically, levels of drowsiness, weakness, and concerns regarding "loss of control" increased along with interest in hastened death across the three groups, but levels of nausea and breathlessness did not. However, because these authors did not apply multivariate models to assess the overlap among these symptoms (no doubt because of the small sample size), the unique contribution of each of these symptoms is unknown.

Chochinov et al. (1999) studied "will to live" among terminally ill cancer patients and found even less consistency with regard to the role of physical symptoms. Although pain was unrelated to will to live in any of the analyses conducted, dyspnea (shortness of breath) was the strongest predictor of will to live in several analyses, with the presence of dyspnea corresponding to the absence of a will to live. Specifically, as patients approached death, this variable became increasingly salient, overtaking the psychological distress variables that had dominated the prediction models earlier in the course of the illness. Chochinov and his colleagues concluded that not only does physical discomfort become more important as death approaches, but dyspnea in particular may be the most feared and distressing physical symptom of all, despite the more common focus on pain as the primary physical symptom driving requests for or interest in physician-assisted suicide.[5]

Dyspnea was also frequently cited by patients who requested physician-assisted suicide in Oregon, according to the survey conducted by Linda Ganzini and her colleagues (Ganzini, Nelson, et al., 2000) discussed above. Dyspnea was cited by more than one quarter of patients requesting physician-assisted suicide in Oregon, representing the third most commonly reported physical

---

[5]Passik et al. (2001) found that cancer patients about to begin chemotherapy expressed substantial fear of pain, fatigue, and anxiety regarding the future but that the nature of these fears changed over time.

symptom (behind pain and fatigue). Similarly, Meier et al. (1998) noted that "physical symptoms other than pain" were far more often reported as a factor driving requests for physician-assisted suicide or euthanasia in their national survey, although they did not specify which specific symptoms were particularly common or distressing.

Despite methodological limitations, the studies by M. Sullivan et al. (1997) and Seale and Addington-Hall (1994) also demonstrated stronger influence for physical symptoms other than pain. Sullivan and his colleagues found that overall symptom burden was significantly associated with interest in hastened death, as was fatigue, sedation, and diminished sexual drive, and that these variables were more highly associated with interest in a hastened death than was pain.[6] Likewise, Seale and Addington-Hall found significant associations between overall symptom burden and several individual symptoms with expressions of a desire for hastened death and request for euthanasia, and these associations were virtually all stronger than were the associations with pain.

Finally, in a recent study of cognitive impairment and desire for hastened death, Pessin, Rosenfeld, Burton, and Breitbart (2003) concluded that this "symptom" adds a unique contribution to our understanding of the factors that influence end-of-life decision making, despite the complex and perhaps nonlinear relationships that probably exist. Pessin et al. analyzed data from an ongoing study conducted by William Breitbart and myself, adding several indices of cognitive functioning to analyze the impact of cognitive deterioration among patients with advanced AIDS. They found that although correlations between cognitive functioning and desire for hastened death were relatively modest, patients classified as having mild cognitive impairment were significantly more likely to express a desire for hastened death than were patients with either no impairment or severe impairment. Pessin et al. concluded that a nonlinear relationship may exist in which worsening cognitive impairment leaves patients unaware of their limitations and eases the frustrations that often accompany deteriorating health and mental functioning. However, when cognitive impairment is still modest and patients are aware of their increasing disability, they may be at the greatest risk for seeking a hastened death. Mild cognitive impairment may also lead to more "black and white" thinking such that terminally ill patients have greater difficulty conceiving solutions to the difficulties they face, raising the appeal of

---

[6]The finding that diminished sexual interest was significantly associated with desire for hastened death is particularly interesting given the failure of most researchers to study this possible predictor. Whether this reflects a discomfort with sexuality among palliative care researchers or discomfort on the part of patients in answering such questions is unknown, but understanding this potentially important variable has certainly been hindered. In our own research, one institutional review board required that we exclude questions about sexual functioning from our in-depth interviews with terminally ill cancer patients (despite having no objection to detailed questioning about end-of-life preferences). Such obstacles, although well-intentioned, clearly affect the ability of researchers to systematically examine potential influences on desire for death.

suicide as a relatively simple alternative. Pessin et al. acknowledged the difficulties inherent in studying patients with severe cognitive impairment, because impaired mental functioning typically precludes valid informed consent to participate in research and often results in meaningless, essentially random data.

Given the range of findings about physical symptoms other than pain, it is certainly premature to offer any firm conclusions regarding which particular symptoms are more or less influential in fueling the desire for hastened death and requests for assisted suicide. Yet several individual symptoms and symptom summary variables have been studied, and a handful have emerged with some consistency as significant predictors or correlates of desire for hastened death or requests for assisted suicide. Of these symptoms, overall physical functioning in general and dyspnea in particular appear to have gained the strongest (although certainly not universal) empirical support with regard to their importance. Measures of overall symptom burden or symptom distress have also emerged as significant correlates in a number of studies, but whether such summary variables would remain significant after considering individual, particularly salient symptoms (e.g., dyspnea) is unclear. Nevertheless, there seems to be little doubt that physical symptoms other than pain can play an integral role in end-of-life decision making, despite the subordination of these "other" physical symptoms in the empirical literature.

SUMMARY

In many ways, the history of the pain–assisted suicide relationship has been more complex than the data would warrant. Early theorists typically cited unresolved pain as a central contributor to requests for euthanasia and assisted suicide. But the empirical literature focused on hypothetical interest in assisted suicide has largely failed to support this hypothesis, leading many researchers to conclude that the role of pain in assisted suicide requests may be more complex (or less important) than was assumed. As this literature has evolved, particularly with a growing emphasis on studying actual desire for hastened death rather than hypothetical interest in assisted suicide, the role of pain has emerged with some (but hardly complete) consistency. In particular, studies that have distinguished patients in moderate to severe pain from those in mild or no pain have generally observed a significant role for pain in end-of-life attitudes. Even in these cases, however, few studies that have used multivariate models have found a unique role for pain; researchers have found that this variable loses its predictive power after effects of psychological factors such as depression are accounted for. Thus, the impact of pain on desire for hastened death or interest in assisted suicide may be an indirect one, with depression playing the role of mediator. Such a model would posit that inadequately treated pain may lead to (or increase) depression, which in turn fuels the desire for hastened death. At present, however, no one has adequately tested this or any other model of end-of-life attitudes or decisions, in part because of the small datasets available to most researchers. As this literature continues to grow, a more complete understanding of the manner by which symptoms such as pain influence the desire for hastened death will no doubt emerge.

Likewise, the literature on other physical symptom and functioning variables remains, to a large degree, in its infancy. Hindered by idiosyncratic methods of studying or even selecting individual physical symptoms or overall symptom burden and distress measures, this literature has been skeletal at best. There is little doubt that a broad perspective on end-of-life care extends well beyond pain, but there has been little consistency in deciding which variables to study or how they should be studied. Nevertheless, a handful of symptoms, including dyspnea, have emerged as most troubling, and overall physical functioning appears to be one of the more important, albeit nonspecific physical influences. However, these variables have not been included consistently enough to allow a clear understanding of their relative importance in end-of-life decisions. Whether physical symptoms also exert a direct influence on the desire for hastened death or are mediated by psychological factors such as depression and hopelessness remains unclear and will no doubt require a great deal of additional study. At present, the empirical literature appears to suggest that a direct relationship may exist between physical functioning and other symptoms and the desire for hastened death despite the lack of support for a direct relationship between that desire and pain. If so, then these "other" physical symptoms and factors would perhaps be distinguished from pain both in terms of the magnitude of their influence as well as the mechanism by which they exert this influence.

7

END-OF-LIFE DECISION MAKING

Many of the most important end-of-life issues, such as physician-assisted suicide, the validity of advance directives, and the right to refuse life-sustaining interventions, center on decision-making capacity. Determining when an individual has sufficient capacity to make valid and legally binding decisions can be a formidable task for treatment providers and mental health consultants, particularly in the context of a severe or terminal illness. The failure to accurately assess decision-making capacity entails a number of risks such as allowing incompetent individuals to make an irreversible decision that may conflict with their long-standing values. At the other extreme, denying individuals the right to make their own decisions simply because others (e.g., family, physicians) disagree with them also has significant costs, both psychologically and legally. Yet, despite the obvious importance of decision-making capacity in end-of-life settings, relatively little guidance has been offered to clinicians who perform these evaluations and even less empirical research has been conducted that might inform the assessment process. This chapter reviews both the clinical aspects of end-of-life decision making and the empirical research on this topic.

ELEMENTS OF DECISION MAKING

Most discussions of end-of-life decision making tend to confound two related but clearly distinct topics: decision-making processes and decision-making abilities. A *decision-making process* refers to the way in which individuals reach decisions; what factors are influential and how these various factors interact with one another in shaping individual decisions. Although an understanding of decision-making processes is crucial to understanding why patients might consider suicide or request assisted suicide, such processes have rarely been the subject of clinical research. As is discussed in subsequent sections, the few studies that have been conducted have been relatively simplistic, such as analyzing preferences for life-sustaining treatments and the factors that influence these preferences. Another body of research has focused on assessing decision-making ability in medically ill individuals or psychiatric patients, although this literature has not focused on patients at the end of life or their ability to make decisions to hasten death. Decision-making ability is generally construed as the individual's understanding of the relevant factors and integration of this information into a coherent whole.

Decision-making ability (or capacity)[1] is intimately intertwined with the legal definition of decision-making competence (itself a requisite element of valid informed consent) and has increasingly been identified as a crucial component of end-of-life care. The term *competence*, however, is a legal determination typically made by a judge, whereas *ability* or *capacity* simply refers to the individual's level of decision-making sophistication. Because many individuals might be legally competent to make decisions despite substantial impairments in their decision-making abilities, the latter terms are used in this chapter whenever decision making is discussed, and the term *competence* is reserved only for those instances in which legal status is at issue. It should be noted, however, that although important legal differences exist between clinical assessments of decision-making capacity and legal determinations of competence, in practice this distinction is often less clear. Because of the practical difficulties inherent in seeking judicial determinations of competence, many clinicians simply turn to family members whenever they, or a consulting clinician, have determined that the patient lacks adequate decision-making capacity. Indeed, many ethicists, lawyers, and health care providers have supported this practice, citing the delays and excessive costs associated with legal determinations of competence that in most instances ultimately mirror the clinician's initial assessment (e.g., Grisso & Appelbaum, 1998).

The importance of decision-making competence in end-of-life situations in general, and physician-assisted suicide in particular, cannot be overstated. Although many arguments have been offered in favor of and in opposition to legalized physician-assisted suicide, virtually all have agreed that

---

[1]The terms *decision-making ability* and *decision-making capacity* are typically used interchangeably in the clinical and research literature, because *capacity* is typically measured in terms of actual performance (i.e., ability) rather than potential (i.e., capacity). This chapter retains this convention by treating ability and capacity as essentially synonymous.

this end-of-life option should apply only to "competent" individuals. Despite concerns about the adequacy of safeguards, the ODDA (1996) specifically requires that any individual requesting physician-assisted suicide be "capable" of making such a decision. The Oregon statute (1996, §127.825 3.03) mandates a mental health evaluation whenever the physician has reason to suspect that a "psychiatric or psychological disorder or depression causing impaired judgment" is present. Guidelines for responding to requests for assisted suicide, developed by the Task Force to Improve the Care of Terminally Ill Oregonians (1998), specify that "the evaluation should focus on assessing the patient's competency and factors that limit competency such as mental disorders, knowledge deficits, and coercion" (p. 30). However, these guidelines acknowledge that "although the Act calls for a decision that the patient is or is not competent to request a lethal prescription, in clinical practice competency exists on more of a continuum. Competency standards specific to the decision to seek a prescription to end life have not been developed" (p. 30). Despite this admitted gap between health care policy guidelines and clinical practice, similar provisions have been included in other guidelines offered by advocates of legalization for assisted suicide (e.g., Baron et al., 1996; Quill, Cassel, & Meier, 1992).

DECISION-MAKING COMPETENCE

The construct of decision-making competence predates the recently renewed interest in end-of-life issues and physician-assisted suicide and is rooted in the legal doctrine of informed consent. Health care practitioners have long had a legal and ethical responsibility to ensure that any patient who consents to a medical intervention does so knowingly, voluntarily, and competently (Faden & Beauchamp, 1986). Although legal and practical definitions of the "knowing" and "voluntary" requirements have been relatively well-established, attempts to define *competence* have proven much more difficult. There is no accepted consensus as to the cognitive criteria of "competence" (Grisso, 2002), but a number of different definitions of competence have been identified and used (Appelbaum & Grisso, 1988; Roth, Meisel, & Lidz, 1977). These "tests" of competence range from relatively simple standards such as the mere expression of a choice or recall of the information one's physician has disclosed, to more complex standards such as an assessment of whether the individual can appreciate the information presented (i.e., recognize the relevance of the risks and benefits as they pertain to his or her situation) or has weighed the risks and benefits of various treatment alternatives in a rational manner. Many, if not most, writers have suggested that more stringent requirements for competence be applied as the importance of the decision increases, although no guidelines exist for deciding which of these standards to apply in any particular situation (Appelbaum & Grisso, 1988; Drane, 1984; Rosenfeld, 2002).

The assessment of decision-making ability in clinical practice is further complicated by a number of practical issues. First, the absence of any standardized procedures for determining when a particular individual is sufficiently impaired as to be considered incompetent forces clinicians to rely on their own judgments, resulting in idiosyncratic methods and variable standards (B. Lo, 1990).[2] Furthermore, decision making is often assessed by clinicians with little or no specialized training or expertise in mental health issues, with most assessments being conducted by the clinician offering the proposed treatment (Grisso & Appelbaum, 1998). Although there are many advantages to having decision-making capacity assessed by one's own treatment provider rather than an independent mental health consultant, there are also important disadvantages. Foremost among the advantages is the potential for the assessment to occur in the context of an ongoing doctor–patient relationship. By framing a patient's decision in the context of his or her past decisions, an evaluator has the opportunity to develop a richer, more thorough understanding of why a particular decision has been reached. Treating clinicians are also in the position to assess the consistency between the current decision and the patient's long-standing values and goals. In addition, the treating clinician is likely to be the most knowledgeable about the relevant factors that might (or should) influence a decision such as the patient's medical condition and the probable outcome of various alternative courses of action (e.g., Fried, Bradley, & Towle, 2002).

However, most clinicians are unfamiliar with either the methods or the issues involved in assessing decision-making capacity, leaving them relatively naive as to precisely what to assess and how to conduct the assessment. Hence, they may base their assessment on idiosyncratic or personal beliefs such as their perception of the appropriateness of the decision (i.e., considering a patient's rejection of a proposed treatment an indication of incompetence) rather than on a reliable and systematic method. In addition, clinicians who lack mental health training are prone to misinterpret or misidentify important psychological changes that may influence decision making. The difficulty most clinicians have in accurately recognizing potentially important psychological conditions, such as depression or delirium, are well-known (e.g., Inouye, Foreman, Mion, Katz, & Cooney, 2001; Passik et al., 1998; Pessin et al., 2003). Clinicians do not identify these potentially important psychological influences for reasons that have not been well established. For example, clinicians may simply fail to inquire about depression or anxiety because of their own discomfort discussing negative emotional states. When they do

---

[2]Although a formal adjudication of incompetence must be made by a judge, clinical input typically forms the primary, if not sole, basis for these decisions. Hence, whereas a clinician will be asked to determine whether a patient is "competent," this assessment encompasses two separate steps: evaluating the patient's decision-making ability and deciding whether this ability is sufficiently impaired as to render the patient incompetent (i.e., to opine to the judge that the patient is "too impaired" to make rational treatment decisions).

observe mental status changes, clinicians often normalize the patient's reactions, projecting their own feelings or expectations onto the patient such as attributing crying and expressions of hopelessness to a "natural reaction" to terminal illness rather than depression. Whatever the reasons for the frequent failure to perceive emerging symptoms, what has become increasingly clear is the need for systematic methods to assess decision making, particularly when the potential for compromised decision making is heightened as it is in end-of-life decision making.

Even for well-trained and experienced clinicians, the lack of generally accepted methods for assessing decision-making ability or established standards for determining how much ability (or which abilities) is sufficient are likely to result in considerable variability in the assessment process. This problem is compounded by the fact that very few of the clinicians who are faced with a patient requesting assisted suicide or cessation of mechanical ventilation have received training in the evaluation of decision-making ability. Few medical schools or residency training programs provide training in the assessment of decision-making ability, and most physicians have little practical experience in these matters, essentially leaving them without guidance when questions of competence arise (or should be raised). Similar limitations apply to most training programs for clinical or counseling psychologists; few if any include coursework or training focused on assessing decision-making ability. Although psychologists are rarely forced to decide whether to permit a patient to make important end-of-life treatment decisions, many psychologists provide consultation services in medical settings where competence assessments arise. Hence, the potential benefits of formal training in the assessment of decision-making abilities are substantial, as these clinicians might provide valuable input when decision-making capacity is questioned.

In response to the need for guidance in assessing decision-making competence, researchers have developed measures to assist in this process. Early attempts to assess competence focused primarily on cognitive functioning, using simplistic cognitive screening tools such as the Mini-Mental State Exam (Folstein, Folstein, & McHugh, 1975) to identify "impaired" patients. More recent efforts have focused on functions more closely linked to decision making and informed consent, such as the Hopkins Competency Assessment Test (HCAT; Janofsky, McCarthy, & Folstein, 1992), which consists of a short essay describing informed consent and the Durable Power of Attorney followed by several questions pertaining to the information disclosed (e.g., "What are the four things a doctor must tell a patient before beginning a procedure?" "What are these instructions to doctors and family called?"). However, this measure still suffers from many of the same shortcomings as the more general measures of cognitive functioning in that the HCAT only addresses one type, or standard of competence (information understanding) and does not address the specific treatment decisions that the patient faces.

The shortcomings of the HCAT, both its lack of specificity and the limited range of functions assessed, were addressed by Grisso and Appelbaum in developing their measure of decision-making capacity, the MacArthur Competence Assessment Tool—Treatment (MacCAT–T). The MacCAT–T has rapidly gained popularity since its publication (Grisso & Appelbaum, 1998), because of its comprehensiveness and flexibility. The MacCAT–T addresses four of the most commonly used standards of decision-making competence: the ability to render a decision, the ability to understand relevant information, the ability to appreciate the significance of that information, and the ability to rationally weigh the risks and benefits of available alternatives.[3] These various abilities are assessed through a semi-structured interview that is developed in accordance with general guidelines but individualized to the patient's unique circumstances.[4] J. Werth, Benjamin, and Farrenkopf (2000) have recommended that the MacCAT–T be used to assess end-of-life decision making (in addition to other data collection techniques) although no empirical research to date has established the utility or validity of the MacCAT–T for this purpose. In fact, given the original purpose of the MacCAT—to assist the clinician in identifying psychiatric patients who are unable to make *rational* treatment decisions—this instrument may still be inadequate to capture the nature of psychological influences on decision making at the end of life. Because the MacCAT focuses primarily on identifying "irrational" decision makers, it would identify few terminally ill patients who request assisted suicide as "incompetent," and those that are may be readily apparent to treating clinicians. Nevertheless, the MacCAT offers a number of advantages, because it quantifies several important aspects of decision making that warrant further investigation. For example, by further developing our understanding of the influence of age, depression, and cognitive impairment on various aspects of decision-making capacity, clinical assessment of the abilities required for meaningful, informed end-of-life treatment decision making can be greatly enhanced.

CLINICIAN'S ABILITY TO ASSESS DECISION-MAKING CAPACITY

The ambiguity in assessing decision-making capacity is evident in several recent studies. Marson, Hawkins, McInturff, and Harrell (1997) asked

---

[3]Although other standards, such as the ability to provide "rational reasons" for one's decision, have been recognized by the courts (Roth et al., 1977), Appelbaum and Grisso have seemingly discouraged this "standard" by omitting it from their writings and the McCAT measures. Nevertheless, the ability to offer a logical explanation for one's decision has intuitive appeal for many evaluating clinicians and remains a theoretically valid alternative "standard" of competence.

[4]Grisso and Appelbaum have also published a companion instrument, the MacCAT–CR, designed for assessing capacity to participate in clinical research (Grisso & Appelbaum, 1998).

five clinicians to evaluate the decision-making capacity of patients with mild Alzheimer's disease based on their review of videotaped interviews. The clinicians, all of whom were geriatricians and neurologists with extensive experience in treating elderly patients and conducting assessments of decisional capacity, had dramatically different opinions as to the competence of the patients evaluated. For example, one clinician considered 90% of the Alzheimer's patients incompetent, whereas another considered the very same patients to be competent. (In fact, one clinician found all the patients in the study to be competent.) The remaining three clinicians fell somewhere between these two extremes, with rates of incompetence ranging from 14% to 52%. It is interesting that the clinicians who considered 52% and 90% of the patients to be incompetent appeared to base their judgment primarily on the verbal memory abilities of patients, whereas the clinicians who found fewer patients to be incompetent (0%, 14%, and 24% rates of incompetence) appeared to be influenced by higher cognitive functions (e.g., executive functioning and reasoning). Given these discrepancies in both conclusions and criteria, the Marson and colleagues concluded that physician assessments of decision-making capacity reflect a "very subjective process" (p. 952).

Similar concerns about the reliability and accuracy of clinician assessments of decision-making capacity were raised in a study of nursing home patients. Barton, Mallik, Orr, and Janofsky (1996) compared clinical judgments of patient's decision-making capacity with ratings based on the HCAT. Of the 20 patients classified as incompetent based on the HCAT, only 7 (35%) were considered incompetent by the treatment staff (based on whether the institution allowed the patient to make treatment decisions for him- or herself).[5] Moreover, even among the most severely impaired patients (i.e., those obtaining a score of 0 on the HCAT), only one had been identified as incompetent by the nursing home clinical staff. However, only 2 of the 24 patients classified as competent by the HCAT were identified by the evaluators as incompetent (i.e., false negatives), and these two cases fell just above the threshold for distinguishing competence. Thus, although the rate of false negatives is reassuringly low, many potentially incompetent individuals may not be recognized as impaired by treatment staff.[6] The failure to recognize impairments in decision-making ability is particularly troubling given the procedures in place in Oregon, where the decision as to whether mental health consultation to assess decision making is needed rests with the attending and consulting physicians who may well have little or no understanding of the issues involved.

---

[5]It should be noted that although informative, this study has important limitations. First, some patients may have been readily identified as having impaired decision-making ability but nevertheless have been permitted to make treatment decisions (and numerous reasons might exist that would, in theory, justify this practice). Also, as noted above, the elements of decision-making capacity measured by the HCAT are general and thus might not optimally tap decision-making ability around a specific treatment decision.

[6]Recent studies have demonstrated that delirium, a common source of confusion in medically ill patients, is typically under-recognized in medical settings (e.g., Inouye et al., 2001).

Given the apparent limitations in expertise and training related to the assessment of decision making among clinicians, it is perhaps reassuring that many clinicians are cognizant of their own limitations in this regard. Ganzini and her colleagues (Ganzini, Fenn, Lee, Heintz, & Bloom, 1996) highlighted this issue in their 1996 survey of Oregon psychiatrists. They found that only 6% of responding psychiatrists were "very confident" that they could determine, in the course of a single evaluation, whether an individual's decision making was impaired. More than half of their sample indicated that they were "not at all confident" that they could make such a determination. Similar findings were observed among a sample of Oregon psychologists (Fenn & Ganzini, 1999); 50% of the respondents indicated that they were "not at all confident" in their ability to assess a patients decision-making capacity in a single session. It is interesting that 40% of the responding psychologists indicated that they would not even participate in evaluations of capacity to make end-of-life decisions (e.g., physician-assisted suicide) and of the psychologists willing to conduct such evaluations, the proportion of "not at all confident" responses dropped to only 28%. However, within the context of an ongoing relationship, 84% of all respondents felt confident in their ability to perform such evaluations. Although there are many reasons to believe that assessments of decision-making capacity made within the context of an ongoing relationship should be more accurate (as noted above), research has yet to address this important question.

In a subsequent study, Ganzini and colleagues (Ganzini, Leong, Fenn, Silva, & Weinstock, 2000) surveyed a national sample of forensic psychiatrists, a group presumed to have much more familiarity with the assessment of decision-making ability.[7] The vast majority of these respondents, most of whom had conducted evaluations of decisional capacity in the past, agreed that at least two independent assessments of decision making should be required of patients who request physician-assisted suicide. It is interesting that most (73%) of the respondents indicated that a finding of a major depressive disorder "should result in an automatic finding of incompetence" regardless of the extent to which depression appears to have influenced decision making. Moreover, 38% indicated that even less severe conditions such as dysthymia or adjustment disorder should result in an automatic finding of incompetence. The physicians who favored an automatic finding of incompetence in the context of depression were also significantly more likely to consider physician-assisted suicide unethical, suggesting that these attitudes may be more reflective of their personal values than an unbiased assessment of the impact of depression on decision making.

---

[7]Because the issue of decision-making capacity is, at core, a legal one, forensic psychiatrists and psychologists are, as a group, more familiar with the psycholegal issues.

FACTORS INFLUENCING DECISION MAKING

Given the importance of decision-making competence, it is perhaps surprising that so little empirical research has focused on determining which factors lead to decisional impairments. This research literature is small and has largely relied on relatively simplistic methods such as studying the amount of information recalled from the informed consent process. Yet a growing number of researchers, spurred by the increasing availability of standardized methods (e.g., the MacCAT–T), have begun to focus on understanding the factors that can impair decision making with particular emphasis on the role of depression and cognitive impairment (often in contrast to normal aging). The elements of this literature that are most relevant to issues of end-of-life decision making are summarized in the following paragraphs.

Age and Cognitive Impairment

One of the most critical issues in understanding and assessing end-of-life decision making pertains to the impact of cognitive impairment. Whether associated with normal age-related declines in cognitive functioning or fueled by pathology (e.g., Alzheimer's dementia), the potential for impaired decision-making capacity due to cognitive limitations clearly rises with advancing age and illness progression. A number of early studies addressed the impact of age on decision-making capacity, but these investigations were often plagued by substantial methodological limitations. For example, several early studies of decision making used elderly samples recruited from nursing homes, presumably because of the frequency with which older adults face medical treatment decisions and the frequent decline in cognitive functioning in this population (Christensen, Haroun, Schneiderman, & Jeste, 1995; Kim, Karlawish, & Caine, 2002). However, most of these studies focused solely on the patient's ability to recall information disclosed during the informed consent process (i.e., memory, often of nonessential or even trivial information) rather than actually assessing ability to make treatment decisions per se. Thus, although one might logically assume that knowledge of the relevant information is a prerequisite for adequate decision making, the relevance of these simplistic studies for understanding the impact of age on decision-making ability is at best limited. Nevertheless, several of these early studies observed significantly lower levels of recall or comprehension among older individuals compared with younger ones, lending some credence to concerns that decision-making ability might decrease with age. However, the basis for the "age effect" found in these cross-sectional studies may be more artifact than real, because age and cognitive impairment are clearly confounded when comparing elderly and nonelderly individuals.[8] Thus, a

---

[8]Inclusion of even a small number of cognitively impaired individuals among the elderly sample (which is considerably more likely than among younger adults) could lead to significant group differences even if most healthy elderly individuals do not show any impairment.

focus on cognitive impairment rather than age is a much more logical choice for investigating factors that might impede decision-making capacity.

Given the relevance of cognitive impairment to decision-making capacity, it should be readily apparent why several investigators have chosen to study the impact of Alzheimer's disease on decision making. Much of this research has been conducted by a single research group led by Daniel Marson. In their first study, Marson, Ingram, Cody, and Harrell (1995) used their own measure of decision-making competence, a vignette-based measure that quantifies decision making along five different legal standards. They compared patients with mild cognitive impairment with those with moderate impairment and a comparison group of cognitively intact elderly. Despite the modest sample size (15 with mild dementia, 14 with moderate dementia, and 15 cognitively intact control participants), they found significant group differences on each element of decision making. Even those patients with mild dementia (defined as MMSE scores of 20 and above) demonstrated significantly poorer decision-making abilities than did the control participants, and patients with moderate dementia performed even worse than the mildly impaired patients. Moreover, as the stringency of the standard for competence increased, the proportion of patients who fell below the threshold for identifying decisional impairment similarly increased (see Figure 7.1). In fact, when the most stringent standard of decision making was used (the capacity to understand the treatment situation and choices), none of the patients with Alzheimer's disease were classified as "competent" (although 1 of the 15 patients with mild impairment was classified as "marginal"), whereas all 15 of the control participants met this standard. Marson et al. (1995) concluded not only that their measure was a reliable and valid instrument for guiding assessments of decision-making capacity but also that even patients with mild cognitive impairment might be incompetent to consent in situations in which the decision is particularly important (i.e., in which the highest standard of competence should apply), such as decisions to terminate life-sustaining intervention or requests for physician-assisted suicide.

In a more recent study of patients with Alzheimer's disease, Scott Kim and his colleagues (Kim, Caine, Currier, Leibovichi, & Ryan, 2001) used the MacCAT–T to quantify decision-making ability. They administered the MacCAT–T to 37 individuals with mild to moderate Alzheimer's disease in an attempt to explore the impact of early stage dementia on decision making.[9] Like Marson et al.'s research, they too found that individuals with Alzheimer's disease were significantly more impaired than a comparison sample of healthy elderly adults (caretakers of the Alzheimer's patients) on all three of the primary MacCAT–T indices, Understanding, Appreciation, and Reasoning. Although roughly half of all participants with Alzheimer's

---

[9]They adapted the MacCAT–T vignettes to describe a scenario in which the individual was offered participation in a low-risk, placebo-controlled, double-blind medication trial.

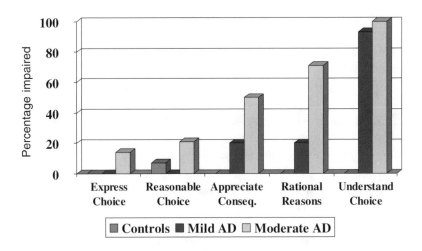

Figure 7.1. Decision-Making Capacity Among Patients With Alzheimer's Disease (AD). Conseq. = consequences. Data from "Assessing the Competency of Patients With Alzheimer's Disease Under Different Legal Standards," by D. C. Marson, K. K. Ingram, H. A. Cody, and L. E. Harrell, 1995, *Archives of Neurology, 52*.

scored in the intact range on the Appreciation and Reasoning subscales (compared with virtually all of the healthy elderly individuals), only one third obtained high scores on the Understanding subscale. However, MacCAT–T scores may have over-estimated the extent of decisional impairment in this sample because an "expert panel" of judges deemed more than half of the patients to be "competent" (10 of 18; ratings were not provided for 19 participants). Unfortunately, although this study provided important data on the utility of the MacCAT–T to assess decision-making capacity in an elderly, cognitively impaired sample, many important questions were left unanswered. For example, the researchers did not address whether any psychological, cognitive, or personal characteristics differentiated competent from incompetent patients, despite the importance of such information in clinical practice. Likewise, they did not address the discrepancy between the MacCAT–T results and clinical judgments (i.e., why some patients were deemed competent by expert evaluators yet performed poorly on the MacCAT–T). Such information might provide important guidance, particularly to health care providers who use the MacCAT–T in their clinical practice. Nevertheless, this study identified important avenues for future research and may offer a much-needed method for assessing capacity to make end-of-life decisions.

Using a dramatically different methodology, my colleagues and I used an experimental decision-making paradigm to assess both decision-making processes and ability in a sample of patients with HIV (Rosenfeld, White, & Passik, 1997). We presented patients with pairs of alternative medications intended to treat HIV including traditional, experimental, and alternative medications, as well as the option to refuse treatment altogether.[10] Treatment alternatives were described in terms of the known risks and benefits, cost, extent of research support (i.e., experimental vs. established medications), dosing requirements–restrictions, and other relevant information. Decision-making ability, as measured by the consistency of decision preferences (an experimental analogy to Grisso and Appelbaum's "rational manipulation of information" standard), was strongly, and significantly associated with severity of HIV dementia. However, there was no relationship between decision-making ability and either anxiety or depression. The lack of an association between decision-making ability and psychological functioning may have been due to the exclusion of patients who had high levels of depression or anxiety, essentially restricting the range of symptom distress. Moreover, although the association between cognitive functioning and decision-making ability was consistent with the studies of Alzheimer's patients described above, our approach did not permit a determination of which participants might be considered "impaired" in their decision making. Nevertheless, this literature, limited though it is, consistently supports the hypothesis that cognitive impairment significantly impedes decision-making ability. Although few would argue that cognitive disorders such as Alzheimer's disease or HIV dementia are common among terminally ill patients considering assisted suicide, the possibility of some cognitive impairment among terminally ill individuals is clearly substantial. Hence, studies of cognitively impaired patients that demonstrate an adverse effect on decision making from even mild levels of impairment have important implications for the assessment of end-of-life decisions. Identifying subtle forms of cognitive impairment, and assessing the extent and manner in which this impairment influences decision making, may help clinicians distinguish end-of-life decisions that are well-reasoned from those that are influenced by cognitive limitations.

Depression

Despite the failure to observe a significant impact for depression or anxiety on decision-making ability in our study (Rosenfeld et al., 1997), the potential for such influence is widely assumed by clinicians who conduct evaluations of decision-making capacity (Ganzini, Leong et al., 2000). Yet empirical research has not been nearly as convincing as the response to Ganzini's survey would suggest, even in studies focusing on patients with high levels of depression. For example, Appelbaum and Grisso, in their studies of decision-making competence, have found few depressed patients to be so impaired as to be found incompetent (based on the MacCAT–T), despite studying indi-

---

[10]The study was conducted before the advent of multidrug regimens.

viduals with relatively severe depressive disorders (Appelbaum, Grisso, Frank, O'Donnell, & Kupfer, 1999; Grisso & Appelbaum, 1995). In one study of decision making among hospitalized psychiatric patients, Grisso and Appelbaum administered an early version of the MacCAT–T to groups of patients diagnosed with schizophrenia, depression, and a comparison sample of patients hospitalized for angina. Although they did not use a cut-off for determining incompetence, they found that roughly one fourth of hospitalized depressed patients had significant impairments in their ability to make treatment decisions compared to nearly half of the schizophrenic sample and virtually none of the medically ill but psychiatrically healthy angina patients (Grisso & Appelbaum, 1995).

Appelbaum and his colleagues (1999) also studied the relationship between depression and competence to consent to research using a sample of female outpatients with moderate levels of depressive symptoms. They too found very few participants who demonstrated significant impairments in decisional capacity, perhaps because the levels of depression in this sample were somewhat more modest (particularly compared with their previous study of depressed inpatients). Moreover, severity of depressive symptoms in this sample was not significantly associated with decisional capacity on any of the MacCAT subscales. They did observe an association between age and decision making; older women obtained lower scores on the "appreciation" subscale compared with younger women, although the implications of this finding are unclear given the modest levels of impairment found overall. Nevertheless, the finding that age may represent a "risk factor" for poorer decision-making abilities is consistent (albeit weak support) for Grisso and Appelbaum's clinical observations (1998) suggesting that elderly and medically ill individuals have an elevated risk of impaired decision making.

Grisso and Appelbaum's findings from samples of depressed patients, coupled with my own research on decision making in patients with HIV (Rosenfeld et al., 1997), demonstrate a relatively weak relationship between severity of depression and decision-making impairment. Among medically ill patients who are not depressed, virtually no impairment in decision-making ability has been observed, whereas a small number of moderately depressed outpatients were found to be impaired and a somewhat greater proportion of depressed inpatients. Thus, as the severity of depression increases, decision making is more likely to be impaired, although this proportion remains relatively small even in cases of severe depression (particularly compared with psychiatric or cognitively impaired individuals). Hence, the belief that depression *necessarily* impairs decision-making abilities may be unfounded, at least as far as the research using systematic assessment measures has shown.

However, whereas the impact of depression on decision-making capacity may be much less pronounced than that of cognitive impairment, depression may be an even more clinically significant factor given the potential for successful treatment of depression. Unlike cognitive impairment, which typi-cally results in a progressive worsening of symptoms (with the exception of delirium, which may resolve with either time or treatment), depression is often successfully treated in medically ill or terminally ill patients, leaving open the possibility that impaired decision making will resolve over time. Indeed, this possibility may explain why Ganzini's survey found that most forensic psychiatrists believed that a major depressive disorder should auto-matically lead to a finding of incompetence. Whether justified or not, there appears to be a general perception that depression impairs decision-making competence.

RESEARCH ON THE DECISION-MAKING PROCESS

Although the research on the influence of depression on decision-mak-ing abilities might lead one to conclude that concerns regarding the influ-ence of depression on end-of-life decision making are exaggerated, such a conclusion is probably premature. Granted, the justification for refusing an individual the right to make treatment decisions is typically premised on incompetence, yet decision-making ability is only one aspect of decision making that might be influenced by depression. More modest levels of de-pression might nevertheless influence the decision-making process by affect-ing the value placed on particular aspects of a decision such as the impor-tance placed on continued life. Despite the importance of studying decision-making processes, few researchers have focused on this aspect of decision making with regard to end-of-life issues.

Linda Ganzini and Melinda Lee (Ganzini et al., 1994; Lee & Ganzini, 1992; M. A. Lee et al., 1998) conducted some of the only studies to system-atically investigate the impact of depression on decision-making processes, focusing their investigation on depressed but physically healthy geriatric pa-tients. In their first study, the authors compared depressed and nondepressed patients' preferences for life-sustaining interventions in a series of hypotheti-cal illness scenarios (Lee & Ganzini, 1992). Although there were few differ-ences in the preferences expressed by these two groups, depressed patients were less likely to desire life-sustaining interventions when the prognosis for recovery was described as good. The authors speculated that this pattern might reflect the "fatalism" that some writers have observed in the decision-making process of depressed patients (e.g., Bursztajn et al., 1991). Several years later, these authors reviewed the medical records of patients who had participated in the study, seeking evidence of actual treatment decisions made by these patients when faced with comparable illnesses or conditions (M. A. Lee et al., 1998). They found that roughly one third of the treatment deci-sions made by these patients differed from the initial preferences they had expressed and most of these changes were in the direction of accepting treatments that they had previously anticipated rejecting. Unfortunately, despite the emphasis on depression in their initial study, the authors did not report whether depressed patients were more or less likely to make decisions that differed from their earlier preferences.

However, a second longitudinal study conducted by this research group focused squarely on the issue of whether depression influences treatment decisions (Ganzini et al., 1994). They assessed preferences for life-sustaining medical therapies in a sample of 43 elderly patients hospitalized for treatment of depression, questioning them before and after antidepressant treatment. Twenty-four of these patients were re-assessed after their depression was in remission. Twenty-five percent of the patients available at follow-up expressed different opinions regarding life-sustaining interventions after successful treatment for depression. Although one might expect that depression would lead patients to decline interventions that would be desired after successful treatment, this assumption was not supported by the data. Contrary to their expectation, a comparable number of patients expressed a desire for life-sustaining interventions that they had previously declined as did those who declined interventions that they had previously wanted. Thus, although depression appeared to influence whether patients sought or declined end-of-life interventions, the nature of this influence was not straightforward. Nevertheless, the authors noted that the subgroup of patients who were the most severely depressed were also the most likely to change their opinions about desiring interventions that they had previously declined. Yet, these results, however intriguing, must be qualified by the extremely limited sample size (only 6 of 24 patients changed their preferences after treatment).

My own research using an experimental decision-making paradigm also focused on the process by which HIV-infected individuals make treatment decisions (Rosenfeld et al., 1997). In addition to studying decision-making ability, we analyzed the factors that influenced these hypothetical treatment decisions. We found that antiviral treatment decisions were primarily influenced by the expected benefits of treatment (e.g., increased CD4+ cell counts) and dosing frequency–constraints, with relatively little emphasis placed on potential side effects or other medication characteristics (e.g., whether the treatment was approved by the Food and Drug Administration). However, no clinical or demographic variables were identified that significantly influenced these decision processes (e.g., the importance of expected benefits), including anxiety, depression, or cognitive impairment, although the failure to include individuals with high levels of anxiety or depression (as well as the small sample size, with only 20 patients) clearly limits the conclusiveness of these null findings.

Although Ganzini's studies and my own offer a conflicting picture of the relationship between depression and decision-making processes, they highlight the possibility that even modest levels of depression might alter an individual's end-of-life treatment preferences. Yet this influence may be less straightforward than some would assume, as some of Ganzini et al.'s participants who sought end-of-life treatment options while depressed chose to forego these interventions when they were less depressed. This change in treatment preferences may not necessarily be due to a resolution of depression, because some retested patients may have had continued depressive symptoms despite treatment. Clearly further research must address decision-making processes and the role of depression in influencing treatment decisions. Without a clearer understanding of this, potentially more subtle, influence of depression, any conclusions regarding the influence of depression on end-of-life decision making would be premature.

More important, the relationship between decision-making processes and ability has never been clearly articulated. One might argue that altered decision-making processes related to depression or other psychological factors should be considered evidence of incompetence even when decisions are not irrational per se. Depression might render a patient unable to perceive the potential benefits of extending life or increase skepticism regarding the likely outcome of treatment, leading to a desire for hastened death or refusal of life-extending interventions. Although not illogical, the presence of such influences on decision making in an individual who, prior to the onset of depression, had been adamant about continuing treatment and extending life as long as possible, is a plausible definition of incompetence. Nevertheless, most courts and theorists have centered conceptualizations of competence on decision-making ability rather than processes, leaving the relevance of decision-making processes somewhat ambiguous. Further attention to this important aspect of decision making clearly is needed.

SUMMARY

Understanding end-of-life decision making is undoubtedly a complex undertaking, and the present state of scientific research provides a crude outline of these issues at best. A growing number of clinicians and researchers have begun to study decision-making ability, aided in part by newly developed instruments designed to facilitate these assessments. Yet studies of decision-making processes, perhaps an even more important issue in end-of-life care, have rarely been undertaken. The possibility that a terminally ill patient might, because of a treatable depression, seek physician-assisted suicide is an indisputable concern for many ethicists, clinicians, and legal scholars. Yet whether evidence of changing decision preferences in the face of psychological symptoms such as depression is indicative of "incompetence" (and therefore should negate a patient's request for assisted suicide) is unclear, as this standard differs substantially from the "tests" typically accepted by the courts (Roth et al., 1977). Theorists have occasionally suggested that individuals who seek to make decisions that stray from their long-held beliefs might be considered incompetent, despite possessing an understanding of the risks and benefits of their proposed decision and an appreciation of the implications of the decision (B. Lo, 1990). Clearly, questions as to what constitutes impaired decision making have implications far beyond end-of-life settings. The possibility that different, potentially more stringent, standards of competence might be applied to decisions to forego life-sustaining interventions or request a prescription for a medication to end one's life is plausible and perhaps justifiable. The true impact such increased restrictiveness would have on actual practices is not yet known.

8

LESSONS LEARNED FROM THE NETHERLANDS

The debate surrounding euthanasia and physician-assisted suicide reached the American spotlight only in the 1990s, but these issues have been prominent for several decades in the Netherlands, where euthanasia was decriminalized in the 1980s and legalized in 2001. Both opponents and advocates of legalization of euthanasia and assisted suicide in the United States cite the practice of euthanasia in the Netherlands in support of their positions. Opponents argue, for example, that data from the Netherlands support their belief that legalization leads to an ever-increasing reliance on death-hastening interventions and fosters a gradual expansion of who might be eligible to elect euthanasia or assisted suicide (the "slippery slope" argument). Advocates of legalization, on the other hand, claim that data from the Netherlands demonstrate the relative infrequency with which euthanasia and assisted suicide are sought despite their widespread availability. However, the appropriateness of examples drawn from the Netherlands may be less clear than either advocates or opponents acknowledge, because of the sociocultural (e.g., availability of health care resources, patient–physician relationships) as well as legal (e.g., requirements for legal assisted suicide or euthanasia) differences between the two countries.

Unlike in Oregon, where state statute has allowed the legal application of physician-assisted suicide since 1997, the practice of euthanasia and assisted suicide was not actually legal in the Netherlands until April 2001.[1] In fact, until recently, two articles of the Dutch criminal code explicitly prohibited both euthanasia and physician-assisted suicide despite the widespread awareness and acceptance of these practices.[2] Nevertheless, both were openly exercised in the Netherlands during the 1970s. In the 1980s, a series of court rulings effectively decriminalized these acts, allowing physicians to practice euthanasia and assisted suicide without fear of criminal prosecution as long as they follow established procedural guidelines (Gevers, 1996; Griffiths, Bood, & Weyers, 1998). Thus, until April 2001, the "legalization" of euthanasia and physician-assisted suicide frequently cited in medical and legal writings was based solely on case law precedent and public policy ("Dutch Legalize Euthanasia, the First Such National Law," 2001). Nevertheless, the legalization was essentially a formality, having little practical impact on medical practice or legal decision making.

Formal clarification of what actions constitute euthanasia in the Netherlands first came in 1985, when the State Commission on Euthanasia defined the term as "intentionally terminating another person's life at the person's request" (Griffiths et al., 1998, p. 69). The State Commission clearly distinguished euthanasia and assisted suicide from other "medical behaviors that shorten life" (termed MBSL in Commission writings) such as withholding or withdrawing life-sustaining interventions or the provision of pain medications which may, as an indirect effect, hasten death.[3] Further distinctions have been drawn between voluntary and nonvoluntary euthanasia, and these distinctions have legal relevance for Dutch physicians. *Voluntary euthanasia* is typically used to describe situations in which the patient is cognitively intact and is able to make a well-considered and thoughtful decision to end his or her life. *Nonvoluntary euthanasia*, on the other hand, refers to cases in which the patient does not have the cognitive capacity to make a

---

[1]Although U.S. policy debates have focused almost exclusively on physician-assisted suicide, euthanasia is far more widely utilized (relative to assisted suicide) in the Netherlands. The reasons for these differing preferences are not altogether clear.

[2]Article 293 of the Dutch criminal code states: "A person who takes the life of another person at the other person's express and earnest request is liable to a term of imprisonment of not more than twelve years or a fine of the fifth category." Article 294 states: "A person who intentionally incites another to commit suicide, assists in the suicide of another, or procures for that other person the means to commit suicide, is liable to a term of imprisonment of not more than three years or a fine of the fourth category, where the suicide ensues." Following the passage of the Termination of Life on Request and Assisted Suicide (Review Procedures) Act, the following amendment was made to Article 293 (and a stipulation that the same applies to Article 294): "The act referred to in the first paragraph shall not be an offence if it is committed by a physician who fulfils the due care criteria set out in section 2 of the Termination of Life on Request and Assisted Suicide Act, and if the physician notifies the municipal pathologist of this act in accordance with the provisions of section 7, subsection 2 of the Burial and Cremation Act (1998)."

[3]Many writers debate whether any death-hastening intervention such as the termination of a life-sustaining intervention can appropriately be termed *indirect*, but this distinction is sufficiently common as to justify the continued use of this term.

decision to end his or her life, because of such conditions as severe dementia, excessive sedation, or coma. Dutch law requires that in cases of nonvoluntary euthanasia the physician prove that the person would have requested euthanasia had he or she been competent and capable of expressing preferences at the time (analogous to the "substituted judgment" standard of surrogate decision making discussed in chap. 3). In the absence of such evidence (i.e., without any evidence of desire for hastened death from the patient), nonvoluntary euthanasia remains illegal and subject to criminal prosecution as murder (Griffiths et al., 1998). The Dutch do not draw any such legal distinctions, however, either in terms of practice requirements or legal status between euthanasia and physician-assisted suicide although euthanasia is by far the more commonly used of the two.

HISTORY OF EUTHANASIA IN THE NETHERLANDS

Public debate of and physician involvement in euthanasia in the Netherlands escalated dramatically in the 1970s following a series of events that brought this issue to the political forefront (Griffiths et al., 1998; van der Waal et al., 1996). The initial catalyst for interest in euthanasia was the 1972 criminal prosecution of a physician (referred to as "Ms. Postma" in legal writings) who admitted having ended her mother's life, reportedly at her mother's request. Ms. Postma's mother, a 78-year-old woman, had been living in a nursing home after suffering a cerebral hemorrhage that left one side of her body paralyzed. She had reportedly expressed her desire to die to family members as well as nursing home staff and had asked her daughter for assistance in dying on several previous occasions. Ms. Postma eventually granted her mother's request and injected her with a lethal dose of morphine.

In February 1973, Ms. Postma was tried for murder. During the course of her trial, the medical inspector testified that it was common practice to administer pain relief to terminally ill patients even when the dosage has the effect of hastening the death of the patient. The medical inspector outlined five specific conditions that, when met, legitimized the practice of hastening death through medications. These conditions were (a) the presence of an incurable illness, (b) the terminal phase of the disease, (c) unbearable physical or mental suffering, (d) the patient's wish to die, and (e) a doctor granting the request (Nederlandse Jurisprudentie, 1973, p. 558). The five conditions, with only minor modifications, have formed the basis for subsequent Dutch case law and legislation.

Despite receiving considerable support from her colleagues, as well as a general consensus that Ms. Postma had met the requirements set forth by the medical inspector, the court ruled that the injection of a lethal dose of morphine was premature because her mother's suffering might have been alleviated with a tolerable level of morphine. Ms. Postma was ultimately sentenced to 1 week in jail and 1 year of probation, effectively a "slap on the wrist" for her conviction of a crime that has been likened to murder by opponents of euthanasia and assisted suicide. The Postma case was widely publicized in newspapers and medical journals, particularly in the Dutch Medical Association's principal journal, *Medisch Contact*. This media and professional attention fueled widespread public debate in the Netherlands much as the actions of Dr. Jack Kevorkian did in the United States two decades later. In addition, the court's decision began the process of specifying legal guidelines under which the practice of euthanasia would be considered permissible.

In 1975, the Dutch Medical Association published a report outlining procedures that should be followed in euthanasia and physician-assisted suicide, and several political parties issued position papers describing their stances on the euthanasia debate (Griffiths et al., 1998). Despite differences on specific recommendations, most of the groups (with the exception of a few strong opponents such as the Dutch Association of Patients and the Roman Catholic Church) agreed in principle that there were circumstances in which euthanasia and physician-assisted suicide were permissible. By the end of the 1970s, the public and political acceptance of euthanasia and physician-assisted suicide as a theoretically permissible action had become well established in the Netherlands despite the lack of clear guidelines or formal legal approval.

MS. WERTHEIM SPURS THE EUTHANASIA MOVEMENT FORWARD

The second catalytic event in the Dutch euthanasia movement occurred in 1981, when a "euthanasia activist," Ms. Wertheim, was tried for the murder of a 67-year-old woman (Griffiths et al., 1998). The deceased woman suffered from both physical and psychological ailments and had made numerous requests of her general practitioner to hasten her death. Her physician had consistently refused and eventually suggested that she contact Ms. Wertheim. On April 19, 1981, Ms. Wertheim directed the woman to ingest Vesparax (a powerful sedative, also referred to as Secobarbital) and then drink alcohol, the combination of which resulted in her death. The court found Ms. Wertheim guilty and sentenced her to a brief period of incarceration and probation, but again it articulated conditions under which euthanasia and assisted suicide would be acceptable. The requirements set forth in this case were only slightly different from those expressed in Ms. Postma's case, essentially eliminating the requirement of a terminal illness and instead emphasizing the need for the patient's request to be stable, voluntary, and informed. These modified requirements were as follows:

1. The physical or mental suffering of the person was such that [the patient] experienced it as unbearable;
2. This suffering as well as the desire to die were enduring;
3. The decision to die was made voluntarily;
4. The person was well informed about his [or her] situation and the available alternatives, was capable of weighing the relevant considerations, and had actually done so;
5. There were no alternative means to improve the situation;
6. The person's death did not cause others any unnecessary suffering. (Nederlandse Jurisprudentie, 1982, p. 223)

The court outlined several additional requirements for the person assisting in the suicide, effectively mandating physician involvement in the practice. Specifically, the judges required that the decision to give assistance must be made by a physician and, if the patient's illness is in the terminal phase, the decision must be discussed with a second physician. If the patient was not terminally ill, the physician was required to consult with a mental health professional. Furthermore, they required that the decision as to the method used to end life must be made by the physician and must also be discussed with another physician (Nesderlandse Jurisprudentie, 1982, p. 223).

Shortly after this decision was published, in July 1982, another case of euthanasia brought these issues to the forefront of Dutch legal policy. In this case, a physician, Dr. Schoonheim, was tried on charges of performing euthanasia on a 95-year-old patient. This woman had experienced a steady decline in her hearing, eyesight, and ability to speak. She also experienced dizzy spells and became permanently disabled and bedridden after she broke her hip. A week before her death her situation so deteriorated that she was unconscious and unable to eat or drink. Her condition improved slightly several days later, when she regained consciousness and appeared coherent and lucid. At that time, she requested that Dr. Schoonheim end her life, a request she had made in the past, both verbally and in writing (Nederlandse Jurisprudentie, 1985).

In May 1983, the District Court acquitted Dr. Schoonheim of all criminal charges, the first time a Dutch doctor charged with performing euthanasia was found not guilty. Despite the widespread acceptance of euthanasia among the Dutch public and lawmakers, a subsequent Court of Appeals ruling reversed this decision and found Dr. Schoonheim guilty. Dr. Schoonheim appealed the reversal and, in November 1984, the Dutch Supreme Court vacated the appellate court's ruling, citing the failure of the Court of Appeals to fully consider Dr. Schoonheim's argument that his actions were the result of a "conflict of duties" (Nederlandse Jurisprudentie, 1985). Specifically, the Supreme Court cited Article 40 of the Dutch Criminal Code, providing an exemption from criminal liability if a person's acts were due to a force he could not be expected to resist, one example of which includes a "conflict of duties." Dr. Schoonheim argued that his conflicting goals of keeping his patient alive and alleviating her suffering represented such a conflict. He claimed that his responsibilities to alleviate his patient's suffering eventually forced him to end the woman's life because of the tremendous physical and emotional burden she faced each day.

In its ruling, the Dutch Supreme Court asserted that the Court of Appeals should have considered the following factors in reaching a decision regarding the appropriateness of Dr. Schoonheim's actions:

1. Whether, and if so to what extent, according to responsible medical opinion it was to be feared that the situation . . . would involve increasing loss of personal dignity and/or worsening of her already unbearable suffering;

2. Whether, taking into account among other things the possibility of further serious collapses, it was to be anticipated that she might soon no longer be in a position to die in a dignified manner, something which, on 16 July 1982, was still possible;

3. And whether, and if so to what extent, there were any remaining ways of relieving her suffering. (Nederlandse Jurisprudentie, 1985)

During the period in which the Dutch Supreme Court was deliberating on the Schoonheim case, the Dutch Medical Association's Executive Board issued a report clarifying the Dutch medical community's official position on the issue of euthanasia that appeared to have considerable influence on the Court's decision (Griffiths et al., 1998). Essentially, the Board declared euthanasia and physician-assisted suicide to be routine aspects of medical practice. Moreover, they outlined their own set of guidelines that physicians should follow in order to meet the "requirements of careful practice" in the performance of euthanasia and physician-assisted suicide. The requirements outlined in this report were roughly comparable to those outlined in Ms. Wertheim's case and have formed the basis for Dutch policy since that time. The requirements outlined by the Royal Dutch Medical Association (1984) were as follows:

1. The request must be voluntary,
2. The request must be well-considered,
3. The desire to die must be a lasting one,
4. The patient must perceive his [or her] suffering as unacceptable,
5. The physician performing euthanasia must consult another colleague.

A number of subsequent legal cases have incorporated these policies, and physicians who have followed these procedures have not been prosecuted. Although the specific procedures required to avoid criminal prosecution have been refined somewhat over time, the basic premises have remained stable. In fact, following a subsequent case, the Dutch Minister of Justice notified the Dutch Medical Association that physicians who comply with the "requirements of careful practice" outlined above would not be prosecuted. The culmination of case law and legislative developments resulted in a gradual refinement of the requirements for "legal" euthanasia and physician-assisted suicide, including procedural and reporting requirements, even though both procedures remained illegal under Dutch law (van der Waal et al., 1996).

Legislation to legalize euthanasia and physician-assisted suicide did not keep pace with either these court rulings or emerging medical practices. The first bill to legalize euthanasia was proposed in April 1984 and required the patient to be in a terminal stage of illness and suffering from unbearable physical and mental anguish, in addition to the "requirements of careful practice" specified by the courts. Neither this bill nor several subsequent bills proposed during the 1980s and 1990s (each of which generated considerable public and political debate) were passed by the Dutch Parliament. However, in 1994 legislation passed that mandated the notification procedures that had been outlined in previous cases. Nevertheless, a survey of Dutch physicians conducted several years later revealed that less than half of all euthanasia/assisted suicide cases were being reported, in part because of lingering fears of possible prosecution (van der Waal et al., 1996). These fears likely diminished in April 2001, when a bill to legalize the practice of euthanasia and physician-assisted suicide was accepted by the Senate.[4] The requirements of this legislation essentially echoed the case law that had been previously articulated in the Schoonheim case described above, requiring unbearable suffering that cannot be resolved by means acceptable to the patient, but with no requirement that the patient be terminally (or even medically) ill.

DUTCH ATTITUDES TOWARD EUTHANASIA

An important question for many legal scholars and ethicists concerns whether the Dutch legal system's treatment of euthanasia and physician-assisted suicide has been a response to public attitudes or whether public attitudes have been shaped by legal changes. This issue was addressed in a study by Paul van der Maas and colleagues (1996) that reviewed several public opinion surveys from a 25-year period beginning in the 1960s. They compared responses to a single question that had been asked as part of a public opinion survey roughly every 5 years: "What should a doctor do when a patient asks him to put an end to his suffering by administering a lethal injection?" Respondents were offered four possible responses to this question ("give

---

[4]The Dutch Parliament had passed this legislation in November 2000. The law did not take effect, however, until April 2002.

the injection," "do not give the injection," "depends," and "do not know,"), but the authors focused primarily on responses that indicate an acceptance of euthanasia ("give the injection" or "depends") versus those that did not ("do not give the injection").

Van der Maas, Pijnenborg, and van Delden (1995) noted a marked decrease in opposition to euthanasia during this period, along with a corresponding rise in the acceptability of euthanasia. In the 1966 survey, nearly half of the respondents (47%) indicated that the physician should not give a lethal injection if asked, whereas 39% thought the doctor should comply with the request and an additional 11% responded with "depends" (3% responded "don't know"). Opposition to euthanasia ("do not give the injection" responses) dropped steadily during the surveys that followed (1970, 1975, 1980), whereas responses indicating an acceptance of euthanasia ("give the injection" and "depends" responses) consistently increased (see Figure 8.1). By 1975, only 9 years after the initial survey, "do not give the injection" responses had dropped to roughly 15% whereas 80% indicated some acceptance of euthanasia, with approximately 50% responding "give the injection" and an additional 30% responding with "depends." In the 1991 survey, only 9% of respondents opposed lethal injection; 57% thought the injection should be given, and 32% responded with "depends." These surveys suggest that public attitudes toward euthanasia began to change even before the changes in legal status occurred. Nevertheless, this pattern clearly demonstrates overwhelming public support for the practice of euthanasia.

FREQUENCY OF EUTHANASIA AND ASSISTED SUICIDE IN THE NETHERLANDS

The first attempt to systematically study the Dutch euthanasia and physician-assisted suicide policies began in 1990 when a commission was appointed to study these practices. This commission has since become known as the Remmelink Commission after Professor Jan Remmelink, the attorney general of the Dutch Supreme Court at the time the study was commissioned. This investigation, first published in 1991 (van der Maas et al., 1991), has become a seminal study in the area of end-of-life care. The Remmelink Commission's study incorporated data from several sources in assessing the frequency and reasons for euthanasia and other end-of-life medical practices. The specific end-of-life medical treatment decisions of interest in this study were the practices of euthanasia and physician-assisted suicide, as well as the withdrawal or withholding of life-sustaining treatment and use of high-dose pain medication at levels that might hasten death.

In the first phase, the Commission reviewed 7,000 death certificates filed in the Netherlands during the preceding year. They then mailed questionnaires to the physicians who completed these certificates in order to gen-

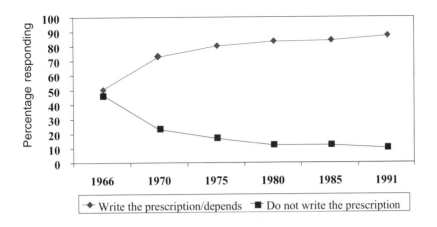

Figure 8.1. Dutch Public Opinion Regarding Euthanasia. Data from "Changes in Dutch Opinions on Active Euthanasia, 1966 Through 1991," by P. J. van der Maas, L. Pijnenborg, and J. J. van Delden, 1995, *Journal of the American Medical Association, 273,* p. 1413.

erate additional medical/clinical data that were not available from the official records (5,000 questionnaires were returned, an impressive 76% response rate). In addition to the "death certificate" data, the authors randomly selected a group of 405 physicians from various disciplines and conducted in-depth interviews with them specifically targeting their experiences with medical decisions concerning the end of life (referred to as MDEL in Commission publications). Each of the physicians interviewed was asked to provide information on all of their patients who died in the 6 months following the interview. This prospective study yielded a third dataset comprising 2,205 patient deaths. By integrating data from these three sources, the Remmelink Commission generated what appear to be reasonably accurate estimates of the frequency with which each of these end-of-life interventions was used.

Combining their data sources, the Commission estimated that 1.8% of all deaths annually were the result of euthanasia and 0.3% involved physician-assisted suicide (see Table 8.1). If extrapolated to the entire nation, these rates would correspond to approximately 1,900 cases of euthanasia or assisted suicide carried out annually in the Netherlands. In addition, approximately 0.8% of all deaths were classified as "life terminating acts without an explicit and persistent request" (i.e., "nonvoluntary" euthanasia), a subgroup of end-of-life interventions that has been particularly troubling to many ethicists and clinicians. In fact, in a subsequent publication, the authors indicated that a large proportion (37%) of patients who received euthanasia without making an explicit request were considered competent to make treatment decisions, although all of these patients had previously expressed their interest in euthanasia should their suffering become "unbearable" (van der Maas

TABLE 8.1
Percentages of Overall Deaths Resulting From
Medical Interventions, 1990

Intervention	Interviews	Certificates	Prospective	Best estimate[a]
Euthanasia	1.9	1.7	2.6	1.8
Physician-assisted suicide	0.3	0.2	0.4	0.3
Nonvolunatry euthanasia	NA	0.8	1.6	0.8
High-dosage opioids	16.3	18.8	13.8	17.5
Decision to forgo treatment	NA	17.9	17.0	17.5

Note. Percentages are based on 128,786 deaths in the Netherlands during 1990.
[a]Estimate reflects a weighting scheme used by the authors.
Data from "Euthanasia and Other Medical Decisions Concerning the End of Life," by P. J. van der Maas,
J. J. M. van Delden, L. Pijnenborg, and C. W. N. Looman, 1991, *Lancet, 338*, p. 672

et al., 1996). Nevertheless, despite the strong likelihood that the physicians carrying out these acts were motivated to reduce their patient's suffering, the question as to why the patients were not offered the opportunity to participate in this life or death decision remains unanswered. Not surprisingly, the Remmelink Commission observed substantially higher rates of opioid use at dosages that might hasten death, as well as withdrawal or withholding of potentially life-extending interventions ("no treatment decisions"), with each of these "interventions" occurring in 17.5% of all deaths.

Of particular interest to students of research methodology is the striking difference in estimates generated by the three different studies (Table 8.1). Indeed, the rates of euthanasia and assisted suicide generated from the prospective study were nearly double those generated by the mailed questionnaire, although the author's "best estimate" was much more closely aligned with the lower estimates. Given the remarkably high response rate for the mailed questionnaires, coupled with the large sample, closer adherence to these estimates is perhaps not surprising (nor inappropriate), yet it certainly leaves open the question as to whether these published data underestimated the actual rate of MDEL that were observed. Van der Maas and colleagues (1991) offered another explanation for this apparent difference in MDEL rates across study methods, suggesting that many deaths described as euthanasia in the prospective study more accurately fit their definition of high-dose opioid administration and were not euthanasia (an explanation that is consistent with the substantially lower estimate of high-dose opioid use generated by the prospective study). Although the logic behind this explanation is compelling, the variability in estimates across different research methods indicates that the frequency with which euthanasia and other MDEL are utilized in the Netherlands remains ambiguous.

Although reasonable people might disagree as to whether 2.9% of all deaths related to euthanasia or assisted suicide (based on the authors' "best estimate") reflect a high, moderate, or low rate, the authors' conclusion that such requests "are not rare in the Netherlands" certainly appears justified. On the other hand, these data were cited in support of maintaining the status quo, leaving Articles 293 and 294 intact, because the existing legal prohibitions were apparently not preventing patients from access to euthanasia should they so desire. Nevertheless, as noted above, subsequent legislation did formalize mandatory reporting requirements following cases of euthanasia and assisted suicide, in part to facilitate future research and in part to monitor these death-hastening interventions more closely.

Five years after the Remmelink Commission, the Ministers of Health and Justice commissioned a second study designed to follow a similar research methodology, although without the prospective element (van der Maas et al., 1996). The goals of the 1995 study were twofold: to update estimates of the incidence of euthanasia and other MDEL and to assess any changes in the rates of end-of-life behaviors over the intervening 5-year period. Like its 1990 counterpart, the 1995 study began with a review of death certificates, and then researchers mailed questionnaires to the 6,060 physicians who had completed the certificates. Remarkably, 4,666 physicians completed the questionnaires, yielding an even higher response rate (77%) than the previous study. These data were then integrated with in-depth interviews with a random sample of 405 physicians who were selected from the larger group of 4,666.

In comparing data from 1990 and 1995, van der Maas and his colleagues (1996) found a notable increase in the rate of euthanasia but little change in the use of other forms of MDEL (e.g., physician-assisted suicide, ending the life of a patient without a specific request; see Table 8.2). The overall number of requests for euthanasia rose from roughly 8,900 to 9,700 per year, a 9% increase. The increase in completed acts of euthanasia was even larger, although the precise increase depends on which of the two methods of data collection was used. According to the data from the physician interviews, the rate of euthanasia rose by roughly 21%, from 1.9% of all deaths in 1990 to 2.3% in 1995. However, data from the mailed questionnaires indicated an increased use of euthanasia of more than 40%, from 1.7% to 2.4%. The actual increase in euthanasia utilization probably lies somewhere between these two estimates (e.g., approximately 30%), and in fact appears to be much closer to the estimates generated by van der Maas et al.'s prospective study.

More recently, a third study of end-of-life interventions in the Netherlands has addressed these same issues, based on data from deaths occurring in 2001 (Onwuteaka-Philipsen et al., 2003). The authors replicated earlier studies, reviewing death certificates and mailing questionnaires to the physician who signed the certificate (n = 5617, a 74% response rate) as well as interviewing a random sample of physicians (n = 410, an 85% response rate). These authors noted a smaller but nonetheless appreciable increase in the rate of euthanasia deaths in their analysis of death certificates and physician questionnaires, from 2.4% to 2.6% of all deaths. Deaths related to physician-

TABLE 8.2
Percentages of Overall Deaths Resulting From Medical Interventions

Intervention	Interview data			Death certificate data		
	1990	1995	2001	1990	1995	2001
Euthanasia	1.9	2.3	2.2	1.7	2.4	2.6
Physician-assisted suicide	0.3	0.4	0.1	0.2	0.2	0.2
Nonvoluntary euthanasia	NA	0.7	0.6	0.8	0.7	0.7
High-dosage opioids	16.3	14.7	NA	18.8	19.1	20.1
Decision to forgo treatment	NA	NA	NA	17.9	20.2	20.2

Note. Percentages are based on the total number of deaths in the Netherlands: 128,824 in 1990; 135,675 in 1995; and140,377 in 2001.
Data are compiled from the following sources: "Euthanasia and Other Medical Decisions Concerning the End of Life," by P. J. van der Maas, J. J. M. van Delden, L. Pijnenborg, and C. W. N. Looman, 1991, *Lancet, 338,* p. 672; "Euthanasia, Physician-Assisted Suicide, and Other Medical Practices Involving the End of Life in the Netherlands, 1990–1995," by P. J. van der Maas et al., 1996, *New England Journal of Medicine, 335,* p. 553; and "Euthanasia and Other End-of-Life Decisions in the Netherlands in 1990, 1995, and 2001," by B. D. Onwuteaka-Philipsen et al., 2003, *Lancet,* online publication available at http://image.thelancet.com/extras/03ART3297web.pdf.

assisted suicide remained stable at 0.2% of all deaths. However, estimates based on physician interviews revealed the opposite pattern, as both euthanasia and assisted suicide deaths decreased (from 2.3% to 2.2% for euthanasia and from 0.4% to 0.1% for physician-assisted suicide). These contradictory results led the authors to conclude that euthanasia and physician-assisted suicide rates are stabilizing, despite the legal changes that had occurred during this time period. It is interesting that the disproportionate preference for euthanasia remained intact despite recommendations from the Royal Dutch Medical Association that physician-assisted suicide is the preferred alternative (Onwuteaka-Philipsen et al., 2003).

WHO UTILIZES EUTHANASIA AND ASSISTED SUICIDE?

A second line of inquiry generated by the Remmelink Commission and its successors has focused on describing the individuals who used the various end-of-life options to hasten death. Although this aspect of the research received considerably less attention than the primary focus of generating prevalence estimates, a number of intriguing findings have nonetheless emerged from the data. For example, women and younger adults appeared more likely to use some form of MDEL to end their lives compared with the overall death rates nationwide. Approximately 61% of the patients utilizing an MDEL were

---

[5]The proportion utilizing euthanasia or physician-assisted suicide has hovered around 50% in each of the surveys conducted.

women, whereas women comprised only 48% of all deaths in 1990,[5] and children and younger adults (under 65) comprised 38% of the MDEL deaths yet only 21% of deaths nationwide. Patients with cancer comprised a particularly large proportion of patients who died by euthanasia or assisted suicide (68%), yet cancer deaths accounted for a much smaller proportion of the overall deaths (27%). Patients with nervous system diseases also appeared to make up a substantially larger proportion of MDEL deaths relative to their proportion of the total deaths (12% of MDEL deaths vs. 2% of deaths overall. Data collected in the 1995 study essentially echoed the 1990 results, although the authors' method of reporting these data precluded clear comparisons with either the earlier results or Netherlands deaths more generally.[6]

The reasons patients offered for requesting hastened death have been described in previous chapters but received only superficial attention in these published reports. In short, the most common reasons offered for seeking euthanasia or assisted suicide were loss of dignity (reported by 57% of all patients), pain (reported by 46% of all patients, but listed as the sole reason for only 10 patients, representing 5% of the patients in which pain was cited as a reason), "unworthy dying" (reported by 46% of patients), dependence on others (reported by 33% of patients), and feeling tired of life (reported by 23% of patients).

Another recent article analyzing the practice of euthanasia in the Netherlands focused exclusively on patients with ALS, a disease that has recently emerged at the forefront of end-of-life research in general, and the physician-assisted suicide debate in particular (Veldink, Wokke, van der Wal, Vianney de Jong, & van der Berg, 2002). The authors surveyed the physicians of more than 200 patients who died between 1994 and 1999 in order to estimate the frequency of euthanasia/assisted suicide among this population and explore their reasons for choosing a hastened death. They found that 20% of the patients chose either euthanasia (17%) or assisted suicide (3%), and an additional 1% (2 patients, both of whom were unconscious and one had previously expressed a desire for euthanasia) received nonvoluntary euthanasia ("ending of life without patient's explicit request"). They also found that 24% received high doses of pain medications that probably hastened death, and 10% chose to forgo life-extending treatments. In total, over half of all ALS patients chose some type of death-hastening intervention (or lack of intervention).

It is interesting that the authors found none of the usual correlates of these decisions to hasten death among ALS patients. Neither the stage of disease nor the extent of physical disability appeared to predict decisions to hasten death, although patients who chose hastened death were less religious

---

[6]They separated euthanasia, assisted suicide, and nonvoluntary euthanasia from one another for some "analyses," but for other analyses they only studied the total pool of MDEL decisions, including high-dose opioid administration and decisions to forgo treatment. No comparable data were reported in the summary of 2001 data.

and less anxious than ALS patients who did not opt to hasten their death. The latter finding, that anxiety was significantly lower among patients who chose hastened death, supports one of the primary arguments in favor of legalization of assisted suicide, as this option may substantially increase a terminally ill patient's feeling of control and thereby greatly improve the quality of their death. Unfortunately these surveys, although important and informative, are insufficient to support any broad conclusions about policy regarding euthanasia.

IS IT A "SLIPPERY SLOPE"?

Perhaps one of the most important and controversial legal developments in Dutch euthanasia and physician-assisted suicide policies occurred in the early 1990s, when the practice of euthanasia was taken fully outside the medical arena and into the psychiatric one. The case that prompted this shift involved a request for physician-assisted suicide that was, for the first time, predicated on psychological suffering in the absence of any physical disorder (Griffiths et al., 1998). The woman making the request, referred to as Ms. B, was 50 years old at the time she sought assistance in dying and was described as being in good health. However, she reportedly suffered chronic psychological distress related to her traumatic family life. Following a turbulent, often violent marriage, Ms. B lost both of her sons within a 5-year period. Her oldest son had committed suicide in the mid 1980s, leading Ms. B to a brief psychiatric hospitalization where she was treated with little apparent benefit. Then in 1991 her youngest son died of cancer following a brief illness. Following his death, Ms. B reportedly became preoccupied with ending her own life, making one unsuccessful suicide attempt and frequently discussing her wish to die with family and friends. She admitted having tried to secure drugs with which she could commit suicide but feared that another failed attempt might result in serious disability or a commitment to a psychiatric hospital. Despite her obvious psychological distress, Ms. B adamantly refused to accept mental health treatment.

In August 1991 Ms. B. was referred to a psychiatrist (Dr. Boudewijn Chabot), by the Dutch Association for Voluntary Euthanasia. Dr. Chabot met with Ms. B on several occasions and reportedly discussed her situation with Ms. B's sister and brother-in-law. He also provided Ms. B's records to several independent consultants, requesting their opinions on her case. Dr. Chabot ultimately concluded that Ms. B was suffering "intense, long-term psychic suffering that, for her, was unbearable and without prospect of improvement" (Nederlandse Jurisprudentie, 1994). Dr. Chabot expressed his belief that the request for assisted suicide and refusal of mental health treatment were well-considered and that Ms. B understood the consequences of her decisions. After reviewing the medical records, the psychiatric consultants agreed with Dr. Chabot, adding that there was relatively little likelihood of successful intervention. On September 28, 1991, in the presence of several witnesses, Dr. Chabot provided Ms. B with a lethal medication that she ingested in his presence.

In April 1993, the District Court acquitted Dr. Chabot of "intentionally assisting another person to commit suicide," and this verdict was upheld by the Court of Appeals. The ruling was ultimately affirmed by the Dutch Supreme Court, citing existing precedents that euthanasia can be justified "when it is proven that the defendant acted in a situation of necessity, that is to say . . . confronted with a choice between mutually conflicting duties, he chose to perform the one of greater weight" (Nederlandse Jurisprudentie, 1994, p. 3154). In fact, the Court specifically rejected the claim that euthanasia cannot be justified in cases where the patient is not diagnosed with a "somatic" condition (i.e., a medical illness) and is not terminally ill. However, the Court did rule that Dr. Chabot had violated proper procedure by failing to insure that an "independent medical expert" had actually seen (rather than merely reviewed records and offered consultation) and examined the patient prior to providing assistance in dying. As a result, the court rejected Dr. Chabot's defense that he was forced to confront a "conflict of duties" in his desire to aid his patient but that treatment was unlikely to reduce her suffering. Because his defense was rejected, Dr. Chabot's case was ultimately returned to the lower court for re-trial where he was eventually found guilty but no punishment was imposed. Instead, he received a "reprimand" from the Dutch Medical Association because his actions were considered to have "undermined the confidence in the medical profession" (Griffiths et al., 1998).

The result of Dr. Chabot's trial generated a firestorm of controversy both within and outside the Netherlands (Hendin, Rutenfrans, & Zylicz, 1997; Schoevers, Asmus, & Van Tilburg, 1998). The extension of "legitimate" euthanasia to nonmedically ill individuals, and to depressed psychiatric patients in particular, has fueled concerns that this precedent might lead to a growing utilization of euthanasia and assisted suicide among individuals suffering from psychiatric disorders. Some authors have responded by arguing that the presence of a psychiatric disorder precludes rational decision making about end-of-life issues (Koerselman, 1994). However, this blanket generalization has not been generally accepted (J. L. Werth, 1996). Nevertheless, given the relative dearth of research focusing on the ability of psychiatric patients to make rational treatment decisions, as well as the imprecise nature of any predictions regarding treatment outcome in psychiatric disorders, the controversy that surrounded this extension of Dutch policy is not surprising (Schoevers et al., 1998).

More recently, the Dutch euthanasia practice was extended to an individual who was not only physically healthy, but did not describe "intolerable suffering." Edward Brongersma, a controversial member of the Dutch Senate (or Dutch Tweede Kamer), sought euthanasia because he was "tired of life" and believed that his life was no longer worth living (Matersvedt, 2003). In

April 1998, he committed suicide using medication prescribed by his doctor, Philip Sutorius, despite failing to meet the requirements set forth by the Dutch Supreme Court in its previous decisions. Dr. Sutorius was subsequently charged with violating Article 294 but was eventually acquitted of all charges after expert witnesses testified that Mr. Brongsma was experiencing unbearable psychological suffering. Upon appeal, Dr. Sutorius's acquittal was overturned on the basis of a distinction drawn by the courts that Mr. Brongsma's psychological pain was not consistent with the intent of Dutch law. However, despite his ultimate conviction, Dr. Sutorius received no sentence because it was believed that he acted out of compassion rather than criminal intent. This case, however, highlights the inherent difficulty in determining where the legal threshold lies for ambiguous referents such as "intolerable pain and suffering."

Despite concerns from many critics, the Royal Dutch Association of Medicine has largely supported the extension of assisted suicide/euthanasia to psychiatric patients and other nonterminally ill individuals, issuing a report that recommended treating requests for assisted suicide similarly regardless of whether the request is made in the context of a psychiatric disorder or a medical illness (Kerkhof, 2000). However, the extent to which this extension truly reflects the "slippery slope" may be less clear than the commentators would acknowledge. Yet the Association suggested that even in cases where patients suffer from intractable symptoms, the presence of severe mental illness does not necessarily invalidate a consistent request.

In a survey of Dutch psychiatrists, (Groenewoud et al., 1997) researchers attempted to evaluate the extent to which the Chabot case has influenced medical or psychiatric practice in the Netherlands. The authors mailed questionnaires to half of the psychiatrists listed in the register of the Royal Dutch Association of Medicine, receiving responses from 552 (an 83% response rate). The vast majority of respondents (64%) indicated that assisted suicide could be "acceptable" for psychiatric patients under some circumstances, and many of those psychiatrists indicated that they could personally conceive of a situation in which they would be willing to provide this assistance. In terms of their own clinical practice, 37% of the psychiatrists reported having received at least one explicit request for euthanasia or assisted suicide, and 12 (2%) reported having acceded to at least one request. Based on the data, the authors estimated that more than 300 psychiatric patients request assisted suicide annually. However, two to five of these roughly 300 annual requests are actually granted each year and many of the fulfilled requests are made by individuals who suffer from both a severe mental disorder as well as a serious physical illness. The most common reasons psychiatrists offered for assisting suicide was the perception that the patient's suffering was unbearable or hopeless and that previous treatments had failed.

Despite raising concerns among psychiatrists and ethicists around the world, the relatively low rate of euthanasia and assisted suicide facilitated by Dutch psychiatrists has been cited as evidence that a stringent standard has been applied to requests by psychiatric patients.[7] Indeed, Kerkhof (2000) concluded that "the data on euthanasia and physician assisted suicide in the Netherlands do not provide support for the slippery slope hypothesis" (p. 454). Nevertheless, virtually all of the psychiatrists surveyed (96%) indicated that psychiatric consultation should always occur whenever a physically ill patient requests euthanasia or assisted suicide primarily because of mental suffering.

SUMMARY

Although the Netherlands' experience has certainly illuminated a number of important issues regarding the practice of euthanasia and assisted suicide, firm conclusions and clear interpretations regarding many of the important issues remain elusive. There appears to be little doubt that the acceptability of euthanasia for both terminally ill and psychiatrically ill individuals has steadily increased as the legal restrictions on both have relaxed. However, it remains unclear whether the easing of such restrictions has led to this growing acceptability or is a response to the public's demand. More important, the limited epidemiological data preclude any firm assessment of whether the practice of euthanasia and assisted suicide has continued to increase and if so, whether an increased reliance on euthanasia and assisted suicide indicates the presence of a problem in the Dutch medico-legal practices. Because determining the "optimal" proportion of euthanasia/assisted suicide deaths is inherently subjective (if not frankly impossible), determinations of whether these interventions are overused or misused are ultimately subjective.

An area that has been less widely discussed is the extension of euthanasia to psychiatric patients and other elderly adults who are not medically ill. The Dutch Supreme Court's ruling that psychiatric patients are not necessarily precluded from legally sanctioned euthanasia/assisted suicide was met by stern opposition from the mental health community and continues to be an issue on which little debate (i.e., near unanimous opposition) has arisen in the United States. Despite the acknowledgment by many mental health professionals that some situations might exist in which assisted suicide or euthanasia would be appropriate, the vast majority of clinicians and ethicists have rejected this extension. Moreover, determinations such as the "untreatability" of a psychiatric disorder seem inherently problematic, particularly in light of the dramatic strides made in mental health treatment in recent years. Nevertheless, given the connection to "slippery slope" arguments, this issue will probably continue to fuel debates both in the United States and in Europe for the foreseeable future.

---

[7]Others would no doubt argue than any euthanasia requests made by a psychiatric patient that are fulfilled demonstrate the failure to adhere to a "stringent" standard.

9

THE OREGON EXPERIMENT

Researchers devoted to the study of assisted suicide and end-of-life care saw a rare opportunity when Oregon voters approved the 1994 ballot initiative legalizing physician-assisted suicide. The passage of the ODDA (1996) has enabled scientists and policymakers to study both the reasons for assisted suicide requests as well as the impact of legalization on health care practices in the United States. Using what Supreme Court Justice Brandeis termed "the laboratory of the states" (*Washington v. Glucksberg*, 1997, p. 2303), this natural experiment in end-of-life care has provided enormous opportunities that scientists, thus far, have only begun to explore. The ability to study actual requests for assisted suicide among terminally ill Americans and to contrast these observations with the existing research literature on desire for hastened death and end-of-life practices has virtually unlimited potential for understanding the psychology of end-of-life care.

The legal history behind the ODDA has already been described in chapter 2 and need not be repeated here, but the application of this act warrants some explication. Although Oregon voters originally approved of the ODDA in 1994, it was not until 1997 that Oregonians were first offered the option to request a prescription for a lethal medication. This delay was in part because of legal challenges raised in the courts (*Lee v. State of Oregon*, 1997; cert. denied, *Lee v. Harcleroad*, 1997) and challenges taken directly to the voters (Batavia, 2000). After all apparent routes to challenge the ODDA had been exhausted (although more would emerge later; J. L. Werth, 2002), and a task force convened to outline practice guidelines had issued their recommendations (Task Force to Improve the Care of Terminally-Ill Oregonians, 1998), the first legally sanctioned requests for assisted suicide in U.S. history occurred. Before discussing the research that has emerged from Oregon thus far, a review of the ODDA's provisions is necessary.

THE ODDA

The ODDA allows any eligible adult to request a prescription for medication to end his or her life provided a number of conditions are met. These requirements for eligibility entail obligations on the part of both the patient and the physician. In order to request a prescription for a lethal medication, the patient must be (a) over 18 years old, (b) a resident of Oregon, (c) diagnosed with a terminal illness with a life expectancy of 6 months or less, and (d) capable of making a reasoned decision (i.e., judgment not impaired by depression or other mental disorders).

The Oregon requirements reflect a significant departure from the criteria used in the Netherlands, where an individual must be experiencing intolerable pain or suffering (but need not be terminally ill) in order to request euthanasia or assisted suicide.[1] Assuming the above conditions are met, the patient must make two verbal requests to his or her physician with at least 15 days elapsing between the requests. In addition, the patient must provide the physician with a written request no less than 48 hours before the prescription is provided and the written request must be witnessed by at least one person who is not a relative, is not employed by the health care facility responsible for the person's care, and is not entitled to any portion of the requesting person's estate. These latter requirements were added to ensure that the request was made voluntarily, without undue coercion from family, health care providers, or those with a financial incentive.

In addition to the requirements placed on patients, physicians are also charged with the following responsibilities:

1. Determining whether the patient's diagnosis and prognosis meet the requisite criteria (i.e., terminal illness with less than 6-month life expectancy).
2. Referring the patient to a consulting physician who must confirm the patient's diagnosis and prognosis.

---

[1] As noted in the previous chapter, intolerable pain or suffering was originally conceived as an additional requirement beyond a terminal prognosis but more recently has been seen as a sufficient basis for physician-assisted suicide and euthanasia in the Netherlands even in the absence of a severe medical illness.

3. Discussing the risks and benefits of the lethal medication with the patient making the request (i.e., that the medication will likely cause immediate death, as well as the possible palliative care alternatives that exist).

4. Determining whether the patient is suffering from any mental disorder that may be impairing his or her judgment. If a mental disorder is suspected, the physician is required to refer the patient for mental health "counseling." After such a referral has been made, no lethal prescription can be provided "until the person performing the counseling determines that the patient is not suffering from a psychiatric or psychological disorder or depression causing impaired judgment."[2]

5. Encouraging the patient to notify his or her next of kin (although patients are not mandated to do so).

6. Documenting that all of the above requirements have been met and specifying which medication has been prescribed. These physician reports, filed with the Oregon Health Division, permit monitoring and evaluation of the ODDA utilization.

Assuming the physician has fulfilled these requirements in good faith, the ODDA provides immunity from any criminal or civil prosecution, as well as from censure, discipline, or loss of privilege from any professional association or organization.

However, in fall 2001, the United States Department of Justice issued a policy statement effectively overruling these legal and administrative protections, classifying the prescription of any controlled substance (i.e., the medication that would be provided under the ODDA) as a violation of the Controlled Substances Act (J. L. Werth, 2002). Had this policy prevailed, physicians who comply with the ODDA could have been subjected to federal criminal prosecution analogous to that of a drug trafficker. This proposed reinterpretation of the Controlled Substances Act engendered considerable debate among medical and mental health professionals, as well as attorneys and civil libertarians, but has not yet been upheld by the U.S. Court of Appeals.[3] Despite this challenge to the ODDA, however, important observations and empirical data have arisen from Oregon with regard to the utilization of legalized assisted suicide.

---

[2]Although this criteria might initially appear as if it requires mental health treatment to resolve the underlying mental disorder, in fact the requirements stipulate only that the patient be deemed "competent" to make the decision (i.e., no longer having "impaired judgment").

[3]This policy statement was immediately followed by a temporary injunction, allowing the ODDA to continue unhindered until the legal issues are resolved (i.e., whether a federal agency can effectively override the legislative authority of an individual state). In April 2002, the U.S. District Court issued a permanent injunction, but as of this writing the case has not yet been heard at the appellate level.

In February 1999, the Oregon Health Division (OHD), in cooperation with the Oregon Department of Human Resources and the Center for Disease Prevention and Epidemiology, published a report documenting the first year's experience with the ODDA. (The report was simultaneously published in a somewhat abbreviated form in the *New England Journal of Medicine*; Chin, Hedberg, Higginson, & Fleming, 1999.)[4] The data for the report were drawn primarily from the documents submitted by physicians as part of their compliance with the Act's requirements. In addition, beginning in January 1998, physicians who provided prescriptions for a lethal medication under the ODDA were interviewed by OHD research staff in order to garner additional information that was not available in the standard reporting forms. The information elicited from these interviews included determining whether the patient actually ingested the prescribed medication, whether the person experienced any unexpected adverse effects (e.g., medication side effects or a significant delay before death occurred), and other potentially relevant information such as insurance status, medical and functional status at the time of death, and end-of-life care and concerns.

During the first year of the ODDA, 24 patients were provided lethal prescriptions, typically a fast-acting barbiturate (secobarbital or pentobarbital), 22 of whom died during 1998 (OHD, 1999). Of the 22, 16 died as a result of ingesting the lethal medication and 6 died of their underlying illness. (Two were still alive as of January 1, 1999.[5]) Only 5 of these 24 individuals had undergone a psychological or psychiatric evaluation prior to receiving the prescription for lethal medication, and none were considered to be suffering from a mental disorder of sufficient magnitude so as to impair their judgment. Supporters of the ODDA have been quick to note that these 16 deaths represented only a tiny fraction of the total deaths in Oregon during the year, as roughly 30,000 deaths occur annually in that state, representing a rate of 5.2 assisted suicides per 10,000 deaths.

In analyzing the characteristics of this small sample, Chin and colleagues (1999) compared 15 patients to a matched (on age, medical illness, and date of death) comparison sample of individuals who died without physician intervention. They found no difference between patients who used the ODDA and the comparison sample in terms of health care coverage, utilization of hospice services, or completion of advance directives. Patients who used the ODDA were significantly more likely to have expressed concerns to their physicians regarding loss of autonomy and loss of control of bodily functions,

---

[4]In fact, the summary of the first year of the ODDA actually encompassed the first 14 months, because the provisions of the ODDA took effect on October 27, 1997.

[5]Chin et al. (1999) reported on a sample of 15 patients, but in subsequent reports (A. D. Sullivan et al., 2000) these data were revised after a 16th death related to the ODDA was recorded.

but they were no more likely to express concerns about being a burden to others or to report an inability to participate in activities. Many of these statements were limited by a reliance on the patient's spontaneous reports rather than a systematic review of problems or concerns. Because patients who requested assisted suicide are required to voice concerns to their physician as a justification for their request whereas other patients are not, differences in the frequency of discomfort or functional limitations may simply be an artifact of the study method rather than genuine differences between patients who request assisted suicide and those who do not. In fact, palliative care researchers have noted that patients often deliberately withhold complaints about their physical functioning and problematic symptoms for fear of distracting their health care provider from the "more important" task of curing their disease (Breitbart et al., 1998; Ward et al., 1993). Nevertheless, on the basis of their findings (or, more accurately, their lack of significant findings), Chin and colleagues concluded that patients who requested assisted suicide were not disproportionately poor, uneducated, members of an ethnic minority, or receiving inadequate health care.

B. C. Lee and Werth (2000) reached roughly similar conclusions from their analysis of individuals requesting assisted suicide. Rather than relying on "official" records from the OHD, they studied utilization of the ODDA using files from a private organization, Compassion in Dying, a nonprofit organization dedicated to providing information, consultation, and support services to terminally ill individuals. This group, one of the plaintiffs in the case that ultimately reached the Supreme Court (*Washington v. Glucksberg*, 1997), has been a vocal advocate of legalization of assisted suicide in Oregon and elsewhere. Originally based in the state of Washington, a branch of Compassion in Dying began operating in Portland, Oregon, in January 1998. Unlike the handful of cases reported to the OHD, Compassion in Dying received more than 350 requests for information in the first year following the enactment of the ODDA, and 56 of these individuals appeared to qualify for assistance in dying under the provisions of the Act.[6] In total, 34 of the individuals who contacted Compassion in Dying died during 1998, 10 of whom ended their lives with a medication prescribed by a doctor. An additional 10 individuals had some form of hastened death, either through termination of nutrition and hydration (4 individuals) or high doses of pain medication (6 individuals); 14 died without having taken any steps to hasten death. It is interesting that Lee and Werth found that requests for assisted suicide often resulted in a "marked improvement" in the quality of palliative care provided by the physician, either in the form of hospice services or more aggres-

---

[6]The basis for this determination was not described in B. C. Lee and Werth (2000). Although Compassion in Dying's staff includes physicians, it is not clear whether these determinations were based on actual medical examinations or patient report of their diagnosis/prognosis. Because many of these "requests for information" appear to be solely telephone encounters, the latter seems more likely.

sive symptom management. In other cases, however, family members reported substantial psychological distress because of the unrelieved discomfort of their dying relative, particularly when that relative's request for assisted suicide was not fulfilled. Furthermore, several patients studied by Lee and Werth perceived their physician's response to their request as "evasive." For example, Lee and Werth described one patient who, after being told of her terminal condition and making her initial request for a lethal prescription, was informed by her physician that he was not (or no longer) convinced of her terminal prognosis and instead ordered further diagnostic testing. When the patient died several weeks later, her family expressed the belief that her physician had deliberately ignored the patient's request and instead pursued his own agenda. Nevertheless, despite these occasional complaints, Lee and Werth concluded that the ODDA "is working as the drafters had planned and that the abuses forecasted by opponents have not materialized" (p. 289). On the other hand, they noted that improvements in doctor–patient communication (and physician honesty) are clearly necessary, particularly among physicians who are not in favor of the act.

Year 2 of the ODDA

A year after Chin's account of the first year's experience, A. D. Sullivan, Hedberg, and Fleming (2000) published a summary of the second year statistics compiled by the OHD (2000). This report echoed and extended many of the findings from the first year, but with a substantially greater number of assisted suicides. Indeed, in 1999 the number of individuals who ended their lives with a medication prescribed under the ODDA was nearly double that of the preceding 14 months (27 in 1999 vs. 16 in 1997/1998), although the actual increase in lethal prescriptions written was not quite as large (33 in 1999 vs. 25 in 1998). These 27 deaths also reflected a larger percentage of the actual prescriptions written; 26 of 33 individuals who received lethal prescriptions used the medication to end their life (the 27th death resulted from a prescription written in 1998). Although this substantial increase in the rate of assisted suicide (roughly 9 per 10,000 deaths compared to 5.2/10,000 in 1998) is certainly noteworthy, even ardent opponents of the ODDA have stopped short of labeling this increase evidence of excessive or inappropriate use of the act. Of the 27 patients who used a lethal prescription to end their life, 10 (37%) had been referred for a psychiatric consultation prior to providing the prescription.

Aside from the increase in actual requests for lethal prescriptions and utilization of these medications to end life, a number of other interesting differences emerged between the 1998 and 1999 reports. For example, the median time elapsed between the provision of a lethal prescription and the utilization of this medication increased fourfold, from a median interval of 22 days in 1998 to 83 days in 1999, including one individual who waited 247 days before ingesting the medication. Moreover, because these data reflect the median, this increase cannot be attributed to a small number of patients who waited an extremely long time before ending their lives. Rather, this increased length of time between the provision of a lethal prescription and its actual use supports the "secondary" benefit of legalized assisted suicide that many clinicians have cited, providing patients with a sense of relief by knowing that they have the ability to end their life when (or if) they so choose. Without actually interviewing these patients who waited to use the medication, it is not possible to conclusively determine what, if any, purpose or result was behind this increased interval between prescription and use of a lethal medication, but one may reasonably conclude that decisions to use a lethal prescription under the ODDA were not taken impulsively.

Another interesting development in the 1999 data was the emergence of patients with ALS as a substantial group of ODDA utilizers. Four of the 27 decedents had been diagnosed with ALS compared to none of the 1998 decedents (almost all of whom were diagnosed with cancer). More important, these four ALS patients represented 5% of all deaths of patients with ALS in Oregon, whereas the rate of assisted suicide among cancer patients was only 0.4%. Also intriguing in the 1999 data was the emergence of a relationship between education and assisted suicide, with the likelihood of requesting assisted suicide increasing with higher levels of education. Of the 27 individuals who ingested a lethal medication in 1999, 13 had at least a college degree and only 2 had less than a high school diploma. No such relationship between education and use of the ODDA was evident in the 1998 data, but it is consistent with studies of patient attitudes and acceptance of assisted suicide (e.g., Brietbart et al., 1996).

Like the 1998 data, however, concerns regarding the loss of autonomy remained the most common reason for patient requests for a lethal medication, with this concern expressed in 81% of all 1999 cases. Another frequently cited rationale for seeking a hastened death was increasing functional disability (phrased as "decreasing ability to participate in activities that make life enjoyable"). On the other hand, pain remained a relatively infrequent reason for requests for assisted suicide; only 7 of 27 patients expressed "concern about worsening pain" (and only 2 of 16 patients expressed this concern in the 1998 study). Family members interviewed as part of the OHD's assessment process perceived relatively similar reasons behind patient requests. Of the 19 family members interviewed, loss of control over bodily functions, loss of autonomy, and physical suffering were the most frequently cited reasons behind decisions to end life.

Year 3: Trends Stabilize, Attention Fades

Data from the third year of the ODDA, although issued in the same manner as in previous years (with an "official" document prepared by the

OHD issued in 2001 simultaneously reported in the *New England Journal of Medicine*), received much less attention and scrutiny. In fact, unlike the two previous reports, only a brief summary comparing Year 3 data to the previous 2 years was published in the *Journal*, and this report received virtually no attention in the lay press. This seeming lack of attention may be partially due to many similarities between the data of the third year to and those of the second year, with another 27 deaths related to lethal medications (A. D. Sullivan, Hedberg, & Hopkins, 2001). These 27 deaths represented two thirds of the total number of lethal prescriptions written in 2000 (26 of 39 prescriptions written; one of the 27 deaths in 2000 resulted from a prescription written in 1999), a rate roughly comparable to those observed in previous years (27 of 33 in 1999 and 16 of 24 in 1998). On the other hand, rates of referral for mental health consultation were somewhat lower in 2000, as only 5 of the 27 (19%) had been referred for a mental health consultation, half the rate observed in 1999. As in previous years, no information was obtained as to what if any mental health interventions took place.

Similar to the 1999 data, most patients who ended their lives with a lethal medication were relatively well-educated. Half of the assisted suicide decedents had at least a college degree compared to only 13% of Oregon deaths among individuals who died from similar diseases without assistance from the ODDA. On the other hand, only 8% of individuals who utilized the ODDA in 1999 (i.e., 2 individuals) had less than a high school degree compared to 26% of Oregon decedents overall. Reasons for requesting assisted suicide remained consistent, with loss of autonomy continuing to be the most common rationale, followed by deteriorating bodily functioning and decreased ability to participate in activities. Unlike in previous years, however, feeling that one was a burden to friends, family, or caregivers emerged as a relatively common explanation for ODDA utilization, with 17 individuals (63%) offering this reason compared to only 9 of 43 (21%) in the previous 2 years. Despite these modest differences (lower rate of mental health consultation and greater prominence of concerns regarding being a burden), the third-year data revealed few other changes or surprises. Hence, most commentators have continued to suggest that the ODDA has been utilized in an appropriate and thoughtful manner, without evidence of either abuse or misuse, and that fears of a growing reliance on assisted suicide over time have simply not been realized thus far.[7]

Year 4: In the Midst of Controversy

The fourth year of the ODDA witnessed the first significant legal challenge since the law was enacted in 1997. The now famous "Ashcroft Direc-

---

[7]See the special issue of *Psychology, Public Policy and Law* devoted to the Oregon Death with Dignity Act, 2000, Volume 6, Issue 2.

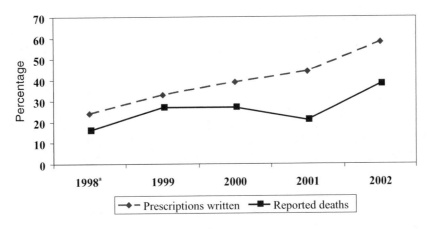

Figure 9.1. Use of the ODDA. ODDA = Oregon Death with Dignity Act.
ªIncludes data from October 1997 through December 31, 1998.

tive," discussed previously, entailed a brief entry in the Federal Register in which Attorney General John Aschroft declared that the use of controlled substances under the ODDA did not constitute a "legitimate medical purpose" and therefore was subject to criminal prosecution and other legal sanctions. Whether this directive, issued November 9, 2001, had any impact on the utilization of the ODDA, which decreased somewhat from previous years, is not yet known but is certainly possible. However, although the number of patients who ended their lives with a prescribed medication decreased somewhat in 2001 (compared to previous years), the actual number of prescriptions written did not (Hedberg, Hopkins, & Southwick, 2002). A total of 44 prescriptions for lethal medication were written in 2001 by 33 different physicians (OHD, 2002), compared to 39 in 2000, 33 in 1999, and 24 in 1998 (see Figure 9.1). On the other hand, only 21 terminally ill individuals ended their lives with these medications in 2001, and only 19 of these were among the 44 prescriptions written. (Two patients who had received a prescription in 2000 did not use the medication until 2001.) Hence, the overall rate of assisted suicide dropped to only 7 per 10,000 for the year, a small decrease from the rate of 9 per 10,000 reported in the preceding 2 years. Fourteen of the patients who received a lethal prescription died of their underlying disease, and 11 were still alive as of December 31, 2001.

Much of the OHD data reported from 2001 support the trends that have now become apparent, as "losing autonomy" and "decreasing ability to participate in activities that make life enjoyable" remained the most common reasons for patient requests for PAS (reported in 94% and 76%, respectively), whereas inadequate pain control was reported by only 1 patient (5%). Only 24% cited feeling a burden to their friends or family as a reason for seeking assisted suicide, and one patient cited the financial implications of continued treatment (5%). Patients who utilized the ODDA continued to be predominantly well-educated, with only 3 of 21 (14%) having less than a high school diploma and 38% having a college or graduate degree. A somewhat larger proportion of patients who died from ingesting a lethal medication were diagnosed with cancer, as this was the primary diagnosis in 18 of 21 cases (86%, compared to 74% in the previous 3 years combined). Other diseases such as ALS and COPD comprised the remaining 3 cases (none were diagnosed with HIV/AIDS). In short, although there were no surprises in the 2001 data, nor any significant reaction from the medical community or general public, the annual report certainly solidified the emerging patterns regarding who utilizes the ODDA and why.

Five Years of Legalized Assisted Suicide

Much of the ODDA's fifth year was mired in the controversy surrounding the Ashcroft directive described above. Although this directive was ultimately overturned in April 2002, when the U. S. District Court issued a permanent injunction ("Federal Judge Upholds Assisted Suicide Law," April 17, 2002), the first several months of 2002 were mired in uncertainty as to how this political quagmire would ultimately be resolved (J. L. Werth, 2002). The extent to which this legal ambiguity influenced the utilization of the ODDA, or whether the findings from 2002 merely reflect emerging trends, will probably not be known for several more years.

Although some writers may have anticipated that physicians would be more reluctant to utilize the provisions of the ODDA because of fear of legal repercussions, the number of prescriptions written jumped dramatically in 2002, to 58 (from a previous high of 44 in the preceding year, see Figure 9.1; Department of Human Services, 2003). This increase continued the rising trend in utilization, although the overall frequency with which dying patients sought a lethal prescription remained low (13 per 10,000 deaths, nearly triple the rate from the ODDA's first year). The number of deaths from lethal prescriptions also increased in 2002, to 38 (including two patients who had received prescriptions in 2001).

Other than the growing number of requests for, and use of lethal medications, patients who sought a lethal prescription in 2002 appeared to be quite similar to patients from previous years (see Table 9.1). The vast majority of patients who sought and used lethal prescriptions were Caucasian (one individual was Asian), raising the 5-year total of ODDA deaths to 125 Caucasians and 4 Asians who died after ingesting a lethal medication. Likewise, patients who used the ODDA tended to be younger than those who died without assistance, were more highly educated, and were more likely to be diagnosed with cancer or ALS.

Reasons for seeking a lethal prescription also remained largely unchanged in 2002 (see Table 9.2), with the majority of patients voicing concerns about

TABLE 9.1
ODDA Utilization Data

Data	1998	1999	2000	2001	2002
Prescriptions written	24	33	39	44	58
Death from medication	16	27	27	23	36
Characteristics of decedents					
Average age (years)	70	71	70	68	69
% Female	50	41	56	62	29
% Caucasian	100	96	96	95	97
Education (%)					
Less than high school	19	7	8	14	10
High school graduate	56	44	42	48	64
College graduate	25	48	50	38	26
Underlying illness (%)					
Cancer	88	63	78	86	84
ALS	0	15	7	5	8
Other[a]	12	23	15	9	8
Enrolled in hospice	73	78	88	76	92
Referred for psych.					
evaluation	31	37	19	14	13

Note. ODDA = Oregon Death with Dignity Act; ALS = amytotrophic lateral sclerosis; psych. = psychological.
[a]More than half of the "other" category are patients diagnosed with chronic obstructive pulmonary disease.

losing autonomy (84%), a decreasing ability to participate in pleasurable activities (84%), and losing control over bodily functioning (47%). Not surprisingly, these concerns are particularly prominent when patients are diagnosed with ALS, perhaps accounting for the relatively higher frequency with which ALS patients seek relief under ODDA.

PHYSICIAN PERSPECTIVES ON THE ODDA

Because the OHD data focused solely on patients who were provided prescriptions for a lethal medication rather than the larger population of individuals who requested them, Ganzini, Nelson, and colleagues (2000) conducted a survey of Oregon physicians in order to better understand the ODDA process from the physician's perspective. They mailed questionnaires to all licensed physicians with relevant specializations (internal medicine, family or general practice, etc.) practicing in Oregon, asking them to provide information about all of their terminally ill patients who had requested a prescription for a lethal medication. Of the 2,649 responding physicians (a response rate of 65%), 144 physicians reported receiving a total of 206 unique requests (excluding cases where more than one physician seemed to have reported the same case). Of these 206 requests, more than half (n = 112) occurred in 1998 (data collection began in spring 1999), confirming the fact

TABLE 9.2
Reasons for Using the ODDA (in Percentages)

Reason	1998	1999	2000	2001	2002
Loss of autonomy	75	81	93	94	84
Less able to participate in activities	69	81	78	76	84
Loss of control of bodily functions	56	59	78	53	47
Burden on family/friends/caregivers	13	26	63	24	37
Inadequate pain control	13	26	30	6	26
Financial implications of treatment	0	0	4	6	3

Note. ODDA = Oregon Death with Dignity Act.

that the 24 prescriptions written in 1998 (described in the OHD reports) reflect a small proportion (21%) of the larger number of individuals requesting a lethal prescription.[8]

Like the OHD reports, the factors seen as precipitating requests for a lethal prescription were largely functional, as nearly 60% of the patients seeking assistance in dying were confined to a bed or chair much of the day and in 41% of cases the request followed a noticeable deterioration in the patient's medical condition. On the other hand, depression was relatively infrequently noted by responding physicians. Only 20% of the patients had "symptoms of depression," and only 3 patients (2%) were considered "incompetent" to make medical decisions. This modest rate of depression is particularly striking given the consistently higher rates of depression observed in studies of desire for hastened death (described in chap. 5), which have typically hovered around 50% (e.g., Breitbart et al., 2000; Chochinov et al., 1995). Given the potential for inaccuracy in physician assessments of depression that should be obvious to anyone who has read the preceding chapters, the low rate of depression reported by Ganzini's sample might elicit concerns regarding the adequacy of the ODDA's requirements for assessing and treating depression and other mental conditions that may impair judgment (see, e.g., Rosenfeld & Breitbart, 2000). By relying on the physician who receives the request to determine whether a mental health referral is necessary, many depressed patients are likely to remain unidentified and untreated.

However, studies of depression and terminal illness have typically generated rates of major depression ranging from 15 to 20%, which is roughly comparable to that observed by Ganzini and her colleagues.[9] Hence, it is

[8]Moreover, if the 65% return rate is considered unbiased (an untestable assumption), the actual number of patients requesting assisted suicide during this period may have been as much as 50% greater.

[9]Ganzini's survey, however, used a substantially lower threshold for identifying depression ("symptoms of depression"), whereas the 15–20% prevalence rates observed in most published studies typically reflect a diagnosis of Major Depressive Disorder.

unclear whether this modest rate of depression reflects the failure of Oregon physicians to recognize depression or merely confirms the relatively modest association between depression and requests for assisted suicide that has been reported in other studies of requests for assisted suicide (e.g., Meier et al., 1998). Furthermore, even if depression was under-recognized, the severity of depression among these unrecognized patients may not have been sufficient to impair judgment (Schwenk, Coyne, & Fechner-Bates, 1996). As discussed in chapter 7, however, the question of whether depression impairs decision-making capacity may depend more on how one defines *decision-making capacity* than on the severity of depression. In any case, Ganzini's data certainly highlight the concern that depression may be underdiagnosed, inadequately treated, and exerting more influence on end-of-life decision making than supporters of the ODDA acknowledge.

The most commonly cited reasons for requesting a lethal prescription reported by Ganzini et al.'s respondents were primarily related to functional abilities and overall quality of life. These factors included a loss of independence (noted in 57% of patient requests), poor quality of life (55%), feeling "ready to die" (54%), and wanting to control the circumstances of one's death (53%). Physical symptoms, such as pain (present in 43% of cases), fatigue (31%), and dyspnea (27%) were relatively common but noticeably less so than the functional factors noted above. Nevertheless, a referral for more adequate palliative care was the most common physician response to requests for lethal medication, as 30% of patients were referred for more aggressive pain management and 30% were referred for treatment of other uncontrolled symptoms. Another 20% of patients were referred for a mental health consultation, and 18% were prescribed psychotropic medication following their request for assisted suicide (typically an antidepressant or anxiolytic medication). Of note, respondents estimated that only half of the recommendations for more aggressive palliative care were ultimately followed.

Perhaps the most striking finding from Ganzini's study was the observation that 35% of the patients who requested a lethal prescription withdrew their request after one or more of the recommended interventions occurred.[10] The interventions most likely to lead to such reversals were symptom management (resulting in 11 cases in which requests were withdrawn), referral to a hospice (8 reversals of the request), general reassurance (another 8 rever-

[10]The proportion of requests for a lethal prescription that were ultimately rescinded (35%) does not account for the large volume of requests that did not result in a prescription being provided. Because only 18% of the patients were ultimately provided the prescription requested, and 35% rescinded their requests, nearly half of all patients who requested physician-assisted suicide remain unaccounted for. This "missing" group includes many patients who died before a prescription was provided (although one might have eventually been given), either of their underlying illness (or another unrelated cause) or through another death-hastening method (e.g., withdrawal of artificial nutrition/hydration), or never completed their request but did not formally rescind their initial request. Although the number of patients who fell into these various categories is unknown, the proportion of patients who reversed their initial decision to end their life likely underestimates the actual number of "reversals" that occurred.

sals), reassurance that a prescription would be provided if desired (8 reversals), treatment of depression (3 reversals), and social work consultation (3 reversals). These data demonstrate what many opponents of legalized assisted suicide have long argued: that a substantial proportion of requests are potentially reversible with the provision of adequate health and mental health palliative care. Yet this conclusion is not the only plausible one that can be drawn from these data. Indeed, one might logically infer from these data that the safeguards contained in the ODDA are both adequate and effective because potentially inappropriate requests (i.e., those that are based solely on inadequate palliative care) were identified and did not result in a hastened death.

PERSPECTIVES OF OTHER HEALTH CARE PROVIDERS

Following their study of physicians who participated in the ODDA, Ganzini and colleagues (2002) conducted a similar survey of nurses and social workers who work with hospice patients. They surveyed 306 nurses and 91 social workers (73% of the total number of potential respondents) who cared for hospice patients in Oregon. Nearly half (45%) of these health care providers had provided care for at least one patient who explicitly requested a lethal prescription, and these respondents were asked to describe the reasons offered by the patient. Of note, 13 of the 82 nurses who provided data indicated that the patient did not receive a lethal medication because he or she could not find a physician willing to provide the prescription.

The most common reasons cited for lethal medication requests were the desire to control the circumstances of one's death, loss of independence (or fear of losing independence), poor quality of life (or fear of poor quality of life), loss of dignity (or fear of losing dignity), and pain or fear of pain. Although depression and lack of social support were noted in the majority of cases, the respondents regarded these factors as much less influential than the other factors. The vast majority of nurses who responded to the survey regarded patients who sought a lethal prescription as more concerned with controlling of the circumstances of their death and more fearful of losing independence than were hospice patients who did not seek a lethal prescription.

DOES THE ODDA WORK?

Given the findings described by the OHD and others, there has been little dissent among supporters of the ODDA as to the "success" of the act. Each published report (and nearly all published commentary) has concluded that the "experiment" thus far appears to be successful. Supporters base this conclusion largely on the relative infrequency with which the Act has been used (particularly in comparison to the Netherlands, where rates of euthanasia and assisted suicide are far greater), the efficacy of medications utilized to end life (i.e., the high success rate and low rate of adverse results), the lack of evidence that patients are either depressed or receiving inadequate palliative care, and the many similarities between those patients who have utilized the act and comparable patients who have not. Yet every political issue that has supporters will inevitably have opposing views. Indeed, several researchers and clinicians opposed to the ODDA have raised important concerns about the "success" of the Act suggesting that it may not be operating as smoothly as its supporters would suggest.

Among the most vocal critics of the ODDA have been Kathleen Foley and Herbert Hendin (1999). Shortly after the OHD first released its findings, Foley and Hendin raised several reservations about the data upon which "unwarranted conclusions" were based. Their criticisms encompassed a wide array of issues, some of which may be less important (e.g., the lack of information regarding the qualifications of telephone interviewers) but others are critical (e.g., the lack of medical data to support diagnosis and/or prognosis). In general, their criticisms center primarily on information that was not obtained rather than the data that were reported. For example, they noted that the conclusion that patients who obtained and utilized a lethal prescription were receiving adequate palliative care was based on the finding that individuals who utilized the ODDA were equally likely to be enrolled in a hospice program or have an advance directive as the comparison sample. Yet OHD data do not reveal the level of competence physicians had at providing palliative care nor the actual care that these patients received. Clearly these "missing" data are far more relevant to the conclusion that adequate palliative care had been provided than the data offered by the OHD reports.

Foley and Hendin also criticized the OHD's attention to economic and social factors, noting that the required documentation did not elicit this information in a systematic manner. Hence, the conclusion that economic factors were not influential in utilization of the ODDA was based on the absence of spontaneous patient reports and the failure to observe a difference in health insurance status between those patients who used the Act and a comparable group of deceased Oregonians. Yet without any systematic assessment of financial or social factors that might have influenced patient decisions, it is impossible to know whether these issues were actually relevant or how important a role they may have played. The financial and social burdens of a terminal illness are obvious and are only partially offset by adequate health insurance and hospice care. Furthermore, it seems unlikely that patients requesting a lethal prescription would cite financial or social burdens as the basis for their request, particularly if they genuinely wanted to end their life, for fear that their physician would find this rationale inadequate. Thus, as Foley and Hendin correctly note, the OHD's data fall far short of providing any clear evidence that financial or social factors were not influential factors for patients who utilized the ODDA.

A final issue raised by Foley and Hendin (as well as others) concerns the OHD's attention (or lack thereof) to mental health factors. Not only do they criticize the ODDA for failing to require formal documentation from psychiatrists and psychologists who have examined patients in conjunction with the Act's provisions, the Act imposes no requirements on the clinicians who conduct these evaluations either with regard to training or to assessment method. These writers suggest that ambivalence may be at the heart of many of the requests for lethal prescription. Although this possibility might be evaluated through interviews with patients, either those who received a prescription but did not use it or those who did in fact end their lives, no such individualized assessments have been made. Rather, in those cases where depression had been identified, Foley and Hendin suggested that patients may have simply sought another physician rather than undergone the required mental health consultation and/or treatment. They attributed this avoidance of mental health involvement to the influence of organizations such as Compassion in Dying, which often provide referral information and recommendations to terminally ill patients. They suggested that these organizations systematically recommend physicians who are supportive of the ODDA and, perhaps, are less likely to carefully scrutinize the appropriateness of individual requests than many physicians would be. Regardless of whether this or other sources of clinician bias do in fact exist, there is little doubt that the psychological or psychiatric status of those patients who seek assisted suicide is poorly understood, and conclusions about the influence (or lack thereof) of depression on the basis of the OHD data are premature.

REMAINING QUESTIONS AND CONCERNS

The ODDA data recorded by the OHD and other sources have left a number of unanswered questions and have raised many concerns. However, one of most striking findings from the Oregon data that has not been widely recognized by either supporters or critics of the Act is the racial disparity among patients receiving a lethal prescription. Of the 129 patients who received and used a lethal medication during the first 5 years, only four were members of an ethnic minority group (and all were Asian), whereas the remaining 125 (97%) were Caucasian and non-Hispanic. Of course, the Oregon population is predominantly Caucasian (approximately 83.5% of the adult population, according to the 2000 U.S. Census), but the absence of any African-American or Hispanic individuals from the ODDA is nonetheless noteworthy. Although many studies have demonstrated significantly more support for legalization of assisted suicide among Caucasians, none has observed a "race effect" of this magnitude. Ganzini's data from their physician survey demonstrated a comparable disparity in requests for a lethal prescription, with 97% of all requests being made by Caucasians. Whatever the explanation for this racial disparity in requests for and utilization of physician-assisted suicide, it does not appear that physicians are any more or less likely to provide a prescription for Caucasians versus minority individuals. Instead, it appears that ethnic minority individuals are simply not inclined to utilize the ODDA. Understanding the possible cultural influences on interest in assisted suicide remains important uncharted territory for future researchers to explore.

A number of writers have speculated that the lack of support for legalization of assisted suicide (and hence, lack of utilization) may reflect a greater mistrust of the medical community on the part of minority individuals (e.g., Crawley et al., 2000). Disenfranchised populations may be naturally skeptical when a physician indicates that the person's prognosis is poor and that no further "curative" treatments are available. In addition, in communities where the ties between patients and their physicians are weak (e.g., where reliance on Medicaid limits a patient's time and sense of connection to the physician), developing the requisite level of trust necessary to engage in a discussion of end-of-life options may simply not exist.

Another means by which ethnicity and culture might influence end-of-life decisions such as assisted suicide pertains to the willingness to discuss illness and prognosis. Many cultures are less supportive of open discussions of end-of-life issues and prefer that patients remain naïve as to the severity of their condition (Bruera, Neumann, Mazzocato, Stiefel, & Sala, 2000). Whether such cultural differences primarily reflect family or physician preferences or extend to the patients themselves has been largely unexplored, although preliminary research has suggested that terminally ill patients may be more motivated to discuss end-of-life issues than their physicians realize (J. A. Lo, Ng, Yap, & Chan, 2000). Whatever the reasons behind these patterns, the racial disparity observed in the OHD reports actually contradicts many expectations that the ODDA would be overutilized by minority and disenfranchised populations because of their more limited access to adequate health care and palliative care resources.

SUMMARY

Data from Oregon have provided ample fodder for both supporters and critics of the ODDA. Supporters have consistently pointed to the low rates of utilization; the seemingly adequate protections offered; and the lack of evidence that patients who seek hastened death are disenfranchised, uneducated, impulsive, or receiving inadequate health care. Indeed, the data currently available suggest precisely the opposite: Patients utilizing the ODDA tend to be white, well-educated, enrolled in hospice care programs, have adequate health insurance coverage, and make their decisions to hasten death over an extended period of time. Nevertheless, opponents of the Act are quick to point out that these data are inconclusive as to the quality of health care these patients have received, the possible role of untreated depression, and as to the clear potential for bias among clinicians who participate in the process. Whether the promise of the ODDA is ultimately realized, both in terms of improving the dying process and our understanding the reasons behind requests for assisted suicide, remains to be seen.

10

WHERE DO WE GO FROM HERE?

Perhaps the most striking theme that has emerged from the previous chapters is the central role played by depression and psychosocial factors in decisions to hasten death. As the literature surrounding assisted suicide and desire for hastened death has grown, the evidence that depression and hopelessness play a critical role in driving patients to consider hastened death has become increasingly apparent. Study after study has demonstrated a substantial role for depression and hopelessness in driving patient desire for hastened death and interest in assisted suicide. Although physical factors such as pain, functional ability, and symptom distress are certainly important components, their role in fueling decisions to hasten death seems to be less direct than that of depression. Physical suffering and disability may leave patients frustrated, fuel depression, and engender a feeling of pessimism or hopelessness about what the future holds, but they do not seem to lead patients to expedite the dying process in the absence of depression and hopelessness.[1] As the scientific literature on assisted suicide has evolved and research methods have become increasingly sophisticated, this pattern of influence has become even more apparent.[2]

---

[1] The exception to this statement may be functional limitations, which have consistently emerged as the leading reasons for using the ODDA, despite having been less powerfully associated with desire for hastened death in the more "experimental" research literature.

[2] Not all commentators would agree with this assessment; many writers, particularly those citing the data from Oregon, continue to emphasize physical symptoms and functioning over psychological and psychosocial factors.

Does the co-occurrence of depression and desire for hastened death or interest in assisted suicide necessarily mean that requests for assisted suicide are "irrational," or can depression serve as yet another rational justification for hastening death? Determining whether a particular decision is "rational" rests on more than the presence or absence of a co-occurring depression because most cases of depression do not deprive the afflicted person of the ability to think rationally. Instead, the influence of depression on decision making appears to be subtle, coloring the lens through which the person views the world such that the future looks bleak, the options limited (i.e., "hopeless"). Thus, the very question that has served as the springboard for many important policy debates and scientific studies, whether requests for assisted suicide are "rational," is perhaps the wrong one.

ARE WE ASKING THE RIGHT QUESTIONS?

Arguably, whether a decision to end one's life is "rational" may be a question that lies outside the scope of a scientific analysis. When an individual is so confused as to be unsure even of what the discussion is about, calling any decision "rational" is absurd. However, actual cases of assisted suicide requests rarely fall at this extreme and when they do, clinical decisions regarding how to respond are often straightforward. More likely, an individual requesting hastened death will have some degree of depression, which the individual (or physician) may or may not see as influencing the decision, but will nevertheless be able to offer a plethora of plausible reasons for ending his or her life. Yet, psychological research has consistently shown the important role of unstated (or unconscious, depending on one's theoretical perspective) factors in decision making, and it seems apparent that depression and hopelessness may be examples of this sort of unstated influence. Empirical research can quantify the importance of various influences such as depression, symptom burden, personality style, and a range of other possible factors, but our ability to determine the extent to which each is relevant in a particular individual's decision is ultimately limited. Thus, as scientists, we may simply be unable to answer the question as to whether an individual's stated reasons are more or less important than the unstated reasons (e.g., depression, hopelessness) in driving his or her desire for death. So, what questions can we ask that will help guide clinical decision making as well as social policy?

Although science may not be able to answer all of the questions that arise around end-of-life issues, many important questions can and should be addressed through empirical research. For example, only in the past few years have researchers begun to understand the range of factors that influence terminal patients' consideration of, or requests for, physician-assisted suicide. This literature has grown (and continues to grow) exponentially over the past decade (much of which was reviewed in chapters 5 through 9); but only recently have we developed a preliminary understanding of what influences end-of-life decisions. The combination of evolving dependent variables and study methods, coupled with varying methods of studying seemingly relevant predictors (e.g., depression, hopelessness, symptom distress, functional disability), has begun to yield some tentative conclusions. Yet, although a handful of variables have emerged as consistent predictors of desire for hastened death, the magnitude of the associations observed has varied substantially. As this literature continues to grow, more and more variables will inevitably be studied and more precise estimates of the magnitude of associations (i.e., effect sizes) will become possible. Moreover, conducting similar studies across a range of populations will likely reveal important differences in predictors and patterns of associations. This process has already begun, with recent studies of ALS patients supplementing the earlier literature on patients with cancer and AIDS that were the focus of most early investigations into assisted suicide and related topics. However, the range of populations for whom end-of-life issues are central extends far beyond cancer, AIDS, and ALS. Patients with Alzheimer's disease have emerged as an important population in studies of decision-making capacity, but no research to date has focused on this population with regard to desire for hastened death. Likewise, patients with Huntington's chorea, Parkinson's disease, chronic obstructive pulmonary disease (or chronic lower respiratory disease), and other progressive or terminal illnesses have rarely been systematically studied yet might help clarify the influences on end-of-life decision making. Expanding the range of populations studied, both in order to identify differences as well as similarities, is an important goal for the next decade of research.

Another set of questions that have been largely absent from the growing empirical and theoretical literature pertain to decision-making capacity. Much of the emerging research on decision making has focused on developing or improving assessment techniques or identifying populations at high risk for decision-making impairments (Kim et al., 2002). However, relatively little attention has been paid to clarifying the nature of competence as a construct. Important questions remain unanswered (and largely unasked), such as which standard of competence should apply in a given situation (e.g., requests for physician-assisted suicide or termination of life-sustaining treatment). Some of the issues surrounding definitions of competence are discussed in chapter 7, such as the extent of impairment necessary in order to consider an individual incompetent, yet these issues have rarely been the focus of scholarly debate in connection with end-of-life issues. Rather, conceptualizations of competence have typically raised issues of incompetence only in cases of severe mental illness or advanced dementia—essentially equating incompetence with irrationality or confusion. Measures of decision-making capacity such as the MacCAT–T mirror this perspective, primarily targeting irrational thinking and impaired memory rather than the decision-making process itself. Given this frame of reference, it is hardly surprising that researchers have found incompetence to be relatively rare among depressed individuals.

Yet an alternative conception of competence might consider individuals to be incompetent when the outcome of their decision-making process or the weight accorded to specific factors is influenced by mental disorder, even when the process itself is not inherently irrational. Thus, individuals whose hopelessness leads them to devalue the possible benefits of life-extending treatment despite a rational understanding of the implications of their decision might be considered by some to be incompetent because their judgment has been influenced by potentially reversible psychological symptoms. Such a conceptualization might lead to markedly different research findings and clinical conclusions with regard to the role of depression in end-of-life decision making. Definitional and conceptual ambiguity in decision-making competence is clearly an area ripe for both theoretical debate as well as empirical research. Studies comparing the impact of different theoretical approaches to competence on clinical practice and patient quality-of-life (or death) and the relationship of different psychological symptoms and conditions to patient decision making are needed to more fully understand the implications of alternative conceptualizations of competence.

A third vein that has yet to be fully mined by social scientists concerns the consistency of end-of-life decisions over time. A handful of studies have now suggested that many elderly and terminally ill patients change their minds about what life-sustaining interventions they would desire (e.g., Ditto et al., 2003; Ganzini et al., 1994). These studies suggest, albeit tentatively, that patient projections as to whether they would want particular interventions and under what circumstances often change as death approaches and they are confronted with the actual decision that was previously only imagined. These tentative conclusions have been drawn in studies of surrogate decision making and advance directives, but they have not been extended to issues such as desire for hastened death and requests for physician-assisted suicide.[3]

A related question is the extent to which end-of-life decisions change among depressed patients who receive mental health treatment. If research demonstrates that aggressive mental health treatment does not influence patient desire for hastened death, many of the questions raised about the conceptualization of competence and the influence of unstated versus stated reasons for seeking a hastened death may be moot. Alternatively, if treatment for depression significantly reduces the desire for hastened death, clini-

---

[3]Chochinov et al. (1995) provided anecdotal information on a handful of terminally ill cancer patients whose desire for hastened death changed over time, but these "data" were purely descriptive, with no empirical analysis of the nature or extent of any changes. Likewise, Ganzini, Nelson et al.'s (2000) description of retracted requests for physician-assisted suicide may represent changing preferences, although the authors framed these changes as reflecting the effect of palliative care interventions.

cal responses to a request for assisted suicide (and public policy recommendations) may change dramatically. Yet this literature, which is still in a nascent stage, has yet to reveal a consistent pattern of changes, let alone enable a differentiation of patients for whom changes are likely versus those unlikely to change their opinions or preferences. These questions, all of which are amenable to (indeed, perhaps ideally suited to) empirical analysis, have been largely ignored by end-of-life researchers.[4]

OBJECTIONS TO ASSISTED SUICIDE (THE SLIPPERY SLOPE?)

One of the principal objections to legalized assisted suicide in the United States has been the concern that legalization would lead to a gradual expansion in terms of both utilization of existing provisions (i.e., the frequency with which assisted suicide occurs) as well as the base of patients for whom legalized assisted suicide applies (i.e., the population of potentially eligible persons). This concern, typically referred to as the "slippery slope" argument, presumes that utilization of assisted suicide and other interventions that hasten death will expand as these interventions become increasingly acceptable to the general public and medical professionals, perhaps even extending to cases in which assisted suicide seems questionable if not overtly inappropriate (e.g., individuals who are not yet severely or terminally ill). Is this fear of the slippery slope justified? Perhaps more important, does a continued prohibition against assisted suicide lead to a better state of affairs for terminally ill patients?

Euthanasia practices in the Netherlands, discussed in chapter 8, can certainly be used to support fears of a slippery slope (Hendin et al., 1997), although firm conclusions are premature. The rate of euthanasia appears to have grown dramatically between the 1970s, when it was first legally tolerated (although still illegal) and the 1990s, when it was first systematically studied. Even between the three large-scale studies of end-of-life interventions in the Netherlands, a time period of only 10 years, rates of euthanasia and assisted suicide rose substantially.[5] Perhaps most important, Dutch policies (and now, Dutch law) have permitted the extension of euthanasia to chronically mentally ill individuals who have no medical illness per se. This extension has been criticized by many as the most extreme and troubling example of the slippery slope (e.g., Hendin & Klerman, 1993), by permitting euthanasia to individuals who, although certainly suffering from a disorder

---

[4]As discussed in chapter 3, Peter Ditto and his colleagues (2003) have conducted an extensive series of studies focusing squarely on end-of-life decision making, including studies of the stability of advance directives and the prediction of patient decisions, but their studies reflect some of the only sophisticated and theoretically grounded empirical research on this topic and have not focused on patients who were terminally ill.
[5]Although there was some debate as to whether the rise in use should raise concerns, there is little dispute that the rates of reported use increased.

(e.g., depression), are not terminally ill or even necessarily untreatable and are, almost by definition, of questionable decision-making competence (regardless of how competence is conceptualized).

On the other hand, data from Oregon have not supported the "slippery slope" hypothesis; rates of assisted suicide have thus far been relatively stable and reassuringly low over the first 5 years since legalization. Furthermore, there has been no discussion in the United States of extending assisted suicide provisions to apply to individuals who are not terminally ill. Whether this level of stability and infrequent utilization are reflective of cultural differences between the United States and the Netherlands or merely represent different points along a similar slope is not yet known.

However, concern that the utilization of assisted suicide will increase because of legalization is only one element of the slippery slope issue. A second important concern pertains to causation: If utilization of assisted suicide increases over time, is this increase due to a growing acceptance or is utilization merely rising to an appropriate homeostasis—rising from a level that is artificially lowered by legal restrictions? Data on this question are also available from the Netherlands, where public opinion surveys have revealed a consistent increase in the acceptability of hastened death in general and euthanasia in particular. This growing public acceptance of hastened death has occurred essentially concurrently with the increased utilization of euthanasia, although these data cannot address issues of causality. Whether Dutch public opinion changed because the legal policy changes essentially sanctioned hastened death, or whether policy changed in response to public opinion cannot be ascertained. An outdated social psychology literature (e.g., Berkowitz & Walker, 1967) once suggested that public opinion of morality changes in response to legislative example, but this limited research base is hardly sufficient to draw any conclusions. Thus, the answer to the question of whether legalization will influence pubic opinion and conception of morality is not yet clear and, given the complexity of the question, may never be.

MAINTAINING THE STATUS QUO

Another important question in debating the legalization of assisted suicide concerns the alternatives to legalization. By maintaining the status quo, policy makers effectively presume that the current state of affairs is preferable to legalization. One might assume that the status quo, in which assisted suicide is illegal in virtually every state, means that assisted suicide does not exist in the United States outside of Oregon. Yet surveys of physicians, nurses, and other health care professionals clearly show that this conclusion is unjustified (e.g., Asch, 1996; Back et al., 1996; Meier et al., 1998; Slome, Mitchell, Charlebois, Benevedes, & Abrams, 1997). Physicians and nurses appear to engage in assisted suicide and euthanasia at rates that, although not precisely known, may actually exceed the rate of legalized assisted suicide reported in Oregon. Although anonymous surveys of physicians and other health care professionals cannot generate accurate estimates,[6] they do show that hastened death is not an infrequent event, despite its illegality.

In the largest national survey of physicians in the United States regarding death-hastening interventions, Diane Meier and her colleagues (Meier et al., 1998) found that 3.3% of responding physicians had provided a patient with a prescription for a lethal medication in response to a specific request for assisted suicide. However, it is not clear from these data what proportion of patients actually filled the prescription, let alone used the lethal medication, and Oregon data suggest that not all patients who receive a lethal prescription ultimately use this medication. An even greater proportion of physicians (4.7%) reported having actually administered a lethal injection at some point during their professional career. These statistics, of course, do not help clarify the frequency with which assisted suicide and euthanasia occur because the events might have taken place years or even decades ago. On the other hand, responding physicians who have engaged in these actions may have done so on more than one occasion and perhaps may even do so with regularity. Slome et al. (1997) surveyed physicians who care for patients with AIDS and found high rates of participation in assisted suicide.[7] More than half of the respondents had provided at least one patient with a prescription for a lethal medication, and some physicians estimated that they have provided dozens of patients with lethal prescriptions.

David Asch's (1996) controversial study of critical care nurses showed that the unsanctioned practice of assisted suicide and euthanasia is not limited to physicians. In his study, a large proportion of critical care nurses acknowledged having provided patients with medication specifically designed to end a patient's life and at times even did so without a specific request from the patient or family. Thus, the illegality notwithstanding, there is little dispute that assisted suicide and euthanasia occur with some frequency in the United States.

Another troubling aspect of the status quo pertains to the limited options available to physicians by way of responses to a request for assisted

---

[6]Although researchers such as Meier et al. (1998) have occasionally asked physicians how often a particular action has occurred in the preceding month (e.g., providing a patient with a prescription for a lethal medication), such data do not reveal how often or when death actually occurred (because many patients who receive a prescription for a lethal prescription may not fill or use the prescription to end their lives). Moreover, even if an accurate estimate of the annual frequency with which patient deaths occurred in the sample of respondents could be determined, this number reflects the numerator of a fraction where the denominator (the number of deaths among these physician's practices during the same year) is unknown and, likely, impossible to estimate. Finally, an estimate of the prevalence of assisted suicide and euthanasia among sample respondents says little about population estimates overall, because sample biases might skew the representativeness of these data.

[7]These data, however, reflect the early history of HIV/AIDS, before the development of more effective medications and/or the changing demographic characteristics of the HIV-infected population appear to have decreased interest in hastened death/assisted suicide.

suicide. Because physicians who disclose such a request increase their risk of liability, there is little incentive to seek counsel from a colleague, request further testing or consultation, or even refer the patient for mental health treatment. Indeed, Meier's national survey of nearly 2,000 physicians found that of those physicians who had received at least one request for assisted suicide or euthanasia, only 30% discussed the request with a colleague and only 2% referred the patient for a psychiatric consultation.[8] The most common response to these requests was to increase the dosage of analgesic medication, reported by 68% of physicians. It is interesting that although physicians rarely sought consultation with a mental health professional, 25% prescribed antidepressant medications to their patient who requested assisted suicide or euthanasia. Whether the low rate of mental health consultation reflects a fear of possible legal sanctions or simply demonstrates a preference among physicians for handling these difficult cases themselves is unknown, but the failure to seek mental health intervention for these patients is striking, particularly given the important role apparently played by depression, hopelessness, and other psychosocial issues in driving patient desire for hastened death.

The data from physician surveys suggest that continued prohibition against physician-assisted suicide may have the unwanted effect of discouraging mental health treatment for terminally ill patients while simultaneously failing to decrease, in any real sense, the frequency with which assisted suicide and euthanasia are actually utilized. Given the low rates of reported utilization of the ODDA (roughly 6–9 cases per 10,000 deaths), it is hard to imagine that the rate of assisted death is substantially lower in states where assisted suicide is illegal. Furthermore, there are few (if any) safeguards for patients in states where assisted suicide is illegal, because the responses patients receive to their requests for assistance in dying are completely dependent on the physicians (i.e., whether or not they seek consultation, change their treatment regimen, etc.). On the other hand, merely legalizing assisted suicide without providing for adequate safeguards does little to improve the unregulated practice of physicians outside of Oregon. Yet, although criticisms can be (and have been) leveled at the ODDA's safeguards, these provisions provide at least a starting point and an opportunity for further discussion and evaluation.

WHAT ABOUT PALLIATIVE CARE?

No discussion of assisted suicide is complete without acknowledging the fear voiced by many opponents of legalization, that legalization of as-

---

[8]These estimates were based on physician descriptions of their responses to the most recent request for assisted suicide or euthanasia.

sisted suicide inevitably hinders efforts to provide adequate palliative care for dying individuals. Unfortunately, virtually no empirical data exist to either support or refute this concern. As noted in the preceding chapter, some writers have attempted to use data from Oregon to dispel fears of an adverse impact on palliative care, but the ODDA data do not actually address this important issue. Data regarding which patients have utilized the ODDA do demonstrate that individuals with inadequate health care or other financial disadvantages are not more likely than other individuals to seek physician-assisted suicide, and this finding has been offered as evidence that legalization has not had the unwanted effect of pushing disadvantaged persons into seeking assisted suicide as their only viable health care option. In fact, most of the existing data suggest precisely the opposite in terms of patient interest in hastened death, as disadvantaged (e.g., less educated) and minority individuals are much less likely to either approve of or seek assisted suicide; only 4 of the 129 individuals who have used the ODDA to end their lives have been of ethnic minority background, and all 4 were Asian. Unfortunately, this crude index of treatment adequacy says little about the real impact that legalized assisted suicide might have on palliative care over the long term.[9]

What of the possibility that physicians will be less aggressive in prescribing palliative care interventions when patients have the option of ending their lives if their condition becomes unbearable? Will insurance companies place greater restrictions on reimbursement for palliative care in an effort to encourage death-hastening interventions? At present, no data exist to address these questions in either Oregon or the Netherlands. There are many opportunities to analyze whether these fears are justified, including studies of physician attitudes and decision making (i.e., the extent to which treatment decisions are influenced by the available options and financial concerns), actual practices of health care providers (e.g., knowledge and practices among palliative care physicians), and patient motives for seeking assisted suicide (expanding upon the simplistic methods that have been used in Oregon and the Netherlands). However, to date none of these avenues has been systematically explored. Given the importance placed on autonomy as a crucial element in end-of-life decisions, particularly in the United States, coupled with the intense scrutiny focused on health care practices in general, these fears seem unlikely to be realized. Nevertheless, the possibility that legalization might adversely affect health care practices on a broader, societal level is sufficiently important as to warrant careful analysis.

---

[9]Research focusing on the impact of poverty and insurance status may, unfortunately, miss a crucial mechanism by which financial burden influences end-of-life decisions. The poor, who typically qualify for Medicaid, are often in a position to receive at least some supportive care for patients with severe disabilities (e.g., home health attendants for several hours per day), whereas middle class individuals who have private insurance may not. Thus, it may be that the greatest caregiver burden is found among middle class families who are not able to afford private home care but do not qualify for Medicaid support. Clearly, greater attention is necessary to clarify the relationships between insurance, financial status, and psychological functioning at the end of life.

WHERE DO WE GO FROM HERE?

It should be clear by now that straightforward answers to most of the difficult questions surrounding physician-assisted suicide do not yet exist. One might suggest, then, that science should move quickly to fill this void in hopes of providing guidance for the important policy issues that have not yet been resolved. Yet the belief that policy decisions should rest on science is undoubtedly reflective of a scientist's bias. Even if a compelling scientific argument can be made for legalized assisted suicide, there is little reason to believe that public policy decisions should necessarily follow suit. Indeed, there are relevant moral, ethical, and political arguments that can be offered for maintaining a legal prohibition against assisted suicide even if scientific data suggest that the well-being of some dying patients may be helped by legalization. Nevertheless, despite the many issues discussed in this volume, as well as the plethora of important questions that have not yet been resolved or at times even addressed in the scientific literature, there appear to be significant adverse consequences for continued, unmonitored, and unregulated assisted suicide in jurisdictions where this practice is illegal. Without adequate safeguards to protect vulnerable patients from irreversible decisions (i.e., death), the potential for untreated depression and inadequate palliative care to lead to assisted suicide is heightened. Would legalized and regulated assisted suicide in other states help identify those patients who are seeking to end their lives because of a depressed, distorted view of their situation, or would it merely create additional bureaucratic requirements that do little to improve patient quality of life?

One of the most important questions to emerge from the empirical research pertains to the appropriate role of mental health professionals. Given the strong possibility that unrecognized depression may drive requests for assisted suicide, some writers have suggested that mental health professionals should have a pivotal role in determining whether a patient's request is fulfilled (Peruzzi, Canapary, & Bongar, 1996). Clearly, mental health professionals are far more skilled at recognizing and treating depression or identifying subtle forms of incompetence than the typical physician. Yet this "gatekeeper" role is troubling for many clinicians and ethicists because it essentially forces mental health clinicians to decide whether a patient's request for assisted suicide will be fulfilled—ultimately giving the clinician power over a patient's life and death (M. D. Sullivan, Ganzini, & Youngner, 1998).

Oregon's Death with Dignity Act specifically avoided the requirement of a mandatory psychological assessment for all individuals seeking physician-assisted suicide, instead giving physicians the discretion to decide. Other proposed guidelines (e.g., Baron et al., 1996; Quill et al., 1992) have suggested that mental health consultation should be a required aspect of any assessment as to the appropriateness of assisted suicide. Given the importance of this decision, coupled with the growing evidence that depression is a central factor, this requirement may be prudent. However, without clear guidance as to how such assessments are to be made, and provisions for how patients are to be treated upon a finding of depression (i.e., should antidepressant therapy be required before acceding to a patient's request for assisted suicide and if so, how extensive must such trials be?), requiring mental health consultation is unlikely to substantially improve the current state of affairs. These issues raise even more questions for clinicians and researchers to tackle, because there is a clear need for improved techniques for screening terminally ill patients for depression and for evidence-based treatment guidelines for treating depression in this population (or, more accurately, these populations).

The role of psychologists and other mental health professionals in the assisted suicide debate has taken many forms and continues to evolve. Many clinical and research questions remain unanswered, and the need for further involvement of psychologists and other social and behavioral scientists is tremendous. Although this book began as a summary of what we know and do not know, it has resulted in a litany of opportunities for contributing to this important and still-evolving social and legal policy issue. Not only are psychologists and other mental health professionals poised to make important contributions through empirical research and clinical practice, but they may be even more influential as ethics consultants, hospital or hospice administrators, or as players of other nontraditional roles that might directly impact health care policy. My hope is that this book serves, at least for some, as a call-to-arms to help bring psychology squarely into the middle of palliative care policy, practice, and research. The expertise of mental health professionals provides us with a special opportunity to positively influence important decisions made during a most critical and vulnerable time in most people's lives.

REFERENCES

Alesandro, J. A. (1994). Physician-assisted suicide and New York Law. *Albany Law Review, 57,* 820–925.

American Medical Association. (1995). Advance directives. Retrieved November 26, 2003, from http://www. ama-assn.org/public/booklets/livgwill.htm

American Medical Association Council on Ethical and Judicial Affairs. (1998). Optimal use of orders not to intervene and advance directives. *Psychology, Public Policy, and Law, 4,* 668–675.

American Psychiatric Association. (1980). *Diagnostic and statistical manual of mental disorders* (3rd ed.). Washington, DC: Author.

Amundsen, D. W. (1978). The physician's obligation to prolong life: A medical duty without classical roots. *Hastings Center Report, 8,* 23–30.

Angell, M. (1998). Helping desperately ill people to die. In L. L. Emanuel (Ed.), *Regulating how we die: The ethical, medical, and legal issues surrounding physician-assisted suicide* (pp. 2–20). Cambridge, MA: Harvard University Press.

Annas, G. J. (1994). Death by prescription: The Oregon initiative. *New England Journal of Medicine, 301,* 1240–1243.

Anonymous (1988). It's over Debbie. *Journal of the American Medical Association, 259,* 272.

Appelbaum, P. S., & Grisso, T. (1988). Assessing patients' capacities to consent to treatment. *New England Journal of Medicine, 319,* 315–336.

Appelbaum, P. S., & Grisso, T. (2001). *MacCAT–CR: MacArthur Competence Assessment Tool for Clinical Research.* Sarasota, FL: Professional Resource Press.

Appelbaum, P. S., Grisso, T., Frank, E., O' Donnell, S., & Kupfer, D. J. (1999). Competence of depressed patients for consent to research. *American Journal of Psychiatry, 156,* 1380–1384.

Asch, D. A. (1996). The role of critical care nurses in euthanasia and assisted suicide. *New England Journal of Medicine, 334,* 1374–1402.

Back, A. L., & Gordon, J. R. (2001, February). *Clinician responses to requests for physician-assisted suicide: What to do and what not to do.* Paper presented at the annual meeting of the American Academy of Forensic Sciences, Seattle, Washington.

Back, A. L., Wallace, J. I., Starks, H. E., & Pearlman, R. A. (1996). Physician-assisted suicide and euthanasia in Washington State. *Journal of the American Medical Association, 275,* 919–925.

Bacon, F. (1937). *Essays, advancement of learning, New Atlantis, and other pieces.* (Ed. R. F. Jones). Garden City, NY: Doubleday.

Baron, C. H., Bergstresser, C., Brock, D. W., Cole, G. F., Dorfman, N. S., Johnson, J. A., Schnipper, L. E., Vorenberg, J., & Wanzer, S. H. (1996). A model state act to authorize and regulate physician-assisted suicide. *Harvard Journal on Legislation, 33,* 1–34.

Barry, R. (1995). The development of the Roman Catholic teachings on suicide. *Notre Dame Journal of Law, Ethics, and Public Policy, 57,* 449–501.

Barton, C. D., Mallik, H. S., Orr, W. B., & Janofsky, J. S. (1996). Clinicians' judgment of capacity of nursing home patients to give informed consent. *Psychiatric Services, 47,* 956–959.

Batavia, A. I. (2000). So far so good: Observations on the first year of Oregon's Death with Dignity Act. *Psychology, Public Policy, and Law, 6,* 291–304.

Batavia, A. I. (2002). Disability versus futility in rationing health care services: Defining medical futility based on permanent unconsciousness: PVS, coma, and anencephaly. *Behavioral Sciences and the Law, 20,* 219–233.

Beck, A. T., Ward, C. H., Mendelson, M., Mock, J., & Erbaugh, J. (1961). An inventory for measuring depression. *Archives of General Psychiatry, 4,* 561–571.

Beck, A. T., Weissman, A., Lester, D., & Trexel, L. (1974). The measurement of pessimism: The Hopelessness Scale. *Journal of Consulting and Clinical Psychology, 42,* 861–865.

Berkman, C. S., Cavallo, P. F., Chesnut, W. C., & Holland, N. J. (1999). Attitudes toward physician-assisted suicide among persons with multiple sclerosis. *Journal of Palliative Medicine, 2,* 51–63.

Berkowitz, L., & Walker, N. (1967). Laws and moral judgments. *Sociometry, 30,* 410–422.

Binding, K. & Hoche, A. (1992). Permitting the destruction of unworthy life. *Issues in Law and Medicine, 8,* 231–265.

Blackstone, W. (1992). *Commentaries on the laws of England.* Buffalo, NY: William Hein. (Original work published 1765)

Blendon, R. J., Szalay, U. S., & Knox, R. A. (1992). Should physicians aid their patients in dying? *Journal of the American Medical Association, 267,* 2658–2662.

Bowling, A. (1997). *Measuring health: A review of quality of life measurement scales.* Berkshire, UK: Open University Press.

Breitbart, W., Passik, S., McDonald, M. V., Rosenfeld, B., Smith, M., Kaim, M., & Funesti-Esch, J. (1998). Patient-related barriers to pain management in ambulatory AIDS patients. *Pain, 76,* 9–16.

Breitbart, W., Rosenfeld, B., & Passik, S. D. (1996). Interest in physician-assisted suicide among ambulatory HIV-infected patients. *American Journal of Psychiatry, 153*, 238–242.

Breitbart, W., Rosenfeld, B., Pessin, H., Kaim, M., Funesti-Esch, J., Galietta, M., Nelson, C. J., & Brescia, R. (2000). Depression, hopelessness, and desire for hastened death in terminally ill patients with cancer. *Journal of the American Medical Association, 284*, 2907–2911.

Brown, J. H., Henteleff, P., Barakat, S., & Rowe, C. J. (1986). Is it normal for terminally ill patients to desire death? *American Journal of Psychiatry, 143*, 208–211.

Bruera, E., Neumann, C. M., Mazzocato, C., Stiefel, F., & Sala, R. (2000). Attitudes and beliefs of palliative care physicians regarding communication with terminally ill cancer patients. *Palliative Medicine, 14*, 287–298.

Bullar, J. (1866). Chloroform in dying. *British Medical Journal, 2*, 10–12.

Bursztajn, H. J., Harding, H. P., Gutheil, T. G., & Brodsky, A. (1991). Beyond cognition: The role of disordered affective states in impaired competence to consent to treatment. *Bulletin of the American Academy of Psychiatry and Law, 19*, 383–388.

Cantor, N. L. (1998). Making advance directives meaningful. *Psychology, Public Policy, and Law, 4*, 629–652.

Carrick, P. (1985). *Medical ethics in antiquity: Philosophical perspectives on abortion and euthanasia.* Boston: Dordrecht.

Chin, A. E., Hedberg, K., Higginson, G. K., & Fleming, D. W. (1999). Legalized physician-assisted suicide in Oregon—the first year's experience. *New England Journal of Medicine, 340*, 577–583.

Chochinov, H. M., Tataryn, D., Clinch, J. J., & Dudgeon, D. (1999). Will to live in the terminally ill. *Lancet, 354*, 816–819.

Chochinov, H. M., Wilson, K. G., Enns, M., & Lander, S. (1994). Prevalence of depression in the terminally ill: Effects of diagnostic criteria and symptom threshold judgments. *American Journal of Psychiatry, 51*, 537–540.

Chochinov, H. M., Wilson, K. G., Enns, M., & Lander, S. (1998). Depression, hopelessness, and suicidal ideation in the terminally ill. *Psychosomatics, 39*, 366–370.

Chochinov, H. M. C., Wilson, K. G., Enns, M., Mowchun, N., Lander, S., Levitt, M., & Clinch, J. J. (1995). Desire for death in the terminally ill. *American Journal of Psychiatry, 152*, 1185–1191.

Christensen, K., Haroun, A., Schneiderman, L. J., & Jeste, D. V. (1995). Decision-making capacity for informed consent in the older population. *Bulletin of the American Academy of Psychiatry Law, 23*, 353–365.

Cleeland, C. S. (1989). Measurement of pain by subjective report. In C. R. Chapman & J. D. Loeser (Eds.), *Advances in pain research and therapy: Vol 12. Issues of pain measurement* (pp. 391–403). New York: Raven Press.

Cleeland, C. S., Gonin, R., Hatfield, A. K., Edmonson, J. H., Blum, R. H., Stewart, J. A., & Pandya, K. J. (1994). Pain and its treatment in outpatients with metastatic cancer. *New England Journal of Medicine, 330*, 592–596.

Commonwealth v. Bowen, 13 Mass. 356 (1816).

Compassion in Dying v. State of Washington, 49 F.3d 586, 79 F.3d 790 (9th cir., 1996).

Coppola, K. M., Ditto, P. H., Danks, J. H., Houts, R. M., & Smucker, W. D. (2001). Accuracy of primary care and hospital-based physicians' predictions of elderly outpatients' treatment preferences with and without advance directives. *Archives of Internal Medicine, 161,* 431–440.

Costello, E. (1983). Information processing for decision making in depressed women: A study of subjective expected utilities. *Journal of Affective Disorders, 5,* 239–251.

Crawley, L., Payne, R., Bolden, J., Payne, T., Washington, P., & Williams, S. (2000). Palliative and end-of-life care in the African American community. *Journal of the American Medical Association, 284,* 2518–2521.

Crone, D. M. (1996). Historical attitudes toward suicide. *Duquesne Law Review, 35,* 7–42.

Cruzan v. Director, Missouri Dept. of Health, 497 U.S. 261, 110 S. Ct. 2841 (1990).

Danis, M., Garrett, J., Harris, R., & Patrick, D. L. (1994). Stability of choices about life-sustaining treatments. *Annals of Internal Medicine, 120,* 567–573.

Darwin, C. (1859). *On the origin of species by means of natural selection.* London: John Murray.

Department of Human Services. (2003). Fifth annual report on Oregon's Death with Dignity Act. Available at http://www.dhs.state.or.us/publichealth/chs/pas/faqs.cfm.

Derogotis, L. R., & Melisaratos, N. (1983). The Brief Symptom Inventory: An introductory report. *Psychological Medicine, 13,* 595–605.

Ditto, P. H., Danks, J. H., Smucker, W. D., Bookwala, J., Coppola, K. M., Dresser, R., Fagerlin, A., Gready, R. M., Houts, R. M., Lockhart, L. K. & Zyzanski, S. (2001). Advance directives as acts of communication: A randomized controlled trial. *Archives of Internal Medicine, 161,* 421–430.

Ditto, P. H., Smucker, W. D., Danks, J. H., Jacobson, J. A., Houts, R. M., Fagerlin, A., et al. (2003). Stability of older adults' preferences for life-sustaining medical treatment. *Health Psychology, 22,* 605–615.

Drane, J. F. (1984). Competency to give an informed consent: A model for making clinical assessments. *Journal of the American Medical Association, 252,* 925–927.

Dutch legalize euthanasia, the first such national law. (2001, April 1). *New York Times,* p. A5.

Edelstein, L. (1967). *Ancient medicine: Selected papers of Ludwig Edelstein* (O. Temkin and C. L. Tempkin, Eds.). Baltimore: Johns Hopkins Press. (Original work published 1943)

Emanuel, E. J. (1994). The history of euthanasia debates in the United States and Britain. *Annals of Internal Medicine, 121,* 793–802.

Emanuel, E. J. (1998). Why now? In L. L. Emanuel (Ed.), *Regulating how we die: The ethical, medical, and legal issues surrounding physician-assisted suicide* (pp. 175–202). Cambridge, MA: Harvard University Press.

Emanuel, E. J., Fairclough, D. L., Daniels, E. R., & Clarridge, B. R. (1996). Euthanasia and physician-assisted suicide: Attitudes and experiences of oncology patients, omcologists, and the public. *Lancet, 347*, 1805–1810.

Emanuel, E. J., Fairclough, D. L., & Emanuel, L. L. (2000). Attitudes and desires related to euthanasia and physician-assisted-suicide among terminally ill patients and their caregivers. *Journal of the American Medical Association, 284*, 2460–2468.

Emanuel, L. L., Barley, M. J., Stoeckle, J. D., Ettelson, L. M., & Emanuel, E. J. (1991). Advanced directives for medical care: A case for greater use. *New England Journal of Medicine, 324*, 889–895.

Emanuel, L. L., & Emanuel, E. J. (1989). The medical directive: A new comprehensive advance care document. *Journal of the American Medical Association, 261*, 3288–3293.

Endicott, J. (1984). Measurement of depression in patients with cancer. *Cancer, 53*, 2243–2249.

Endicott, J., & Spitzer, R. L. (1978). A diagnostic interview: The Schedule for Affective Disorders and Schizophrenia. *Archives of General Psychiatry, 35*, 837–844.

Faden, R., & Beauchamp, T. L. (1986). *A history and theory of informed consent.* New York: Oxford University Press.

Federal judge upholds assisted suicide law. (2002, April 17). Retrieved November 26, 2003, from http://www.cnn.com/2002/LAW/04/17/oregon.assisted.suicide/index.html

Fenn, D. S., & Ganzini, L. (1999). Attitudes of Oregon psychologists toward physician-assisted suicide and the Oregon Death with Dignity Act. *Professional Psychology: Research and Practice, 30*, 235–244.

First, M. B., Spitzer, R. L., Gibbon, M., & Williams, J. B. W. (2001). *Structured Clinical Interview for DSM–IV–TR Axis I Disorders.* New York: Biometrics Research, New York State Psychiatric Institute.

Foley, K. M. (1991). The relationship of pain and symptom management to patient requests for physician-assisted suicide. *Journal of Pain and Symptom Management, 6*, 289–297.

Foley, K. M. (1995). Pain, physician-assisted suicide, and euthanasia. *Pain Forum, 4*, 163–178.

Foley, K., & Hendin, H. (1999). The Oregon Report: Don't ask, don't tell. *Hastings Center Report 29*(3), 37–42.

Folstein, M. F., Folstein, S. E., & McHugh, P. R. (1975). "Mini-mental state." A practical method for grading the cognitive state of patients for the clinician. *Journal of Psychiatric Research, 12*, 189–198.

Fried, T. R., Bradley, E. H., & Towle, V. R. (2002). Assessment of patient preferences: Integrating treatments and outcomes. *Journal of Gerontology, 57*, S348–354.

Fye, W. B. (1978). Active euthanasia: An historical survey of its conceptual origins and introduction into medical thought. *Bulletin of the History of Medicine, 52,* 492–502.

Ganzini, L., Fenn, D. S., Lee, M. A., Heintz, R. T., & Bloom, J. D. (1996). Attitudes of Oregon psychiatrists toward physician-assisted suicide. *American Journal of Psychiatry, 153,* 1469–1475.

Ganzini, L., Havrath, T. A., Jackson, A., Goy, E. R., Miller, L. L., & Delorit, M. A. (2002). Experiences of Oregon nurses and social workers with hospice patients who requested assistance with suicide. *New England Journal of Medicine, 347,* 582–588.

Ganzini, L., Johnston, W., McFarland, B. H., Tolle, S. W., & Lee, M. A. (1998). Attitudes of patients with amyotrophic lateral sclerosis and their caregivers toward assisted suicide. *New England Journal of Medicine, 339,* 967–973.

Ganzini, L., Lee, M. A., Heintz, R. T., Bloom, J. D., & Fenn, D. S. (1994). The effect of depression treatment on elderly patients' preferences for life-sustaining medical therapy. *American Journal of Psychiatry, 51,* 1631–1636.

Ganzini, L., Leong, G. B., Fenn, D. S., Silva, J. A., & Weinstock, R. (2000). Evaluation of competence to consent to assisted suicide: Views of forensic psychiatrists. *American Journal of Psychiatry, 157,* 595–600.

Ganzini, L., Nelson, H. D., Schmidt, T. A., Kraemer, D. F., Delorit, M. A., & Lee, M. A. (2000). Physicians' experiences with the Oregon Death with Dignity Act. *New England Journal of Medicine, 342,* 557–563.

Garrad, J., Rolnick, S. J., Nitz, N. M., Luepke, L., Jackson, J., Fischer, L. R., Leibson, C., Bland, P. C., Heinrich, R., & Waller, L. A. (1998). Clinical detection of depression among community-based elderly people with self-reported symptoms of depression. *Journal of Gerontology: Biological Science and Medical Science, 53,* M92–101.

Gevers, S. (1996). Euthanasia: Law and practice in the Netherlands. *British Medical Bulletin, 52,* 326–333.

Gillon, R. (1969). Suicide and voluntary euthanasia: Historical perspective. In B. A. Downing (Ed.), *Euthanasia and the right death: The case for voluntary euthanasia* (pp. 173–192). London: Peter Owen.

Gorsuch, N. L. (2000). Psychology of religion. *Annual Review of Psychology, 39,* 201–221.

Gorsuch, N. M. (2000). The right to assisted suicide and euthanasia. *Harvard Journal of Law and Public Policy, 23,* 599–645.

Gready, R. M., Ditto, P. H., Danks, J. H., Coppola, K. M., Lockhart, L. K., & Smucker, W. D. (2000). Actual and perceived stability of preferences for life-sustaining treatment. *Journal of Clinical Ethics, 11,* 334–346.

Griffiths, J., Bood, A., & Weyers, H. (1998). *Euthanasia and law in the Netherlands.* Amsterdam: Amsterdam University Press.

Grisso, T. (2002). Evaluating competencies: Forensic assessments and instruments (2nd ed.). New York: Kluwer Academic/Plenum.

Grisso, T., & Appelbaum, P. S. (1995). The McArthur Treatment Competence Study III: Abilities of patients to consent to psychiatric and medical treatments. *Law and Human Behavior, 19,* 149–174.

Grisso, T., & Appelbaum, P. S. (1998). *Assessing competence to consent to treatment: A guide for physicians and other health professionals.* New York: Oxford University Press.

Groenewoud, J. H., van der Maas, P. J., van der Waal, G., Hengeveld, M. W., Tholen, A. J., Schudel, W. J., & van der Heide, A. (1997). Physician-assisted suicide in psychiatric practice in the Netherlands. *New England Journal of Medicine, 336,* 1795–1801.

Hammes, B. J., & Rooney, B. L. (1998). Death and end-of-life planning in one midwestern community. *Archive of Internal Medicine, 158,* 383–390.

Hedberg, K., Hopkins, D., & Southwick, K. (2002). Legalized physician-assisted suicide in Oregon, 2001. *New England Journal of Medicine, 346,* 605–607.

Helms, J. E., & Parham, T. A. (1996). The development of the racial identity attitude scale. In R. L. Jones (Ed.), *Handbook of tests and measurements for Black populations* (pp. 167–174). Hampton, VA: Cobb and Henry.

Henderson, M. (1990). Beyond the living will. *The Gerontologist, 30,* 480–485.

Hendin, H., & Klerman, G. (1993). Physician-assisted suicide: The dangers of legalization. *American Journal of Psychiatry, 150,* 143–145.

Hume, D. (1980). Of suicide. In R. H. Popkin (Ed.), *Dialogues concerning natural religion and the posthumous essays* (pp. 100–110). Indianapolis, IN: Hackett Publishing. (Original work published 1771)

Humphry, D. (1991). *Final exit: The practicalities of self-deliverance and assisted suicide for the dying.* New York: Dell.

In Re Quinlan, 355 A. 2d 647 (N.J. 1976), cert. denied, 429 U.S. 922 (1976).

Inouye, S. K., Foreman, M. D., Mion, L. C., Katz, K. H., & Cooney, L. M., Jr. (2001). Nurses' recognition of delirium and its symptoms: Comparison of nurse and researcher ratings. *Archives of Internal Medicine, 161,* 2467–2473.

Janofsky, J. S., McCarthy, R. J., & Folstein, M. F. (1992). The Hopkins Competency Assessment Test: A brief method for evaluating patients' capacity to give informed consent. *Hospital and Community Psychiatry, 43,* 132–136.

Jost, A. (1895). *Das Recht auf den Tod* [The right to die]. Gottingen, Germany.

Karnofsky, D. A., & Burchenal, J. H. (1949). The clinical evaluation of chemotherapeutic agents in cancer. In C. M. MacLoed (Ed.), *Evaluation of chemotherapeutic agents* (pp. 191–205). New York: Columbia University Press.

Kerkhof, A. J. F. M. (2000). How to deal with requests for assisted suicide: Some experiences and practical guidelines from the Netherelands. *Psychology, Public Policy, and Law, 6,* 452–466.

Kim, S. Y. H., Caine, E. D., Currier, G. W., Leibovichi, A., & Ryan, J. M. (2001). Assessing the competence of persons with Alzheimer's disease in providing informed consent for participation in research. *American Journal of Psychiatry, 158,* 712–717.

Kim, S. Y. H., Karlawish, J. H. T., & Caine, E. D. (2002). Current state of research on decision-making competence of cognitively impaired elderly persons. *American Journal of Geriatric Psychiatry, 10,* 142–150.

Koerselman, F. (1994). Rational suicide as a myth. *Maandblad Geestelijke Volksgezondheid, 49,* 515–527.

Landrine, H., & Klonoff, E. A. (1994). The African-American Acculturation Scale: Development, reliability, and validity. *Journal of Black Psychology, 20,* 104–127.

Larsen, G. (1999). Family members' experiences with Do-Not-Resuscitate (DNR). *Journal of Family Issues, 20,* 269–289.

Lavery, J. V., Boyle, J., Dickens, B. M., Maclean, H., & Singer, P. A. (2001). Origins of the desire for euthanasia and assisted suicide in people with HIV-1 or AIDS: A qualitative study. *Lancet, 358,* 362–367.

Lee v. State of Oregon, 107 F.3d 1382 (9th Cir., 1997), cert. denied, Lee v. Harcleroad, 118 S.Ct. 328, 1997.

Lee, B. C., & Werth, J. L., Jr. (2000). Observations on the first year of Oregon's Death with Dignity Act. *Psychology, Public Policy, and Law, 6,* 268–290.

Lee, M. A. (1992). Depression in the elderly: Effect on patient attitudes toward life-sustaining therapy. *Journal of the Geriatric Society, 40,* 983–988.

Lee, M. A., & Ganzini, L. (1992). Depression in the elderly: Effect on patient attitudes toward life-sustaining therapy. *Journal of the Geriatric Society, 40,* 983–988.

Lee, M. A., Smith, D. A., Fenn, D. S., & Ganzini, L. (1998). Do patients' treatment decisions match advance statements of their preferences? *Journal of Clinical Ethics, 9,* 258–262.

Lo, B. (1990). Assessing decision-making capacity. *Law, Medicine, and Health Care, 18,* 193–201.

Lo, J. A., Ng, W. C., Yap, K. B., & Chan, K. M. (2000). End-of-life issues: Preferences and choices of elderly Chinese subjects attending a day care center in Singapore. *American Academy of Medicine in Singapore, 29,* 50–56.

Lynch, M. (1995). The assessment and prevalence of affective disorders in advanced cancer. *Journal of Palliative Care, 11,* 10–18.

Marson, D. C., Hawkins, L., McInturff, B., & Harrell, L. E. (1997). Cognitive models that predict physician judgments of capacity to consent in mild Alzheimer's disease. *Journal of the American Geriatric Society, 45,* 458–464.

Marson, D. C., Ingram, K. K., Cody, H. A., & Harrell, L. E. (1995). Assessing the competency of patients with Alzheimer's disease under different legal standards. *Archives of Neurology, 52,* 949–954.

Massie, M. J., Gagnon, P., & Holland, J. C. (1994). Depression and suicide in patients with cancer. *Journal of Pain and Symptom Management, 9,* 325–340.

Matersvedt, L. J. (2003, July). Physician-assisted suicide for mental suffering in the Netherlands: In light of "the ideology of autonomy." Paper presented at the International Conference on Psychology and Law, Edinburgh, Scotland.

Matersvedt, L. J., Clark, D., Ellershaw, J., Førde, R., Boeck Gravgaard, A. -M., Müller-Busch, H. C., Porta I Sales, J., & Rapin, C. -H. (2003). Euthanasia and physician-assisted suicide: A view from an EAPC Ethics Task Force. *Palliative Medicine, 17*, 97–101.

McClain, C., Rosenfeld, B. & Breitbart, W. (2003). The influence of spiritual well-being on end-of-life despair among terminally ill cancer patients. *Lancet, 361*, 1603–1607.

McDonald, M. V., Passik, S. D., Dugan, W., Rosenfeld, B., Theobald, D. E., & Edgerton, S. (1999). Nurses' recognition of depression in their patients with cancer. *Oncology Nursing Forum, 26*, 593–599.

McKinney's Consolidated Laws of New York. (1993). St. Paul, MN: West Publishing.

Meier, D. E., Emmons, C., Wallenstein, S., Quill, T., Morrison, R. S., & Cassel, C. K. (1998). A national survey of physician-assisted suicide and euthanasia in the United States. *New England Journal of Medicine, 338*, 1193–1201.

Meisel, A. (1999). Managed care, autonomy, and decision-making at the end of life. *University of Houston, 35*, 1292–1436.

Meisel, A., Snyder, L., & Quill, T. (2000). Seven legal barriers to end-of-life care: Myths, realities, and grains of truth. *The Journal of the American Medical Association, 284*, 2495–2501.

Misbin, R. I., O'Hare, D., Lederberg, M. S., & Holland, J. C. (1993). Compliance with New York State's do-not-resuscitate law at Memorial Sloan-Kettering Cancer Center: A review of patient deaths. *New York State Journal of Medicine, 93*, 165–168.

Molloy, D. W., Guyatt, G. H., Russo, R., Goeree, R., O'Brien, B. J., Bedard, M., et. al., (2000). Systematic implementation of an advance directive program in nursing homes: A randomized controlled trial. *Journal of the American Medical Association, 283*, 1437–1444.

More, T. (1965). *Utopia* (E. Surtz & J. H. Hexter, Eds.). New Haven, CT: Yale University Press. (Original work published 1516)

Murphy, D. J., Murray, A. M., Robinson, B. E., & Campion, E. W. (1989). Outcomes of cardiopulmonary resuscitation in the elderly. *Annals of Internal Medicine, 111*, 199–205.

Nederlandse Jurisprudentie (1973) 183.

Nederlandse Jurisprudentie (1982) 63.

Nederlandse Jurisprudentie (1985) 106.

Nederlandse Jurisprudentie (1994) 656.

Onwuteaka-Philipsen, B. D., van der Heide, A., Kroper, D., Keij-Deerenberg, I., Reitjens, J. A. C., Rurup, M. L., Vrakking, A. M., Georges, J. J., Muller, M. T., van der Wal, G., & van der Maas, P. J. (2003). Euthanasia and other end-of-life decisions in the Netherlands in 1990, 1995, and 2001. *Lancet,* online publication available at http://image.thelancet.com/extras/03ART3297web.pdf

Oregon Death with Dignity Act, Or. Rev. Stat. 13 (1996).

Oregon Health Division. (1999). *Oregon's Death with Dignity Act: The first year's experience*. Portland: Author.

Oregon Health Division. (2000). *Oregon's Death with Dignity Act: The second year's experience*. Portland: Author.

Oregon Health Division. (2001). *Oregon's Death with Dignity Act: Three years of legalized physician-assisted suicide*. Portland: Author.

Oregon Health Division. (2002). *Fourth annual report on Oregon's Death with Dignity Act*. Portland: Author.

Oregon Health Division. (2003). *Fifth annual report on Oregon's Death with Dignity Act*. Portland: Author.

Owen, C., Tennant, C., Levi, J., & Jones, M. (1992). Suicide and euthanasia: Patient attitudes in the context of cancer. *Psycho-oncology, 1,* 79–88.

Passik, S. D., Kirsch, K. L., Rosenfeld, B., McDonald, M. V., & Theobald, D. E. (2001). The changeable nature of patients' fears regarding chemotherapy: Implications for palliative care. *Journal of Pain and Symptom Management, 21,* 113–120.

Passik, S. D., Lundberg, J. C., Rosenfeld, B., Kirsch, K. L., Donaghy, K., Theobold, D., Lundberg, E., & Dugan, W. (2000). Factor analysis of the Zung Self-Rating Depression Scale in a large ambulatory oncology sample. *Psychosomatics, 41,* 121–127.

Passik, S. D., McDonald, M. V., Dugan, W., Lundberg, J., Rosenfeld, B., & Edgerton, S. (1998). Oncologists' recognition of depression in their patients with cancer. *Journal of Clinical Oncology, 16,* 1594–1600.

Peruzzi, N., Canapary, A., & Bongar B. (1996). Physician-assisted suicide: The role of mental health professionals. *Ethics and Behavior, 6,* 353–366.

Pessin, H., Galietta, M., & Rosenfeld, B. (2002, May). *Burden and benefit of end-of-life research in the terminally ill.* Paper presented at the annual meeting of the European Association of Palliative Care, Lyon, France.

Pessin, H., Rosenfeld, B., Burton, L., & Breitbart, W. (2003). The role of cognitive impairment in desire for hastened death. *General Hospital Psychiatry, 25,* 194–199.

Pliny, (1969). *The letters of the younger Pliny* (B. Radice, Trans.). New York: Penguin.

Portenoy, R. K., Thaler, H. T., Korblith, A. B., McCarthy, L., Lepore, J., Friedlander-Klar, H., Kiyasu, E., Sobel, K., Coyle, N., Kemeny, N., Norton, L., & Scher, H. (1994). The Memorial Symptom Assessment Scale: An instrument for the evaluation of symptom prevalence, characteristics, and distress. *European Journal of Cancer, 30A,* 1326–1326.

President's Commission for the Study of Ethical Problems in Medicine and Biomedical and Behavioral Research. (1982). *Making health care decisions: The ethical and legal implications of informed consent in the patient–practitioner relationship.* Washington, DC: Government Printing Office.

Preston, T. A. (1995). Physician involvement in life-ending practices. *Seattle University Law Review, 18,* 531–544.

Quill, T. E. (1993). Doctor, I want to die: Will you help me? *Journal of the American Medical Association, 270,* 870–873.

Quill, T. E., Cassel, C. K., & Meier, D. E. (1992). Care of the hopelessly ill: Proposed clinical criteria for physician-assisted suicide. *New England Journal of Medicine, 327,* 1380–1384.

Quill v. Vacco, 80 F.3d 716 (2nd Cir., 1996).

Rabkin, J. G., Wagner, G. J., & Del Bene, M. (2000). Resilience and distress among amyotrophic lateral sclerosis patients and caregivers. *Psychosomatic Medicine, 62,* 271–279.

Radloff, L. (1977). The CES-D scale: A self-report depression scale for research in a general population. *Journal of Applied Psychological Measurement, 1,* 385–401.

Rich, B. A. (1998). Personhood, patienthood, and clinical practice: Reassessing advance directives. *Psychology, Public Policy, and Law, 4,* 610–628.

Robins, L. N., Helzer, J. E., Croughan, J., & Ratcliff, K. S. (1981). National Institute of Mental Health Diagnostic Interview Schedule: Its history, characteristics and validity. *Archives of General Psychiatry, 38,* 381–389.

Rosenfeld, B. (2000a). Assisted suicide, depression, and the right to die. *Psychology, Public Policy, and Law, 6,* 529–549.

Rosenfeld, B. (2000b). Methodological isuues in assisted suicide and euthanasia research. *Psychology, Public Policy, and Law, 6,* 559–574.

Rosenfeld, B. (2002). The psychology of competence and informed consent: Understanding decision-making with regard to clinical research. *Fordham Urban Law Journal, 22,* 173–185.

Rosenfeld, B., & Breitbart, W. (2000). Physician-assisted suicide and euthanasia. *New England Journal of Medicine, 343,* 151.

Rosenfeld, B., Breitbart, W., Galietta, M., Kaim, M., Funesti-Esch, J., Pessin, H., & Nelson, C. (2000). The schedule of attitudes toward hastened death: Measuring desire for death in terminally ill cancer patients. *Cancer, 88,* 2868–2875.

Rosenfeld, B., Breitbart, W., McDonald, M. V., Passik, S. D., Thaler, H., & Portenoy, R. K. (1996). Pain in ambulatory AIDS patients—II: Impact of pain on psychological functioning and quality of life. *Pain, 68,* 323–328.

Rosenfeld, B., Breitbart, W., Stein, K., Funesti-Esch, J., Kaim, M., Krivo, S., & Galietta, M. (1999). Measuring desire for death among patients with HIV/AIDS. *American Journal of Psychiatry, 156,* 94–100.

Rosenfeld, B., Galietta, M., Breitbart, W., & Krivo, S. (1998, March). *Interest in physician-assisted suicide among terminally ill AIDS patients: The impact of depression on desire for hastened death.* Paper presented at the American Psychology–Law Society Biennial Convention, Redondo Beach, CA.

Rosenfeld, B., Gibson, C., Kramer, M., & Breitbart, W. (2002). *Hopelessness and terminal illness: The construct of hopelessness in patients with advanced AIDS.* Manuscript submitted for publication.

Rosenfeld, B. D., White, M., & Passik, S. D. (1997). Making treatment decisions with HIV infection: A pilot study of patient preferences. *Medical Decision Making, 17,* 308–314.

Roth, L. H., Meisel, A., & Lidz, C. W. (1977). Tests of competency to consent to treatment. *American Journal of Psychiatry, 134,* 279–284.

Royal Dutch Medical Association. (1984). Position on euthanasia. *Medisch Contact, 31,* 990–997.

Schafer, J. L., & Olsen, M. K. (1998). Multiple imputation for multivariate missing data problems: A data analysts perspective. *Multivariate Behavioral Research, 33,* 545–571.

Schloendorff v. Society of New York Hospitals, 211 NY 125 (1914).

Schoevers, R. A., Asmus, F. P., & Van Tilburg, W. (1998). Physician-assisted suicide in psychiatric developments in the Netherlands. *Psychiatric Services, 49,* 1475–1480.

Schonwetter, R. S., Teasdale, T. A., Taffet, G., Robinson, B. E., & Luchi, R. J. (1991). Educating the elderly: Cardiopulmonary resuscitation decisions before and after intervention. *Journal of the American Geriatric Society, 39,* 372–377.

Schwenk, T. L., Coyne, J. C., & Fechner-Bates, S. (1996). Differences between detected and undetected patients in primary care and depressed psychiatric patients. *General Hospital Psychiatry, 18,* 407–415.

Seale, C., & Addington-Hall, J. (1994). Euthanasia: Why people want to die earlier. *Social Science and Medicine, 39,* 647–654.

Shelley, S. I., Zahorchak, R. M., & Gambrill, C. D. S. (1987). Aggressiveness of nursing care for older patients and those with Do-Not-Resuscitate orders. *Nursing Research, 36,* 157–162.

Slome, L. R., Mitchell, T. F., Charlebois, E., Benevedes, J. M., & Abrams, D. L. (1997). Physician-assisted suicide and patients with human immunodeficiency virus disease. *New England Journal of Medicine, 336,* 417–421.

Smucker, W. D., Ditto, P. H., Moore, K. A., Druley, J. A., Danks, J. H., & Townsend, A. (1993). Elderly outpatients respond favorably to a physician-initiated advance directive discussion. *Journal of the American Board of Family Practice, 6,* 473–482.

Smucker, W. D., Houts, R. M., Danks, J. H., Ditto, P. H., Fagerlin, A., & Coppola, K. M. (2000). Modal preferences predict elderly patients' life-sustaining treatment choices as well as patients' chosen surrogates do. *Medical Decision Making, 20,* 271–280.

State v. Bouse, 264 P. 2d 800 (Or. 1953).

Stephens, R. L., Babb, A. K., & Castleman, T. A. (1991). Cancer patient perception of the living will: Report of a pilot survey. OMEGA, *23,* 181–189.

Sullivan, A. D., Hedberg, K., & Fleming, D. W. (2000). Legalized physician-assisted suicide in Oregon—the second year. *New England Journal of Medicine, 342,* 598–604.

Sullivan, A. D., Hedberg, K., & Hopkins, D. (2001). Legalized physician-assisted suicide in Oregon, 1998–2000. *New England Journal of Medicine, 344,* 605–607.

Sullivan, M. D., Ganzini, L., & Youngner, S. J. (1998). Should psychiatrists serve as gatekeepers for physician-assisted suicide? *Hastings Center Report, 28,* 24–31.

Sullivan, M., Rapp, S., Fitzgibbon, D., & Chapman, C. R. (1997). Pain and the choice to hasten death in patients with painful metastatic cancer. *Journal of Palliative Care, 13*, 18–28.

SUPPORT Principle Investigators. (1995). A controlled trial to improve care for seriously ill hospitalized patients: The Study to Understand Prognoses and Preferences for Outcomes and Risks of Treatments. *Journal of the American Medical Association, 274*, 1591–1598.

Suri, D. N., Egleston, B. L., Brody, J. A., & Rudberg, M. A. (1999). Nursing home resident use of care directives. *Journal of Gerontology, 54*, M225–M229.

Task Force to Improve the Care of Terminally-Ill Oregonians. (1998). *The Oregon Death with Dignity Act: A guidebook for health care providers.* Portland: Oregon Health Division.

Uhlmann, R. F., Pearlman, R. A., & Cain, K. C. (1988). Physicians and spouses' predictions of elderly patients' resuscitation preferences. *Journal of Gerontology, 43*, M115–M121.

Vacco v. Quill, 117 S. Ct. 2293 (1997).

van der Maas, P. J., Pijnenborg, L., & van Delden, J. J. (1995). Changes in Dutch opinions on active euthanasia, 1966 through 1991. *Journal of the American Medical Association, 273*, 1411–1414.

van der Maas, P. J., van Delden, J. J. M., Pijnenborg, L., & Looman, C. W. N. (1991). Euthanasia and other medical decisions concerning the end of life. *Lancet, 338*, 669–674.

van der Maas, P. J., van der Waal, G., Haverkate, I., de Graaff, C. L., Kester, J. G., Onwuteaka-Philipsen, B. D., van der Heide, A., Bosma, J. M., & Willems, D. L. (1996). Euthanasia, physician-assisted suicide, and other medical practices involving the end of life in the Netherlands, 1990–1995. *New England Journal of Medicine, 335*, 1699–1705.

van der Waal, G., van der Maas, P. J., Bosma, J. M., Onwuteaka-Philipsen, B. D., Willems, D. L., Haverkate, I., & Kostense, P. J. (1996). Evaluation of the notification procedure for physician-assisted death in the Netherlands. *The New England Journal of Medicine, 335*, 1706–1711.

Veldink, J. H., Wokke, J. H., van der Wal, G., Vianney de Jong, J. M., & van der Berg, L. H. (2002). Euthanasia and physician-assisted suicide among patients with amyotrophic lateral sclerosis in the Netherlands. *New England Journal of Medicine, 346*, 1638–1644.

Ward, S. E., Goldberg, N., Miller-McCauley, C., Mueller, C., Nolan, A., Pawlik-Plank, D., Robbins, A., Stormoen, D., & Weissman, D. E. (1993). Patient related barriers to management of cancer pain. *Journal of Pain, 52*, 319–324.

Washington v. Glucksberg, 117 S. Ct. 2258 (1997).

Werth, J. L. (1996). *Rational suicide? Implications for mental health professionals.* Washington, DC: Taylor & Francis.

Werth, J. L. (2002). Reinterpreting the Controlled Substances Act: Predictions for the effect on pain relief. *Behavioral Sciences and the Law, 20*, 287–305.

Werth, J., Benjamin, G., & Farrenkopf, T. (2000). Requests for physician-assisted deaths: Guidelines for assessing mental capacity and impaired judgment. *Psychology, Public Policy, and Law, 6*, 348–372.

Williams, S. D. (1873). The euthanasia. *Medical and Surgical Reporter, 29*, 122–123.

Wilson, K. G., Scott, J. F., Graham, I. D., Kozak, J. F., Chater, S., Viola, R. A., de Faye, B. J., Weaver, L. A., & Curran, D. (2000). Attitudes of terminally ill patients toward euthanasia and physician-assisted suicide. *Archives of Internal Medicine, 160*, 2454–2460.

Winick, B. J. (1998). Foreward: Planning for the future through advance directive instruments. *Psychology, Public Policy, and Law, 4*, 579–609.

Wolf-Klein, G., Wagner, C. S., & Silverstone, J. A. (1992). The do-not-resuscitate order in a nursing home: Patient's choice or staff's decision. *New York State Journal of Medicine, 92*, 131–134.

Zigmund, A. S., & Snaith, P. R. (1983). The Hospital Anxiety and Depression Scale. *Acta Psychiatrica Scandinavica, 67*, 361–370.

INDEX

Delirium, 117n.6
Dementia, 120, 122
Demographic variables, 71–72
Dependence on others, 88, 102, 141. *See also*
    Loss of independence
Depression, 77–93
    in cancer patients, 90–91
    and competence, 118
    and desire for hastened death, 82–87,
        165–166
    as factor in decision making, 122–124
    and interest in assisted suicide, 78–82
    and ODDA use, 158–159, 162
    and physical symptoms, 105
    and reasons behind requests for PAS,
        88–92
    and research, 70–71
    treatment for, 168
Desire for Death Rating Scale (DDRS), 65–
    66, 83
Desire for hastened death, 65–66, 82–87, 99–
    101
Deteriorating bodily functioning, 154
Diagnosis, medical, 17–18
*Diagnostic and Statistical Manual of Mental
    Disorders (DSM–III)*, 82, 83
Diagnostic Interview Schedule, 80
Dialysis, refusal of, 7
Disability, 165
Discomfort other than pain, 90, 102–103
Ditto, P., 56, 57, 169n.4
DNR order. *See* Do-not-resuscitate order
Doctors. *See* Physician(s)
Do Not Resuscitate (DNR) order, 31, 42, 43–
    50
Drowsiness, 106
DSM–III. *See Diagnostic and Statistical Manual
    of Mental Disorders*
Due Process Clause, 34–37
Durable power of attorney, 42, 43, 55, 115
Dutch Association for Voluntary Euthana-
    sia, 142
Dutch Association of Patients, 132
Dutch Medical Association, 132, 134, 135,
    140, 143
DWDA. *See* Oregon Death with Dignity Act
Dyspnea, 86, 103, 104, 106–108, 159

Eastern Cooperative Oncology Group rating
    scale, 104
Economic depression, 23
Economic factors, 23, 161

Education levels, 153, 154, 156
Elderly patients, 47, 49, 57
Emanuel, Ezekiel, 23, 53, 63, 79, 81, 82, 96,
    98–100, 103, 106
Emanuel, L. L., 53
Emotional factors, 56
End-of-life discussions, 46, 163
England, medieval, 25–26
English law, 27
Epicurus, 14
Equal Protection Clause, 34–37
Eugenics, 5, 21
Europe, 8, 16, 21
Euthanasia, 5–9
    ancient meanings of, 14
    definition of, 5
    Dutch legal status of, 130
    percentages of Dutch deaths resulting
        from, 138, 140
    reasons behind requests for, 88–92
Evolution, theory of, 17, 18
Existential issues, 103
Extraordinary treatments, 52

Family members, 49, 56, 102, 153
Farrenkopf, T., 116
Fatalism, 124
Fatigue, 97, 103, 104, 107, 159
Fear of uncontrollable symptoms, 90, 103
Federal District Court, 36
Federal Register, 155
Final Exit (D. Humphry), 80, 101
Financial considerations, 90, 155
Fleming, D. W., 152
Foley, Kathleen, 160–161
Forensic psychiatrists, 118, 124
14th Amendment, 34, 35
Framing biases, 46
Freedom of religion, 29
Functional impairment, 100, 101, 153, 159,
    165
Future loss of control, 89
Fye, W. B., 17

Ganzini, Linda, 62–64, 73, 80, 82, 90, 97,
    103, 106, 118, 124–126, 157–160,
    162, 168n.3
Gatekeeper role, 174
GDI (Global Distress Index), 105
Germany, 21
Gillon, R., 14
Global Distress Index (GDI), 105

and desire for hastened death, 99–101, 165

and ODDA users, 153, 155

and palliative care, 100

as reason behind request for PAS, 88, 90, 141, 159, 160

research on, 63, 68

research on role of, 96–104

Pain expectancies, 98

Palliative care, 10

and assisted suicide, 172–173

and desire for hastened death, 82, 83, 86

lack of complaints seen in, 151

and ODDA requests, 159, 161

pain management in, 95, 100

and requests for hastened death, 90

Parker, Alton Brooks, 27

Parkinson's disease, 167

Parliament (United Kingdom), 21

PAS. *See* Physician-assisted suicide

Passik, Steven, 78, 106n.5

Passive euthanasia, 7

Patient autonomy. *See* Autonomy, patient

Patient rights, 20

Patient Self-Determination Act (1990), 44, 50

Pearlman, R. A., 56

Penal Law revision (1881), 28

Pennsylvania, 26

Pentobarbital, 150

Peregrinus, 15

Person identity theory, 51

Person's right to choose what to do with his or her own life, 97n.2

Pessimism, 87

Pessin, H., 107, 108

Physical disability, 95

Physical functioning, 104–108

Physical health, ideal of, 14

Physical suffering, 165

Physical Symptom Distress Index, 105

Physical symptoms, 159

Physician-assisted suicide and Hippocratic Oath, 16

Physician-assisted suicide (PAS), 6–9

definition of, 6–7

Dutch legal status of, 130

percentages of Dutch deaths resulting from, 138, 140

reasons behind requests for, 88–92

Physician(s)

and end-of-life discussions, 46

ODDA perspectives of, 157–160

ongoing patient relationship with, 114, 118

PAS prescriptions written by, 171–172

patient communication with, 152

patient discussions with, 91

Physicians Order for Life Sustaining Treatment, 42, 43

Pijnenborg, L., 136

Plato, 14

Pliny the Younger, 15

Poisons, 15

Popular Science Monthly, 19

Portability (of directives), 48

Postma, Ms., 131–132

Poverty, 173n.9

Privacy, right to, 29–30, 44

Prognostic assessments, 17–18

Proposition 161 (California), 38–39

Prosperity, 23

Protection against cruel and unusual punishment, 29

Proxy decision-maker, 42, 53

Psychiatrists, 118, 144–145

Psychological benefits, 48–49

Psychological distress, 67, 70–71, 142–145

Psychological Symptom Distress Index, 105

Psychological well-being, 104

Psychologists, 118

Psychosocial factors, 88, 101

Psychotropic medications, 159

Ptolemy, King, 15

Public opinion, 137, 170

Qualified patients (term), 39

Qualitative research, 74, 85

Quality of life, 88–90, 103, 104, 159, 160

Quill, Timothy, 33, 35

Quinlan, Karen Ann, 29–31

Rabkin, Judith, 84

Racial disparities, 50, 71, 72, 156, 162–163, 173

"Rational manipulation of information" standard, 122

Rational (term), 166

"Rationing" decisions, 55

"Ready to die," 159

Refusal of treatment, 7, 31

Rehnquist, William, 32, 37

Reinhardt, Stephen, 34–35

ABOUT THE AUTHOR

Barry Rosenfeld, PhD, is an associate professor of psychology at Fordham University, where he teaches in the doctoral program in clinical psychology and directs the specialization in forensic psychology. He received his doctorate in clinical psychology from the University of Virginia and completed a postdoctoral fellowship in bio-ethics and consultation–liaison psychology at the Memorial Sloan-Kettering Cancer Center. His research has encompassed a wide array of psychology and public policy issues, including numerous articles in leading psychology and medical journals. For the past decade, he has been studying issues related to physician-assisted suicide, medical decision making, and informed consent, and his work has culminated in this book. In addition to his diverse research interests, he maintains a private practice in clinical and forensic psychology and is a diplomate in forensic psychology of the American Board of Professional Psychology. He lives in New York City with his wife and three beautiful daughters.